2024
SUN SIGN
BOOK

Forecasts by
Alice DeVille

Cover design by Kevin R. Brown
Gettyimages.com/1191314895/©Ali Kahfi
Gettyimages.com/695276506/©PeterHermesFurian
Interior illustration on page 19 by the Llewellyn Art Department

Contents

2023

SEPTEMBER
S	M	T	W	T	F	S
					1	2
3	4	5	6	7	8	9
10	11	12	13	14	15	16
17	18	19	20	21	22	23
24	25	26	27	28	29	30

OCTOBER
S	M	T	W	T	F	S
1	2	3	4	5	6	7
8	9	10	11	12	13	14
15	16	17	18	19	20	21
22	23	24	25	26	27	28
29	30	31				

NOVEMBER
S	M	T	W	T	F	S
			1	2	3	4
5	6	7	8	9	10	11
12	13	14	15	16	17	18
19	20	21	22	23	24	25
26	27	28	29	30		

DECEMBER
S	M	T	W	T	F	S
					1	2
3	4	5	6	7	8	9
10	11	12	13	14	15	16
17	18	19	20	21	22	23
24	25	26	27	28	29	30
31						

2024

JANUARY
S	M	T	W	T	F	S
	1	2	3	4	5	6
7	8	9	10	11	12	13
14	15	16	17	18	19	20
21	22	23	24	25	26	27
28	29	30	31			

FEBRUARY
S	M	T	W	T	F	S
				1	2	3
4	5	6	7	8	9	10
11	12	13	14	15	16	17
18	19	20	21	22	23	24
25	26	27	28	29		

MARCH
S	M	T	W	T	F	S
					1	2
3	4	5	6	7	8	9
10	11	12	13	14	15	16
17	18	19	20	21	22	23
24	25	26	27	28	29	30
31						

APRIL
S	M	T	W	T	F	S
	1	2	3	4	5	6
7	8	9	10	11	12	13
14	15	16	17	18	19	20
21	22	23	24	25	26	27
28	29	30				

MAY
S	M	T	W	T	F	S
			1	2	3	4
5	6	7	8	9	10	11
12	13	14	15	16	17	18
19	20	21	22	23	24	25
26	27	28	29	30	31	

JUNE
S	M	T	W	T	F	S
						1
2	3	4	5	6	7	8
9	10	11	12	13	14	15
16	17	18	19	20	21	22
23	24	25	26	27	28	29
30						

JULY
S	M	T	W	T	F	S
	1	2	3	4	5	6
7	8	9	10	11	12	13
14	15	16	17	18	19	20
21	22	23	24	25	26	27
28	29	30	31			

AUGUST
S	M	T	W	T	F	S
				1	2	3
4	5	6	7	8	9	10
11	12	13	14	15	16	17
18	19	20	21	22	23	24
25	26	27	28	29	30	31

SEPTEMBER
S	M	T	W	T	F	S
1	2	3	4	5	6	7
8	9	10	11	12	13	14
15	16	17	18	19	20	21
22	23	24	25	26	27	28
29	30					

OCTOBER
S	M	T	W	T	F	S
		1	2	3	4	5
6	7	8	9	10	11	12
13	14	15	16	17	18	19
20	21	22	23	24	25	26
27	28	29	30	31		

NOVEMBER
S	M	T	W	T	F	S
					1	2
3	4	5	6	7	8	9
10	11	12	13	14	15	16
17	18	19	20	21	22	23
24	25	26	27	28	29	30

DECEMBER
S	M	T	W	T	F	S
1	2	3	4	5	6	7
8	9	10	11	12	13	14
15	16	17	18	19	20	21
22	23	24	25	26	27	28
29	30	31				

2025

JANUARY
S	M	T	W	T	F	S
			1	2	3	4
5	6	7	8	9	10	11
12	13	14	15	16	17	18
19	20	21	22	23	24	25
26	27	28	29	30	31	

FEBRUARY
S	M	T	W	T	F	S
						1
2	3	4	5	6	7	8
9	10	11	12	13	14	15
16	17	18	19	20	21	22
23	24	25	26	27	28	

MARCH
S	M	T	W	T	F	S
						1
2	3	4	5	6	7	8
9	10	11	12	13	14	15
16	17	18	19	20	21	22
23	24	25	26	27	28	29
30	31					

APRIL
S	M	T	W	T	F	S
		1	2	3	4	5
6	7	8	9	10	11	12
13	14	15	16	17	18	19
20	21	22	23	24	25	26
27	28	29	30			

MAY
S	M	T	W	T	F	S
				1	2	3
4	5	6	7	8	9	10
11	12	13	14	15	16	17
18	19	20	21	22	23	24
25	26	27	28	29	30	31

JUNE
S	M	T	W	T	F	S
1	2	3	4	5	6	7
8	9	10	11	12	13	14
15	16	17	18	19	20	21
22	23	24	25	26	27	28
29	30					

JULY
S	M	T	W	T	F	S
		1	2	3	4	5
6	7	8	9	10	11	12
13	14	15	16	17	18	19
20	21	22	23	24	25	26
27	28	29	30	31		

AUGUST
S	M	T	W	T	F	S
					1	2
3	4	5	6	7	8	9
10	11	12	13	14	15	16
17	18	19	20	21	22	23
24	25	26	27	28	29	30
31						

Meet Alice DeVille

Alice DeVille is known internationally as an astrologer, consultant, and writer. She has been writing articles for the Llewellyn annuals since 1998. Her contributions have appeared in Llewellyn's *Sun Sign Book*, *Moon Sign Book*, and *Herbal Almanac*. Alice discovered astrology in her late teens when she was browsing the book section of a discount department store and found a book that had much more astrology detail in it than simple Sun sign descriptions. Bells of recognition went off immediately. She purchased the book and knew she had to have more.

Alice is a former analyst for the USDA Forest Service in Washington, DC. She later held credentials as a Realtor for twenty-two years in the Commonwealth of Virginia and earned real estate appraisal credentials and certifications in diverse real estate specialties. Her knowledge of feng shui led to the development of numerous workshops and seminars including those that provided Realtors with tips to enhance selling homes and working with buyers.

Alice specializes in relationships of all types that call for solid problem-solving advice to get to the core of issues and give clients options for meeting critical needs. Her clients seek solutions in business practices, career and change management, real estate, relationships, and training. Numerous websites and publications have featured her articles, including StarIQ, Astral Hearts, Llewellyn, Meta Arts, Inner Self, and ShareItLiveIt. Quotes from her work on relationships have appeared in books, publications, training materials, calendars, planners, audio tapes, and world-famous quotes lists. Often cited is "Each relationship you have with another reflects the relationship you have with yourself." Alice's Llewellyn material on relationships has appeared in *Something More* by Sarah Ban Breathnach and *Through God's Eyes* by Phil Bolsta and on Oprah's website.

Alice is available for writing books and articles for publishers, newspapers, and magazines, as well as conducting workshops and doing radio or TV interviews. For information, contact her at DeVilleAA@aol.com or alice.deville27@gmail.com.

How to Use This Book

by Kim Rogers-Gallagher

Hi there! Welcome to the 2024 edition of *Llewellyn's Sun Sign Book*. This book centers on Sun sign astrology—that is, the set of general attributes and characteristics that those of us born under each of the twelve particular Sun signs share. You'll find descriptions of your sign's qualities tucked into your sign's chapter, along with the type of behavior you tend to exhibit in different life situations—with regard to relationships, work situations, and the handling of money and possessions, for example. Oh, and there's a section that's dedicated to good old-fashioned fun, too, including what will bring you joy and how to make it happen.

There's a lot to be said for Sun sign astrology. First off, the Sun's sign at the time of your birth describes the qualities, talents, and traits you're here to study this time around. If you believe in reincarnation, think of it as declaring a celestial major for this lifetime. Sure, you'll learn other things along the way, but you've announced to one and all that you're primarily interested in mastering this one particular sign. Then, too, on a day when fiery, impulsive energies are making astrological headlines, if you're a fiery and/or impulsive sign yourself—like Aries or Aquarius, for example—it's easy to imagine how you'll take to the astrological weather a lot more easily than a practical, steady-handed sign like Taurus or Virgo.

Obviously, astrology comes in handy, for a variety of reasons. Getting to know your "natal" Sun sign (the sign the Sun was in when you were born) can most certainly give you the edge you need to ace the final and move on to the next celestial course level—or basically to succeed in life, and maybe even earn a few bonus points toward next semester. Using astrology on a daily basis nicely accelerates the process.

Now, there are eight other planets and one lovely Moon in our neck of the celestial woods, all of which also play into our personalities. The sign that was on the eastern horizon at the moment of your birth—otherwise known as your *Ascendant*, or *rising sign*—is another indicator of your personality traits. Honestly, there are all kinds of cosmic factors, so if it's an in-depth, personal analysis you're after, a professional astrologer is the only way to go—especially if you're curious about relationships, past lives, future trends, or even the right time to schedule an important life event. Professional astrologers calculate your birth chart—again, the "natal" chart—based on the date, place, and exact time of your birth—which allows for a far more personal and specific reading. In the meantime, however, in addition to reading up on your Sun sign, you can use the tables on pages 8 and 9 to find the sign of your Ascendant. (These tables, however, are approximate and tailored to those of us born in North America, so if the traits of your Ascendant don't sound familiar, check out the sign directly before or after.)

There are three sections to each sign chapter in this book. As I already mentioned, the first section describes personality traits, and while it's fun to read your own, don't forget to check out the other Sun signs.

The second section is entitled "The Year Ahead" for each sign. Through considering the movements of the slow-moving planets (Jupiter, Saturn, Uranus, Neptune, Pluto), the eclipses, and any other outstanding celestial movements, this segment will provide you with the big picture of the year—or basically the broad strokes of what to expect, no matter who you are or where you are, collectively speaking.

The third section includes monthly forecasts, along with rewarding days and challenging days. These pages provide information about each month of the year related to your sign. They are a general interpretation based on solar charts, but they may not address the actual activity in your birth chart, which is based on your time, date, and location of birth. If you are interested in learning more about how the current cycles affect you, consult your astrologer for clarification via a personal consultation or a coaching session.

At the end of every chapter you'll find an Action Table, providing general information about the best time to indulge in certain activities. Please note that these are only suggestions. Don't hold yourself back or rush into anything your intuition doesn't wholeheartedly agree with—and again, when in doubt, find yourself a professional.

Well, that's it. I hope that you enjoy this book, and that being aware of the astrological energies of 2024 helps you create a year full of fabulous memories!

Kim Rogers-Gallagher has written hundreds of articles and columns for magazines and online publications and has two books of her own, *Astrology for the Light Side of the Brain* and *Astrology for the Light Side of the Future*. She's a well-known speaker who's been part of the UAC faculty since 1996. Kim can be contacted at KRGPhoenix313@yahoo.com for fees regarding readings, classes, and lectures.

Ascendant Table

Your Sun Sign	Your Time of Birth					
	6–8 am	8–10 am	10 am–Noon	Noon–2 pm	2–4 pm	4–6 pm
Aries	Taurus	Gemini	Cancer	Leo	Virgo	Libra
Taurus	Gemini	Cancer	Leo	Virgo	Libra	Scorpio
Gemini	Cancer	Leo	Virgo	Libra	Scorpio	Sagittarius
Cancer	Leo	Virgo	Libra	Scorpio	Sagittarius	Capricorn
Leo	Virgo	Libra	Scorpio	Sagittarius	Capricorn	Aquarius
Virgo	Libra	Scorpio	Sagittarius	Capricorn	Aquarius	Pisces
Libra	Scorpio	Sagittarius	Capricorn	Aquarius	Pisces	Aries
Scorpio	Sagittarius	Capricorn	Aquarius	Pisces	Aries	Taurus
Sagittarius	Capricorn	Aquarius	Pisces	Aries	Taurus	Gemini
Capricorn	Aquarius	Pisces	Aries	Taurus	Gemini	Cancer
Aquarius	Pisces	Aries	Taurus	Gemini	Cancer	Leo
Pisces	Aries	Taurus	Gemini	Cancer	Leo	Virgo

Your Sun Sign	Your Time of Birth						
	6–8 pm	8–10 pm	10 pm–Midnight	Midnight–2 am	2–4 am	4–6 am	
Aries	Scorpio	Sagittarius	Capricorn	Aquarius	Pisces	Aries	
Taurus	Sagittarius	Capricorn	Aquarius	Pisces	Aries	Taurus	
Gemini	Capricorn	Aquarius	Pisces	Aries	Taurus	Gemini	
Cancer	Aquarius	Pisces	Aries	Taurus	Gemini	Cancer	
Leo	Pisces	Aries	Taurus	Gemini	Cancer	Leo	
Virgo	Aries	Taurus	Gemini	Cancer	Leo	Virgo	
Libra	Taurus	Gemini	Cancer	Leo	Virgo	Libra	
Scorpio	Gemini	Cancer	Leo	Virgo	Libra	Scorpio	
Sagittarius	Cancer	Leo	Virgo	Libra	Scorpio	Sagittarius	
Capricorn	Leo	Virgo	Libra	Scorpio	Sagittarius	Capricorn	
Aquarius	Virgo	Libra	Scorpio	Sagittarius	Capricorn	Aquarius	
Pisces	Libra	Scorpio	Sagittarius	Capricorn	Aquarius	Pisces	

How to use this table: 1. Find your Sun sign in the left column.

2. Find your approximate birth time in a vertical column.

3. Line up your Sun sign and birth time to find your Ascendant.

This table will give you an approximation of your Ascendant. If you feel that the sign listed as your Ascendant is incorrect, try the one either before or after the listed sign. It is difficult to determine your exact Ascendant without a complete natal chart.

Astrology Basics

Natal astrology is done by freeze-framing the solar system at the moment of your birth, from the perspective of your birth place. This creates a circular map that looks like a pie sliced into twelve pieces. It shows where every heavenly body we're capable of seeing was located when you arrived. Basically, it's your astrological tool kit, and it can't be replicated more than once in thousands of years. This is why we astrologers are so darn insistent about the need for you to either dig your birth certificate out of that box of ancient paperwork in the back of your closet or get a copy of it from the county clerk's office where you were born. Natal astrology, as interpreted by a professional astrologer, is done exactly and precisely for you and no one else. It shows your inherent traits, talents, and challenges. Comparing the planets' current positions to their positions in your birth chart allows astrologers to help you understand the celestial trends at work in your life—and most importantly, how you can put each astrological energy to a positive, productive use.

Let's take a look at the four main components of every astrology chart.

Planets

The planets represent the needs or urges we all experience once we hop off the Evolutionary Express and take up residence inside a human body. For example, the Sun is your urge to shine and be creative, the Moon is your need to express emotions, Mercury is in charge of how you communicate and navigate, and Venus is all about who and what you love—and more importantly, how you love.

Signs

The sign a planet occupies is like a costume or uniform. It describes how you'll go about acting on your needs and urges. If you have Venus in fiery, impulsive Aries, for example, and you're attracted to a complete stranger across the room, you won't wait for them to come to you. You'll walk over and introduce yourself the second the urge strikes you. Venus in intense, sexy Scorpio, however? Well, that's a different story. In this case, you'll keep looking at a prospective beloved until they finally give in, cross the room, and beg you to explain why you've been staring at them for the past couple of hours.

Houses

The houses represent the different sides of our personalities that emerge in different life situations. For example, think of how very different you act when you're with an authority figure as opposed to how you act with a lover or when you're with your BFF.

Aspects

The aspects describe the distance from one planet to another in a geometric angle. If you were born when Mercury was 90 degrees from Jupiter, for example, this aspect is called a square. Each unique angular relationship causes the planets involved to interact differently.

Meet the Planets

The planets represent energy sources. The Sun is our source of creativity, the Moon is our emotional warehouse, and Venus describes who and what we love and are attracted to—not to mention why and how we go about getting it and keeping it.

Sun

The Sun is the head honcho in your chart. It represents your life's mission—what will give you joy, keep you young, and never fail to arouse your curiosity. Oddly enough, you weren't born knowing the qualities of the sign the Sun was in when you were born. You're here to learn the traits, talents, and characteristics of the sign you chose—and rest assured, each of the twelve is its own marvelous adventure! Since the Sun is the Big Boss, all of the other planets, including the Moon, are the Sun's staff, all there to help the boss by helping you master your particular area of expertise. Back in the day, the words from a song in a recruitment commercial struck me as a perfect way to describe our Sun's quest: "Be all that you can be. Keep on reaching. Keep on growing. Find your future." The accompanying music was energizing, robust, and exciting, full of anticipation and eagerness. When you feel enthused, motivated, and stimulated, that's your Sun letting you know you're on the right path.

Moon

If you want to understand this lovely silver orb, go outside when the Moon is nice and full, find yourself a comfy perch, sit still, and have a nice long look at her. The Moon inspires us to dream, wish, and sigh, to reminisce, ruminate, and remember. She's the Queen of Emotions, the astrological purveyor of feelings and reactions. In your natal chart, the condition of the Moon—that is, the sign and house she's in and the connections she makes with your other planets—shows how you'll deal with whatever life tosses your way—how you'll respond, how you'll cope, and how you'll pull it all together to move on after a crisis. She's where your instincts and hunches come from, and the source of every gut feeling and premonition. The Moon describes your childhood home, your relationship with your mother, your attitude toward childbearing and children in general, and what you're looking for in a home. She shows what makes you feel safe, warm, comfy, and loved. On a daily basis, the Moon describes the collective mood.

Mercury

Next time you pass by a flower shop, take a look at the FTD logo by the door. That fellow with the wings on his head and his feet is Mercury, the ancient Messenger of the Gods. He's always been a very busy guy. Back in the day, his job was to shuttle messages back and forth between the gods and goddesses and we mere mortals—obviously, no easy feat. Nowadays, however, Mercury is even busier. With computers, cell phones, social media, and perhaps even the occasional human-to-human interaction to keep track of—well, he must be just exhausted. In a nutshell, he's the astrological energy in charge of communication, navigation, and travel, so he's still nicely represented by that winged image. He's also the guy in charge of the five senses, so no matter what you're aware of right now, be it taste, touch, sound, smell, or sight—well, that's because Mercury is bringing it to you, live. At any rate, you'll hear about him most when someone mentions that Mercury is retrograde, but even though these periods have come to be blamed for all sorts of problems, there's really no cause for alarm. Mercury turns retrograde (or, basically, appears to move backwards from our perspective here on Earth) every three months for three weeks, giving us all a chance for a do-over—and who among us has never needed one of those?

Venus

So, if it's Mercury that makes you aware of your environment, who allows you to experience all kinds of sensory sensations via the five senses? Who's in charge of your preferences in each department? That delightful task falls under the jurisdiction of the lovely lady Venus, who describes the physical experiences that are the absolute best—in your book, anyway. That goes for the music and art you find most pleasing, the food and beverages you can't get enough of, and the scents you consider the sweetest of all—including the collar of the shirt your loved one recently wore. Touch, of course, is also a sense that can be quite delightful to experience. Think of how happy your fingers are when you're stroking your animal companion's fur, or the delicious feel of cool bed sheets when you slip between them after an especially tough day. Venus brings all those sensations together in one wonderful package, working her magic through love of the romantic kind, most memorably experienced through intimate physical interaction with an "other." Still, your preferences in any relationship also fall under Venus's job description.

Mars

Mars turns up the heat, amps up the energy, and gets your show on the road. Whenever you hear yourself grunt, growl, or grumble—or just make any old "rrrrr" sound in general—your natal Mars has just made an appearance. Adrenaline is his business and passion is his specialty. He's the ancient God of War—a hot-headed guy who's famous for having at it with his sword first and asking questions later. In the extreme, Mars is often in the neighborhood when violent events occur, and accidents, too. He's in charge of self-assertion, aggression, and pursuit, and one glance at his heavenly appearance explains why. He's the Red Planet, after all—and just think of all the expressions about anger and passion that include references to the color red or the element of fire: "Grrr!" "Seeing red." "Hot under the collar." "All fired up." "Hot and heavy." You get the idea. Mars is your own personal warrior. He describes how you'll react when you're threatened, excited, or angry.

Jupiter

Santa Claus. Luciano Pavarotti with a great big smile on his face as he belts out an amazing aria. Your favorite uncle who drinks too much, eats too much, and laughs far too loud—yet never fails to go well above and beyond the call of duty for you when you need him. They're all perfect examples of Jupiter, the King of the Gods, the giver of all things good, and the source of extravagance, generosity, excess, and benevolence in our little corner of the Universe. He and Venus are the heavens' two most popular planets—for obvious reasons. Venus makes us feel good. Jupiter makes us feel absolutely over-the-top excellent. In Jupiter's book, if one is good, it only stands to reason that two would be better, and following that logic, ten would be just outstanding. His favorite words are "too," "many," and "much." Expansions, increases, and enlargements—or basically, just the whole concept of growth—are all his doing. Now, unbeknownst to this merry old fellow, there really is such a thing as too much of a good thing—but let's not pop his goodhearted bubble. Wherever Jupiter is in your chart, you'll be prone to go overboard, take it to the limit, and push the envelope as far as you possibly can. Sure, you might get a bit out of control every now and then, but if envelopes weren't ever pushed, we'd never know the joys of optimism, generosity, or sudden, contagious bursts of laughter.

Saturn

Jupiter expands. Saturn contracts. Jupiter encourages growth. Saturn, on the other hand, uses those rings he's so famous for to restrict growth. His favorite word is "no," but he's also very fond of "wait," "stop," and "don't even think about it." He's ultra-realistic and quite pessimistic, a cautious, careful curmudgeon who guards and protects you by not allowing you to move too quickly or act too recklessly. He insists on preparation and doesn't take kindly when we blow off responsibilities and duties. As you can imagine, Saturn is not nearly as popular as Venus and Jupiter, mainly because none of us like to be told we can't do what we want to do when we want to do it. Still, without someone who acted out his part when you were too young to know better, you might have dashed across the street without stopping to check for traffic first, and—well, you get the point. Saturn encourages frugality, moderation, thoughtfulness, and self-restraint, all necessary habits to learn if you want to play nice with the other grown-ups. He's also quite fond of building things, which necessarily starts with solid foundations and structures that are built to last.

Uranus

Say hello to Mr. Unpredictable himself, the heavens' wild card—to say the very least. He's the kind of guy who claims responsibility for lightning strikes, be they literal or symbolic. Winning the lottery, love at first sight, accidents, and anything seemingly coincidental that strikes you as oddly well-timed are all examples of Uranus's handiwork. He's a rebellious, headstrong energy, so wherever he is in your chart, you'll be defiant, headstrong, and quite unwilling to play by the rules, which he thinks of as merely annoying suggestions that far too many humans adhere to. Uranus is here to inspire you to be yourself—exactly as you are, with no explanations and no apologies whatsoever. He motivates you to develop qualities such as independence, ingenuity, and individuality—and with this guy in the neighborhood, if anyone or anything gets in the way, you'll 86 them. Period. Buh-bye now. The good news is that when you allow this freedom-loving energy to guide you, you discover something new and exciting about yourself on a daily basis—at least. The tough but entirely doable part is keeping him reined in tightly enough to earn your daily bread and form lasting relationships with like-minded others.

Neptune

Neptune is the uncontested Mistress of Disguise and Illusion in the solar system, beautifully evidenced by the fact that this ultra-feminine energy has been masquerading as a male god for as long as gods and goddesses have been around. Just take a look at the qualities she bestows: compassion, spirituality, intuition, wistfulness, and nostalgia. Basically, whenever your subconscious whispers, it's in Neptune's voice. She activates your antennae and sends you subtle, invisible, and yet highly powerful messages about everyone you cross paths with, no matter how fleeting the encounter. I often picture her as Glinda the Good Witch from *The Wizard of Oz*, who rode around in a pink bubble, singing happy little songs and casting wonderful, helpful spells. Think "enchantment"—oh, and "glamour," too, which, by the way, was the old-time term for a magical spell cast upon someone to change their appearance. Nowadays, glamour is often thought of as a rather idealized and often artificial type of beauty brought about by cosmetics and airbrushing, but Neptune is still in charge, and her magic still works. When this energy is wrongfully used, deceptions, delusions and fraud can result—and since she's so fond of ditching reality, it's easy to become a bit too fond of escape hatches like drugs and alcohol. Still, Neptune inspires romance, nostalgia, and sentimentality, and she's quite fond of dreams and fantasies, too—and what would life be like without all of that?

Pluto

Picture all the gods and goddesses in the heavens above us living happily in a huge mansion in the clouds. Then imagine that Pluto's place is at the bottom of the cellar stairs, and on the cellar door (which is in the kitchen, of course) a sign reads "Keep out. Working on Darwin Awards." That's where Pluto would live—and that's the attitude he'd have. He's in charge of unseen cycles—life, death, and rebirth. Obviously, he's not an emotional kind of guy. Whatever Pluto initiates really has to happen. He's dark, deep, and mysterious—and inevitable. So yes, Darth Vader does come to mind, if for no other reason than because of James Earl Jones's amazing, compelling voice. Still, this intense, penetrating, and oh-so-thorough energy has a lot more to offer. Pluto's in charge of all those categories we humans aren't fond of—like death and decay, for example—but on the less drastic side, he also inspires recycling, repurposing, and reusing. In your chart, Pluto represents a place where you'll be ready to go big or go home, where investing all or nothing is a given. When a crisis comes up—when you need to be totally committed and totally authentic to who you really are to get through it—that's when you'll meet your Pluto. Power struggles and mind games, however—well, you can also expect those pesky types of things wherever Pluto is located.

A Word about Retrogrades

"Retrograde" sounds like a bad thing, but I'm here to tell you that it isn't. In a nutshell, retrograde means that from our perspective here on Earth, a planet appears to be moving in reverse. Of course, planets don't ever actually back up, but the energy of retrograde planets is often held back, delayed, or hindered in some way. For example, when Mercury—the ruler of communication and navigation—appears to be retrograde, it's tough to get from point A to point B without a snafu, and it's equally hard to get a straight answer. Things just don't seem to go as planned. But it only makes sense. Since Mercury is the planet in charge of conversation and movement, when he's moving backward—well, imagine driving a car that only had reverse. Yep. It wouldn't be easy. Still, if that's all you had to work with, you'd eventually find a way to get where you wanted to go. That's how all retrograde energies work. If you have retrograde planets in your natal chart, don't rush them. These energies may need a bit more time to function well for you than other natal planets, but if you're patient, talk about having an edge! You'll know these planets inside and out. On a collective basis, think of the time when a planet moves retrograde as a chance for a celestial do-over.

Signs of the Zodiac

The sign a planet is "wearing" really says it all. It's the costume an actor wears that helps them act out the role they're playing. It's the style, manner, or approach you'll use in each life department—whether you're being creative on a canvas, gushing over a new lover, or applying for a management position. Each of the signs belongs to an element, a quality, and a gender, as follows.

Elements

The four elements—fire, earth, air, and water—describe a sign's aims. Fire signs are spiritual, impulsive energies. Earth signs are tightly connected to the material plane. Air signs are cerebral, intellectual creatures, and water signs rule the emotional side of life.

Qualities

The three qualities—cardinal, fixed, and mutable—describe a sign's energy. Cardinal signs are tailor-made for beginnings. Fixed energies are solid, just as they sound, and are quite determined to finish what they start. Mutable energies are flexible and accommodating but can also be scattered or unstable.

Genders

The genders—masculine and feminine—describe whether the energy attracts (feminine) or pursues (masculine) what it wants.

The Twelve Signs

Here's a quick rundown of the twelve zodiac signs.

Aries

Aries planets are hotheads. They're built from go-getter cardinal energy and fast-acting fire. Needless to say, Aries energy is impatient, energetic, and oh-so-willing to try anything once.

Taurus

Taurus planets are aptly represented by the symbol of the bull. They're earth creatures, very tightly connected to the material plane, and fixed—which means they're pretty much immovable when they don't want to act.

Sequence	Sign	Glyph	Ruling Planet	Symbol
1	Aries	♈	Mars	Ram
2	Taurus	♉	Venus	Bull
3	Gemini	♊	Mercury	Twins
4	Cancer	♋	Moon	Crab
5	Leo	♌	Sun	Lion
6	Virgo	♍	Mercury	Virgin
7	Libra	♎	Venus	Scales
8	Scorpio	♏	Pluto	Scorpion
9	Sagittarius	♐	Jupiter	Archer
10	Capricorn	♑	Saturn	Goat
11	Aquarius	♒	Uranus	Water Bearer
12	Pisces	♓	Neptune	Fish

Gemini

As an intellectual air sign that's mutable and interested in anything new, Gemini energy is eternally curious—and quite easily distracted. Gemini planets live in the moment and are expert multitaskers.

Cancer

Cancer is a water sign that runs on its emotions, and since it's also part of the cardinal family, it's packed with the kind of start-up energy that's perfect for raising a family and building a home.

Leo

This determined, fixed sign is part of the fire family. As fires go, think of Leo planets as bonfires of energy—and just try to tear your eyes away. Leo's symbol is the lion, and it's no accident. Leo planets care very much about their familial pride—and about their personal pride.

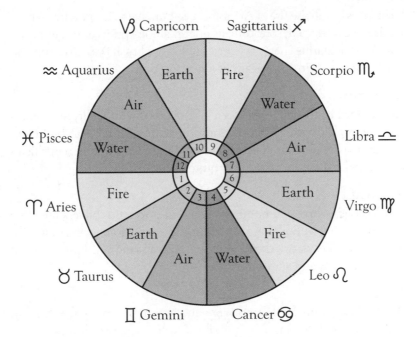

Virgo

Virgo is mutable and therefore easily able to switch channels when necessary. It's part of the earth family and connected to the material world (like Taurus). Virgo energy loves to work, organize, and sort, but most of all, to fix what's broken.

Libra

This communicative air sign runs on high. It's cardinal, so when it comes to making connections, Libra is second to none. Libra planets are people pleasers and the honorary cruise directors of the zodiac, and are as charming and accommodating as the day is long.

Scorpio

Scorpio is of the water element and a highly emotional creature. Scorpio energy is fixed, too, so feelings are tough to shake and obsessions are easy to come by. Planets in this sign are devoted and determined and can be absolutely relentless.

Sagittarius

Sagittarius has all the fire of Aries and Leo but, due to its mutable nature, tends to be distracted, spreading its energy among projects and interests. Think of Sagittarius energy as a series of red-hot brush fires, firing up and dying down and firing up again in a new location.

Capricorn

As the third earth sign, Capricorn is concerned with reality and practicality, complete with all the rules and regulations it takes to build and maintain a life here on Planet Number Three. Capricorn energy takes charge and assumes responsibility quite easily.

Aquarius

The last of the three communicative air signs, Aquarius prefers mingling and interacting with a group via friendships. Freedom-loving Aquarius energy won't be restricted—not for long, anyway—and is willing to return the favor, in any and all relationships.

Pisces

Watery Pisces runs on its emotions—and even more so on its intuition, which is second to none. This mutable, flexible sign is aptly represented by the constant fluctuating movements of its symbol, the two fish.

Aspects

Astrological aspects describe the relationships between planets and important points in a horoscope chart. Basically, they're the mathematical angles that measure the distance between two or more planets. Planets in square aspect are 90 degrees apart, planets in opposition are 180 degrees apart, and so forth. Each of these aspect relationships seems to link energies in a very different way. For example, if two planets are in square aspect, think of what you know about "squaring off," and you'll understand exactly how they're interacting. Think of aspects as a way of describing the type of conversation going on between celestial bodies.

Here's a brief description of the five major aspects.

Conjunction

When two planets are within a few degrees of each other, they're joined at the hip. The conjunction is often called the aspect of "fusion," since the energies involved always act together.

Sextile
Planets in sextile are linked by a 60-degree angle, creating an exciting, stimulating astrological "conversation." These planets encourage, arouse, and excite each other.

Square
The square aspect is created by linking energies in a 90-degree angle—which tends to be testy and sometimes irritating but always action-oriented.

Trine
The trine is the "lazy" aspect. When planets are in this 120-degree angle, they get along so well that they often aren't motivated to do much. Trines make things easy—too easy, at times—but they're also known for being quite lucky.

Opposition
Oppositions exist between planets that are literally opposite one another. Think about seesaws and playing tug of war, and you'll understand how these energies get along. Sure, it can be a power struggle at times, but balance is the key.

2024 at a Glance

Look at the lineup of planets as the new year gets off to a rollicking start. On the first day of the new year, Mercury, the Messenger of the Gods, turns direct in Sagittarius, setting the stage for the 2024 Mercury retrograde periods that will occupy fire signs. On April 1, Mercury turns retrograde in innovative Aries through April 25, a time when you may wish to postpone plans to initiate exciting new projects. Although the Mercury retrograde period that occurs in August starts out with the planet in early Virgo, Mercury spends most of its time in effervescent Leo. The final Mercury retrograde starts on November 25 in Sagittarius and returns to direct motion on December 15.

The rambunctious planet Uranus, which has been retrograde in Taurus since August 28, 2023, is hoping to get feisty when it turns direct on January 27. Uranus streaks along on its disruptive mission until September 1, when it hiccups loudly and backs up in retrograde motion until January 30, 2025, sending those born between May 8 and 18 into discovery mode as they look for answers to determine what went wrong in their usually reliable worlds. Other fixed signs that feel the impact of this Uranus transit include members of Aquarius, Leo, and Scorpio with planets at 19–27 degrees. Pluto is another planet that bears watching this year as it nears completion of its journey in Capricorn, the sign it has occupied since 2008. This slow-moving planet enters Aquarius on January 20, the same day the Sun enters Aquarius, giving those born on that day a personality sparked by spontaneity, humanity, and deep introspection. Pluto advances only two degrees into Aquarius before it stations to move retrograde on May 2. It backs up into Capricorn on September 1 and resumes direct motion on October 11 in the last degree of Capricorn. Pluto finally finishes its tour of Capricorn and embraces Aquarius for good on November 19, staying in this sign through March 2043.

Another planet that is going full blast is Saturn in Pisces, which entered this sign in March 2023 with plans to revolutionize our spiritual world, awaken our intuition, and lead us away from confusing mental patterns. This year, Saturn occupies 3–19 degrees of Pisces, going retrograde on June 29 and resuming direct motion on November 15. Neptune, which is also in Pisces, starts out the year at 25 degrees and turns retrograde on July 2 in the last degree of Pisces, moving forward again on December 7. Members of Pisces born between March 14 and 19 feel the strongest impact from transiting Neptune in 2024 as it slides toward its final leg in Pisces that began in 2011 and then scratches the surface of a brief teaser in Aries in spring of 2025.

Jupiter travels through luxurious Taurus until May 25, when it moves into curious Gemini, taking on multiple interests and enjoying the adventures until October 9, when it makes its first retrograde station of the cycle at 21 degrees. By touching the Suns of two-thirds of the Gemini population, Jupiter spreads its wings and adds numerous experiences to the resumes and life experiences of those born under the sign of communication. This year, Mars makes waves by turning retrograde in entrepreneurial Leo on December 6. Schedules are bound to be disrupted by erratic energy patterns. In 2024, four eclipses grace the heavens: a Lunar Eclipse and a Solar Eclipse in Libra on March 25 and October 2, respectively, and a Solar Eclipse in Aries on April 8, with the final Lunar Eclipse of the year in Pisces on September 17. Check your birth chart to determine the location of each eclipse, noting the proximity of any natal planets to eclipse activity. If present, that house could become a zone of intensity or surprises in 2024.

2024 SUN SIGN BOOK

Forecasts by

Alice DeVille

Aries

The Ram
March 20 to April 20

♈

Element: Fire

Quality: Cardinal

Polarity: Yang/masculine

Planetary Ruler: Mars

Meditation: I build
on my strengths

Gemstone: Diamond

Power Stones: Bloodstone,
carnelian, ruby

Key Phrase: I am

Glyph: Ram's head

Anatomy: Head, face, throat

Colors: Red, white

Animal: Ram

Myths/Legends: Artemis,
Jason and the Golden Fleece

House: First

Opposite Sign: Libra

Flower: Geranium

Keyword: Initiative

The Aries Personality

Strengths, Talents, and the Creative Spark

You have been traveling the world as a passionate cardinal fire sign and enjoy being the first in the zodiac. Very few have the initiative you own, along with an abundance of assertiveness that you eagerly ignite to implement the plans you have developed, doing so without delay. Those who know you seldom have to prod you to get things going, because your goal is to get to your destination fast and teach others a few tricks along the way. Your fertile mind is constantly processing new ideas that you shape into the big picture. While you take ownership of your inventions, you prefer to save the refinement of your products and some of the grunt work for your colleagues. Capitalizing on the influence of Mars, the energetic planetary ruler of your sign, you recognize that time is precious, and you don't waste it wondering if you can avoid barriers and roadblocks. Aries, you love to be in the driver's seat, and you enjoy driving, especially a decked-out vehicle that makes a statement.

A preoccupation with developing your personality and expressing your individuality leads you to the discovery of impressive occupations where you have the opportunity to rise above the achievements of the other signs, especially in those fields where you manage the team, own the company, or operate independently. Recognition of your identity is important to you. When one of your creative ideas is accepted and implemented, you become powerfully motivated to do more to promote the strength of your team and establish expertise in your chosen field. As an Aries, you frequently find satisfaction in more than one career in your work lifetime. Initiating new trends and showing others how to remain upbeat in the face of challenges is part of your charm. Many an Aries knows how to tame impulsive decision-making and a quick temper by selling others on new ways to develop or adapt successful business or social strategies. You're very goal-oriented and believe you can do anything that holds your interest. "I can't" is a cop-out in your eyes.

Intimacy and Personal Relationships

As a fan of self-discovery, you place considerable emphasis on how you choose partners and value intimate partners, business partners, and friendships. At times you fly solo and don't have a love partner in your life until you realize that it is unappealing to do all the fun things by yourself. Your love of adventure and risk-taking means that you like to indulge in activities that are physically challenging. Sometimes it seems as though you are interviewing prospective partners to make sure they tick off most of the boxes that describe the perfect mate to share your wide variety of interests. You feel an inner warmth when you are drawn to someone who stops you in your tracks when you first become aware of their magnetism. You'll want to lavish them with your gifts of passion and devotion. You adore time spent with your loved one and will find yourself greeting life with a more open mind and wholesome attitude because you have learned how much fun it is to share.

You place considerable value on friendships and acquaintances and succeed in accumulating many of them. Those in your inner circle sing high praises about the quality of your friendship and the many kindnesses you show others. Friends and intimate partners are likely to include members of the fire signs (Aries, Leo, Sagittarius) and air signs (Gemini, Libra, Aquarius). Aries often marry more than once and learn many valuable lessons from that initial union. When they remarry, Aries gets it right and the marriage is usually a keeper. Children adore you, and you generally let them know how important they are in your life by becoming an active participant in their interests.

Values and Resources

Aries, you value freedom when it comes to managing your workload. You despise having others look over your shoulder and prefer to take the lead in implementing an action plan and monitoring your timeline. Having a positive self-image is one of your priorities, and you do all you can to protect it. Responsibility is important to you, and you go after it competitively. Your attitude toward money is complex—you like to spend it and wave away the new debt you accumulate by rationalizing that you'll pay it off with your next paycheck or the quarterly bonus you're expecting. Generous to a fault in giving gifts, you also make sure your wish list is honored and update your wardrobe and vehicles regularly. You admire the aptitude of others to take on do-it-yourself projects and have considerable success in remodeling your own home or customizing your car. A smaller number of Aries watch what they spend to the point of appearing miserly, seldom treating friends to a dinner or a drink.

Blind Spots and Blockages

An impulsive type, you are known for going after a job that offers prestige, a generous salary, and the opportunity to get ahead quickly. Once you see the truth and realize the position doesn't suit you, you are out of there and seldom look back, even if the situation calls for some assessment and a thorough search for greener pastures first. Poor performers and lazy types annoy you. You show little tolerance for those who miss deadlines or keep you waiting when you have a date, a plane to catch, or a dentist appointment. While your reaction is often justified, your delivery of an admonition stimulates a chilly response from the recipient and those within earshot. Little do they know that your temper is quick to cool, and you don't carry a grudge after the incident occurs.

Goals and Success

Taking risks appeals to you and ties in with your sign's affiliation with Mars. Very few Aries stick with the same occupation throughout their career. You stay fit to make sure you can get the job done with courage and stamina when sudden events disrupt your community. You are highly skilled at working with your hands and may excel as a dentist, mason, soldier, or surgeon. Many Aries drive for a living and are master mechanics, owning a large collection of tools to get the job done. You gravitate toward work that calls for a uniform, such as the medical field (including ambulance drivers and EMTs), military careers, firefighting, police work, or protective services involving onsite security work or the installation of sophisticated security systems.

Aries Keywords for 2024

Accessible, action-oriented, approachable

The Year Ahead for Aries

With an eclipse in your sign on April 8 in your solar first house, you'll be in the spotlight, especially if it falls near your birthday. Your solar seventh house of personal and business partners will buzz with activity hosting two eclipses this year in Libra, one on March 25 and the other on October 2. If you are anticipating positive change and forward-moving activity, you'll be happy that Mercury starts off the year by turning direct in Sagittarius in your solar ninth house of long-distance activity, giving the okay to reschedule travel that had to be postponed last year. Jupiter continues its journey in Taurus, the sign of good taste and impeccable bargain hunting, and your solar second house of income and resources until May 25, when it moves into Gemini and your solar third house of communication and community. Saturn continues its introspective passage through Pisces and your solar twelfth house throughout 2024, putting you in touch with private movements and behind-the-scenes planning. In its final degrees of Taurus, Uranus keeps company with Jupiter in your solar second house of money and resources, turning direct on January 27 and adding a few surprises along the way before it leaves this sign in 2025. Be optimistic in holding out for a windfall.

Spiritually driven Neptune drifts through your solar twelfth house all year in Pisces, reminding you to assess your mental and physical health by scheduling checkups and getting more sleep as you explore the mysteries that interest your deep psyche. Pluto in Capricorn has dominated your solar tenth house of career and ambition since 2008, aiding your quest to make major life decisions or change the scope of your work. The big news in 2024 is that Pluto makes a teaser entrance into Aquarius on January 20, where it begins to influence friendships and bonds that develop with professional associations that interest you. On September 2, Pluto moves back into Capricorn, ready to launch the final regeneration stage of your life status by reminding you how well you have assimilated the lessons of productivity and success, before it transits back into Aquarius for good on November 19.

Jupiter

Aren't you the lucky one, Aries! You're entering a year where you complete the passage of Jupiter in Taurus in your solar second house of assets, money acquired, money spent, and self-development. If you can avoid a few bumps from transiting Uranus in Taurus in this same house, you will no doubt accumulate an increase in funds in the form of bonuses, raises, or speculative ventures. Despite challenges in the economic sphere, you earned diverse opportunities for increasing your net worth and adding to your retirement account. Enjoy the extra cash while you can and keep investing it wisely. While Jupiter is in Taurus, those of you born between March 26 and April 19 experience the greatest potential for financial growth.

Then Jupiter heads into a new sign, Gemini, on May 25, where it occupies your solar third house of communication, presenting you with a new perspective and tempting you with many options for enjoying prosperity. Aries born between March 19 and April 11 reap considerable benefits from Jupiter in this compatible sign through the end of the year. You may be heavily involved in community activities, upgrading electronic equipment, signing contracts, or writing creative or business material for publication. Local travel or short trips are likely to increase. Hopefully gasoline prices will level off and take a smaller bite out of your paycheck. Be sure to focus on improving communication goals by connecting with neighbors and forming friendly relationships while simultaneously bonding more with siblings and cousins. In 2024, Jupiter goes retrograde on October 9 and goes direct on February 4, 2025, in Gemini.

Saturn

Saturn, the great ringed planet, arrived in Pisces and your solar twelfth house in March 2023 and continues its rigorous journey in the company of Neptune in Pisces. These two planets couldn't be more opposite in outlook: Saturn wants you to adhere to a strict routine and obey all the rules, while dreamy Neptune advocates for making yourself approachable, cutting loose, playing, and tapping into your sensitive, psychic mind. While Saturn is nestled in your solar twelfth house of laid-back routines, you have a chance to do some deep reflective thinking and ponder your next moves, which could include researching opportunities for more inspiring employment and wrapping up loose ends that allow you to shed angst over health concerns, employment disruptions, or personal relationship loss. Developing new goals could be high on your agenda, even if you're not ready to share plans with others until next year. Many of you have hospital visits (planned and unplanned) with relatives and friends who are confined as part of your temporary routine in 2024. The presence of Neptune in Pisces in this same solar twelfth house may lessen the tendency to overthink perplexing issues and give your mind a break from wallowing in the energy of setbacks. While in Pisces this year, Saturn most affects Aries born between March 27 and April 10. Saturn's retrograde phase begins on June 29 and ends on November 15.

Uranus

Uranus, the planet of the unexpected, seems to charge through the universe at an erratic pace, as it has done since May 2018 in Taurus and your solar second house of assets, developmental opportunities, financial affairs, money you earn, and things you value. This year Uranus starts out in retrograde motion and goes direct on January 27, keeping an urgent, action-oriented pace through September 1, when it turns retrograde and remains so until January 30, 2025. In light of unpredictable economic trends, many of you are engaging in belt-buckling tactics to stretch your dollars as you cope with shrinking bargains for goods and services. You may be discarding, selling, or giving away material goods that have outlived their presence in your life. You may have experienced upheavals in the workplace that led to job loss, layoffs, or salary cuts, especially if you have planets in the second house of your birth chart. Just as swiftly, you're likely to receive a reassignment, a job offer, or an opportunity to move. Aries born between April 8 and 18 see the most activity from this Uranus transit in 2024. Use your enterprising wit and performance excellence to draw attractive new employment ventures your way.

Neptune

Watery Neptune travels a dreamy path that it started in April 2011 in Pisces and your solar twelfth house. Aries born between April 14 and 19 feel the most pressure to investigate Neptune's allure this year. When you focus on the twelfth house, think of sabbaticals, recuperation, and retreats that are conducive to dealing with complex people, places, and themes. Charitable interests may drive your passion this year, along with executing a program to help others recover from health, household, or economic setbacks that arose over bouts of illness, loss of income, rising inflation that affected purchasing power, and confidential knowledge of impending change that is unfolding in the operation of your work organization. With Saturn also in your solar twelfth house now, choices are challenging, and more corners of your life need careful consideration to make the right decisions. Metaphysics appeals to a good number of Aries, and the interest seems to peak in 2024 with quests to develop your psychic mind, open your third eye, and learn to take meditation to the next level. Opt for classes or online programs that specialize in these pursuits. Neptune goes retrograde on July 2 and resumes direct motion on December 7.

Pluto

In the resilient sign of Capricorn, Pluto continues its journey of knocking on your door to loosen resistance to inner change in a year that gives you a brief preview of what is coming when this planet finally enters Aquarius for the long haul in 2025. On January 20, Pluto arrives in Aquarius and dips its toes in the first two degrees of the Water Bearer's flowing realm of mutual interests and points you toward recognizing your need for togetherness and companionship. Only Aries born between March 19 and 22 are likely to feel the subtle shift in energy that speaks to your soul as if the plight of humanity were resting on your shoulders.

This short run in nonconforming Aquarius falls appropriately in your solar eleventh house until September 1, when the stickler side of Pluto retreats safely back into Capricorn. While this planet is in the collaborative realm of your solar eleventh house, you'll have a chance to scope out the value and integrity of new relationships, groups, and organizations. The arenas of politics, pressing for justice for unpopular causes, and redefining the economy in terms of the labor market could represent emerging interests for your curious mind. The 2024 retrograde period for Pluto starts on May 2 in Aquarius and concludes on October 11 in the last degree of Capricorn. In riding out Pluto's transit of this last loaded degree, only those born between April 18 and 20 are likely to have any skin in the game. Celebrate your success in ridding yourself of old burdens and approach life with new excitement.

How Will This Year's Eclipses Affect You?

This year's four eclipses, two lunar (Full Moon) and two solar (New Moon), are ready to generate intense periods that start to manifest a few months before their actual occurrence. The Libra/Aries cycle wraps up in March 2023 to make way for the Pisces/Virgo eclipses, the first of which makes its debut in September of 2024. Eclipses unfold in cycles involving all twelve signs of the zodiac and usually occur in pairs about two weeks apart. Never fear eclipses—just think of them as opportunities for growth that allow you to release old patterns. Expect surprises that elicit both positive and perplexing feelings and outcomes. The closer an eclipse is to a planet or point in your birth chart, the greater the importance it has in your life, especially if one of those planets is in the same degree as the eclipse.

The first Lunar Eclipse of 2024 falls on March 25 in your opposite sign of Libra and your solar seventh house of business and personal partners, spouses, collaborators, roommates, doctors, lawyers, therapists, advisers, consultants, enemies, and the public. You could be overwhelmed by what you discover about the status of current personal or professional relationships. Work on strengthening existing bonds, communicating freely with integrity, and fulfilling mutual goals. If you are aware of challenges, address them to release tension and modify the provocative direction the partnership is taking. If this eclipse highlights the strengths of your romantic relationship, you could be headed for the altar. Enjoy the bliss.

The year's first Solar Eclipse occurs on April 8 in Aries and your solar first house of appearance, assertive behavior, enterprise, personality, and self-development. You are consciously aware of your image and are likely to have goals to improve it through better health practices, fitness, nutrition, and counsel with grooming or medical specialists. Sometimes an eclipse here brings a windfall that allows you to splurge on a new wardrobe or invest in education to make you more competitive in your career. Take some before-and-after photos to highlight this phase.

On September 17, a Lunar Eclipse occurs in Pisces and your solar twelfth house of healing, metaphysical interests, privacy, retreats, and secrets. This powerful eclipse could lead to arguing relentlessly, over-talking or rambling, making accusatory statements, acting paranoid, misunderstanding the message, or overspending without consideration for budget limits. Practice self-control when you feel the pangs of anger welling up deep in your soul.

The final Solar Eclipse of 2024 takes place on October 2 in Libra and your solar seventh house of business and personal partners, significant others, collaborators, housemates, legal and medical professionals, consultants, enemies, and the public. If you have been on the fence about addressing any partnership issues that have come to light over the past year, here is your chance to acknowledge the source of your discomfort, decide on a solution, discuss options by engaging with involved partners, and use the expertise of neutral advisers to help you through the rough spots. If this eclipse is the clincher in your decision to marry, get engaged, or buy property, contact your attorney about updating your will or setting up a prenuptial agreement. Then celebrate new events and honor your success by offering a toast to your favorite inspirations.

Aries | January

Overall Theme

As the new year dawns, retrograde Mercury goes direct in Sagittarius and your solar ninth house, opening up options for the travel you postponed over the holidays. The year's first New Moon falls on January 11 in Capricorn and your solar tenth house of career, giving you a boost of confidence for advancing goals for job growth and showcasing your expertise via new responsibilities that could lead to a promotion or raise.

Relationships

If you are single, mingle with work pals and friends early in the month while passionate Venus and Mars occupy your solar tenth house and the possibility of romance sparks optimism. Set aside time for family gatherings on the 24th, when the Moon in Cancer sends loving vibes your way and gives you opportunities to bond with your partner and children as you enjoy favorite entertainment venues.

Success and Money

Visibility is key for expanding your career options this month, especially around the 11th. Share ideas with management and your team. Accept an assignment that puts you on the map to demonstrate your leadership style. Post-holiday sales net huge savings on wish-list items. Target savings when reviewing your 2024 budget.

Pitfalls and Potential Problems

Energy gets hectic when Uranus in Taurus goes direct in your solar second house on the 27th. Jupiter stabilizes a desire to binge on household goods, especially when your partner firmly nixes any impulse spending. Avoid a standoff on the January 25th Leo Full Moon over an old disagreement that resurfaces.

Rewarding Days

1, 11, 15, 24

Challenging Days

2, 16, 21, 25

Aries | February

Overall Theme

Pluto moved into early Aquarius last month and in February joins transiting Venus and Mars in this sign. Those of you with a newly formed romance may feel the magnetism of a quickly growing love cycle. Assess it. If you are already in a love relationship, take the time to examine what is working well and what needs help.

Relationships

The Moon is in your sign early on Valentine's Day, perfect for eliciting warmth and adoration for your love partner. The first half of the month spotlights those in charge in your workplace and the talented team you work with to get the job done. Save time for family on the 20th by planning a special off-night treat that includes a meal and a favorite game or movie.

Success and Money

The absence of retrograde planets this month makes for smoother collaboration on work projects and compliments from your boss. Satisfy customers by building trust and keeping them informed of timeline changes and progress in meeting milestones. Share recent project success with coworkers and review assignments to make use of unique talents that add value to work accomplishments. Accept a dinner invitation with an old friend on the 18th.

Pitfalls and Potential Problems

A power lunch with a colleague planned for February 9 might not get off the ground due to work demands. Reschedule for the 13th. Address a communication problem with a child on the 22nd that needs immediate attention. Deliver a straightforward message and omit the "maybes."

Rewarding Days

7, 13, 18, 20

Challenging Days

1, 9, 22, 24

Aries | March

Overall Theme

The keyword for the month is *action-oriented*, as the vernal equinox welcomes spring on March 19 and the first Lunar Eclipse of 2024 occurs on March 25 in Libra and your solar seventh house of partners. Venus and Mars conjunct in Aquarius aid engaged couples in setting a date and planning their wedding. You could feel more mentally restless than you usually do.

Relationships

Enjoy harmonious interactions with siblings, cousins, and neighbors on March 16 by hosting a family or neighborhood get-together. Schedule meetings with bosses on the 5th, when lunar aspects favor receptivity to new ideas and productive communication. Relatives at a distance may visit you starting on March 18.

Success and Money

Money sources work favorably for you this month, with offers from bankers for better mortgage rates and investment firms announcing new products. A salary increase is possible after the 13th following a favorable performance review that highlights your outstanding accomplishments. Spoil your partner with a surprise gift around the 22nd.

Pitfalls and Potential Problems

Midweek travel on the 3rd could be a bust when flight delays or cancellations work against you to get you to a conference on time. An invitation to a meal with a friend on the 7th might turn out to be a push to get you to contribute time and money to a cause that does not interest you. Overpriced recreational costs could lead to an argument on March 20.

Rewarding Days

5, 13, 16, 18

Challenging Days

3, 7, 20, 25

Aries | April

Overall Theme

Expect more than a few communication mix-ups this month with Mercury launching a retrograde cycle on the 1st and wrapping it up on the 25th in your sign, Aries. Your workplace is the site of increased activity, so expect to correct a fair share of errors or make adjustments to project components.

Relationships

Venus spends most of April in your sign, giving you opportunities for loving moments with your significant other. If you're a single Aries born between April 18 and 21, you have become more approachable and receptive this year to getting married. Stimulated by the April 8th Solar Eclipse in your sign, you are likely to agree to marry the love of your life.

Success and Money

On the 4th you could be the center of attention at your workplace when you receive news that a promotion or raise is on the way. Show gratitude for staff support by hosting a catered meal or invite them to a trendy lunch spot. Reserve April 10 as a good date for a birthday celebration and enjoy the cake and thoughtful gifts.

Pitfalls and Potential Problems

Mercury goes retrograde in your sign on April 1 in your solar first house, alerting you to watch for more April Fools' pranks than usual. A working lunch on the 4th related to pending project changes might yield disappointing results if participants are unable to agree on proposed alternative directives to meet the implementation date later this month.

Rewarding Days

2, 6, 10, 26

Challenging Days

1, 9, 21, 23

Aries | May

Overall Theme
You could be itching for a break from an intense routine by the time the fiery Full Moon in Sagittarius arrives on the 23rd in your solar ninth house of education and distant places. Why not make plans to travel to explore exciting new horizons? Keep an eye on Pluto as it makes its first retrograde station in early Aquarius and your solar eleventh house on May 2. Associations or group dealings in process could slow down or become less of a priority, or a friendship could cool down after showing promise.

Relationships
The planetary aspects for Mother's Day, May 12, are light and loving, perfect for honoring those special women in your life while the Moon is in Cancer. Bombard them with loving tributes and fill your mind with loving memories. Your relationship with your management team picks up momentum by the end of May.

Success and Money
Accomplishments tied to meeting goals earlier than expected draw you into an important conversation with your boss around the 27th. Enjoy the feedback and assimilate the shared information because it is leading to another step up the ladder of success. A surplus of money puts a smile on your face on May 7. If you are shopping, you'll do well in landing a desirable bargain.

Pitfalls and Potential Problems
Table contract negotiations on the 10th, when full disclosure of terms may not be included in the document. Read it over and list your questions. Review any issues you're having with professional affiliates or friends. Look for ways to clear up misunderstandings and resolve differences.

Rewarding Days
3, 7, 12, 27

Challenging Days
1, 10, 15, 25

Aries | June

Overall Theme

The New Moon on the 6th in Gemini and your solar third house has you dealing with community affairs, social invitations from neighbors, finalizing contract negotiations, and local travel. If your job makes traveling out of the area impossible, scope out a local vacation spot and make reservations for an enjoyable alternative. Compatible Mercury, Venus, and Jupiter in Gemini drive your lighter spirit.

Relationships

Siblings contact you about scheduling summer vacation time together, which has been difficult in recent years due to travel and economic hardships and lingering national health issues. Look for venues that accommodate all ages and plan a reunion for family members who want to attend. Get opinions from parents regarding preferred entertainment.

Success and Money

Around the 1st, spend money from a bonus to complete a makeover for a room in your home that is looking a bit tired. Higher earned interest on an investment around the 4th prompts you to look for additional places to accumulate cash. Your boss taps you for a supervisory position and recommends a few helpful training courses you can complete online.

Pitfalls and Potential Problems

Postpone buying a vehicle on the 3rd if you're shopping for a new car. You'll find a better deal toward the end of next month. Saturn turns retrograde on June 29 in Pisces and your solar twelfth house, giving you a chance to polish a speech, rethink project goals, and take care of a health matter.

Rewarding Days

1, 4, 23, 27

Challenging Days

3, 7, 13, 25

Aries | July

Overall Theme

Until July 20, your ruling planet, Mars, is moving through Taurus and your solar second house of money in the company of transiting Uranus in Taurus. Guard your assets and curb impulse spending. You're likely to have a friend or an ex-lover pop into your life out of the blue. Venus occupies Cancer and your solar fourth house of domestic affairs through the 11th, reminding you to cherish the love at home base.

Relationships

When the New Moon in Cancer on the 5th creates the momentum for hosting a festive gathering, enjoy the company of family members who extend their holiday visit for a few more days. Fun and celebrations create mood-elevating moments and memories of past Fourth of July activities. Treat your partner to a night out on the 12th and include a romantic interlude.

Success and Money

Jupiter in Gemini raises the stakes for high achievement, as the month focuses on performance in your solar third house of contracts and communication. The skillful negotiation you demonstrate nets you a bonus around the 30th, when the Moon meets Jupiter and highlights your professional activity and reputation.

Pitfalls and Potential Problems

Don't get sloppy with your work on the 9th by approving an expense that requires a higher level of review. The July 21st Full Moon in Capricorn opposes the Sun in Cancer, which could indicate collaborative friction over how to manage a prominent work project. Use diplomacy to put out the fireworks.

Rewarding Days

1, 5, 12, 30

Challenging Days

3, 9, 19, 21

Aries | August

Overall Theme

With Mars and Jupiter in Gemini this month, you'll enjoy many sociable moments and receive just as many invitations that you turn down due to an overcrowded calendar. The Leo New Moon on the 4th promises adventure and romance in your love-oriented solar fifth house with favorable aspects from the planets of love and friendship Venus, Jupiter, and Mars. Consider the first few days of August for a quick getaway.

Relationships

A weekend of family fun and games is a perfect way to bond on August 2–3 if you travel within driving distance of your home. Spend time with your honey on the 9th listening to music at a favorite entertainment venue. If relatives arrive for a short visit, be sure you're prepared to show them local attractions that include water sports.

Success and Money

If you're refinancing your home, the perfect day to have it appraised is August 11, when it shows its best assets and scores well. The last week of the month features an increase in investment dividends that encourages you to add more to the savings plan you initiated recently.

Pitfalls and Potential Problems

The third of this year's Mercury retrograde periods starts on August 5 in Virgo, moves back into Leo on the 14th, and turns direct in Leo on August 28. Use the time productively to edit reports you have been working on, and delay starting new projects or applying for a loan. Travel around the 14th could result in delays and detours.

Rewarding Days

3, 9, 11, 24

Challenging Days

12, 14, 19, 26

Aries | September

Overall Theme

Your social life continues to be highly active this month with Venus in party-loving Libra in aspect to Jupiter in Gemini. On the 15th, connect with friends you haven't seen in a while and invite them for a weekend visit. The second Lunar Eclipse of the year occurs in Pisces and your solar twelfth house on September 17, giving you a chance to recover from excessive celebrating.

Relationships

Workplace relationships take center stage this month through teaming up with colleagues to manage upcoming deadlines and satisfying your task-oriented boss. Later in the month, touch base with siblings and create bonds with new neighbors, getting to know those who recently moved to your community.

Success and Money

The New Moon on Labor Day, September 2, in Virgo and your solar sixth house reminds you to put in a requisition to purchase upgraded equipment when you return to work. Mercury moves into Virgo on the 9th, highlighting recent acquisitions such as work contracts, grants, and new hires. Medical issues could lead you to discover competent doctors to treat long-standing problem areas.

Pitfalls and Potential Problems

Uranus, the planet of the unexpected, starts off the month going retrograde in Taurus in your solar second house of money. Long-distance travel is likely to be canceled on the 11th. Excessive telephone tag is likely to occur for a couple of weeks. Lunar aspects on the 27th could stifle smooth communication and lead to misunderstandings. You may discover that a backlog of mail was lost or undelivered.

Rewarding Days

2, 13, 15, 22

Challenging Days

3, 11, 17, 27

Aries | October

Overall Theme

Expansive Jupiter turns retrograde on October 9. Then the veteran of transformation, Pluto, moves direct on October 11 in Capricorn and your solar tenth house of career and authority. The last Solar Eclipse of 2024 falls on October 2 in Libra and your solar seventh house, highlighting personal and business partners and how you interact with them.

Relationships

Interactions with a variety of people occupy your time in October, revolving around cousins and siblings, neighbors, and teachers. Matters connected with your partner and relatives at a distance call for your attention, and plans will come together for the enjoyment of all. Invite nearby family members for a meal on the 23rd and enjoy the chatter and compliments on your delicious menu.

Success and Money

Camaraderie gels on the 8th, putting you in a happy mood to tackle innovative humanitarian projects and engage the attention of backers who support the missions. A follow-up meeting finalizes details of a business proposal. Legal matters and travel get the green light on the 8th.

Pitfalls and Potential Problems

If you haven't had enough sleep around the Aries Full Moon on the 17th, you'll benefit from an impromptu day off to recharge your internal battery. Say no to a party on the 4th, but accept a romantic dinner invitation on the 5th. Moderation pays off.

Rewarding Days

2, 5, 8, 23

Challenging Days

4, 10, 20, 25

Aries | November

Overall Theme
By November 8, you'll start receiving holiday invitations for the upcoming round of festive parties scheduled over the next two months. You could be inspired to host one of them yourself. See what happens when you get your network of eclectic partygoers together to savor the fine food and toast the merriment of the occasion.

Relationships
In addition to relatives from near and far, you will also host a couple of close friends at your Thanksgiving table. Children show excitement over holiday celebrations and want to help with food preparation and related tasks. Remember your favorite charity with a generous gift for covering the cost of holiday foods.

Success and Money
The November 1st New Moon in Scorpio highlights your cash on hand to cover extra treats for holiday meals and purchase gifts on the wish lists of loved ones. Discuss menu plans for hosting Thanksgiving with your spouse on the 19th, and place your order for specialty foods and desserts. Savor the inner joy you're feeling over the anticipated reunion with loved ones.

Pitfalls and Potential Problems
Saturn in Pisces stations to move direct on the 15th, granting leeway to resume your plans for business and personal expansion. The head of your organization could be in a testy mood on the 7th, so don't rock the boat with bad news. Be sure out-of-town guests arrive before the 25th to avoid Mercury retrograde travel delays.

Rewarding Days
1, 8, 19, 30

Challenging Days
7, 10, 17, 26

Aries | December

Overall Theme

This month features two New Moons, the first in Sagittarius on December 1 and the second in Capricorn on December 30. If you have a case of wanderlust, look for bargain airfares and book a holiday trip after the 15th to surprise your spouse with a relaxing adventure in a bucket-list locale. Attend a party on the 14th and enjoy toasting old friends.

Relationships

December is all about nurturing family ties as the holiday season brings you closer to your significant other, children, siblings and their offspring, grandparents, cousins, and those who feel like family. You savor intimate moments with your spouse at a lovely restaurant around the 23rd, toasting each other with endearing sentiments.

Success and Money

Business partners and company authorities compliment your stellar productivity on the 3rd as they hand you a check as a performance bonus. Use the money to replace an appliance that could use an upgrade. Finalize plans for holiday entertaining by the 21st, and invite new neighbors to your holiday meal to welcome them to the area. Toast your guests and wish them the best holiday ever.

Pitfalls and Potential Problems

Mars stations to move retrograde in Leo on December 6, while Neptune in Pisces turns direct on the 7th. Early on the 15th, the Full Moon in Gemini occurs opposite Mercury going direct in Sagittarius. Avoid travel on that day. The 11th is a day to keep cool and avoid impulsively causing a blowup.

Rewarding Days

3, 9, 14, 23

Challenging Days

2, 11, 15, 21

Aries Action Table

These dates reflect the best—but not the only—times for success and ease in these activities, according to your Sun sign.

	JAN	FEB	MAR	APR	MAY	JUN	JUL	AUG	SEP	OCT	NOV	DEC
Move			16				30				30	
Romance		13					12			2		23
Seek counseling/ coaching	24			2	12	27			15			
Ask for a raise	11	7		26		23		11				3
Vacation					7				22	8		
Get a loan			13					24			1	

Taurus

**The Bull
April 20 to May 21**

♉

Element: Earth	Glyph: Bull's head
Quality: Fixed	Anatomy: Throat, neck
Polarity: Yin/feminine	Color: Green
Planetary Ruler: Venus	Animal: Cattle
Meditation: I trust myself and others	Myths/Legends: Isis and Osiris, Ceridwen, Bull of Minos
Gemstone: Emerald	House: Second
Power Stones: Diamond, blue lace agate, rose quartz	Opposite Sign: Scorpio
	Flower: Violet
Key Phrase: I have	Keyword: Conservation

The Taurus Personality

Strengths, Talents, and the Creative Spark

Resourcefulness becomes you, Taurus. You were born ready, willing, and able to express yourself through the accumulation of knowledge that you apply to obtain financial success. You are the zodiac sign most concerned with the income-oriented second house of earning power, which includes money you have at your disposal, the way you earn your income, how you prefer to spend your assets, the types of goods and amenities you value, and the material benefits you seek. You cultivate relationships with individuals who offer financial services, such as bankers, builders, investors, loan officers, and real estate specialists. The vision you hold about personal success includes lucrative, prestigious work that makes you stand out from the crowd in a way that leads those who seek your expertise to feel at ease with what you offer, exuding a feeling of trust and honesty. As a member of the sign of the Bull, you are both an earth sign and the first of the four fixed signs known for a passion to succeed and the determination to overcome any petty annoyance or barrier that stands in the way.

You are endowed with a wide array of career choices, and once you decide on the path you want to take, you are seldom dissuaded from following it and manifest growth through self-development options that keep you marketable in the talent pool. If you own the management of a project, you focus on it intently and see it through to completion. With Venus as the planetary ruler of your sign, you have endless ways to apply your charm. Creative work appeals to many a Taurus, covering a broad spectrum, such as food and fine dining, from a chef to a restaurant owner; decorating and design enterprises related to furnishing homes and offices, consulting with remodeling experts, or painting the interiors and exteriors of homes; and the world of glamor, including hair, makeup, color coordination, and fashion. Musically inclined Tauruses emulate Venus with a classically trained voice or mastery of multiple musical instruments. You could be a writer of lyrics, composer of the score, or choreographer of dance moves. I know a few Tauruses who travel worldwide with a troupe bringing Broadway shows to the masses.

Intimacy and Personal Relationships

Potential partners undergo a great deal of scrutiny once your heart tells you this is the one to pursue. You can't take a chance on disrupting the rhythm of the love that is simmering inside your caring heart, so you opt to pursue your loved one in a variety of settings, making sure they have all the right moves. You take love seriously, often placing the object of your affection on a high perch to worship and adore. If you have ever loved and lost, you never forget the lessons you learned and look for assurance that trust is present, along with mutual attraction, love, and affection. If you are unsure of your place in your significant other's universe, you can become possessive and uneasy in your skin. Sometimes that is a signal to let go because the relationship is not working. Friendships could also run the course due to a lackluster response to getting together. Whether male or female, you know all the right romantic gestures and specialize in settings that allow you to pamper your prospective partner with expensive flowers, wine, music, and gourmet food. Find an adoring Virgo, Cancer, Capricorn, or Pisces who wants to share your loyalty and love.

Values and Resources

You wrote the book on autonomy when it comes to valuing ownership of your work and the products you create to keep the organizational environment running smoothly. Working alone appeals to you, even though you participate fully in a group setting. When you're finished with your product, you're willing to show your stuff. Any boss worth their salt treasures the way your structured routines and solid reliability showcase your contributions and give your team visibility and prestige. Security is one of your drivers, and you expect to be amply compensated to pay the bills and have money left over to fund retirement, savings, and vacation spending. As a Taurus, you really prefer to wait until you have saved money to purchase the quality and type of home, furnishings, and accessories you cherish rather than spend cash on inferior products that won't last and don't meet your standards. You can be patient up to a point in training new employees, but the lazy ones don't cut it for you, especially when they watch others do most of the work and chime in near deadlines to add points that others have already made. Nothing makes you feel more at ease than paying off loans quickly and maintaining a high credit rating.

Blind Spots and Blockages

One of the continuous battles you fight is finding a balance between an obsessive need to accumulate material abundance (and the demands this quest places on your psyche) and the need to acquire inner happiness as you work on increasing spiritual progress that affects the true picture of your self-worth. Personal assets and your passion for preserving them can drive a wedge that prevents you from achieving balance in personal and professional relationships. If you are too much of a workaholic, you might be squandering the emotional depth that you could be sharing with your cherished loved ones and sacrificing quality time that is precious to enriching your relationships. Find the words to let others know how you feel and offer praise to children, workmates, and your significant other. Learn the true meaning of give and take.

Goals and Success

The number-one motivator in your list of goals is lifelong stability, which includes a steady, secure position in a firm that pays well, offers superior benefits, and has a compensation plan to ensure steady raises and promotions that keep up with inflation and encourage loyalty to the organization's mission and philosophy. You are multitalented and desire a job that lets you use your well-honed skills and bring your expertise to the table. In both your home and work life, you prefer pleasant surroundings that are orderly and clean, so clutter is never an issue. Along with having a doting partner whom you love to spoil and pamper, you cherish family and favorite traditions affiliated with it. You prefer to invest in innovative electronic equipment that gets the job done and minimizes do-overs. Keeping an eye on budget allocation and efficiency is paramount to your career success.

Taurus Keywords for 2024
Resources, revenue, riches

The Year Ahead for Taurus

As you enter 2024, Jupiter, the planet of benevolence and expansion, occupies your sign and your solar first house through May 25, giving you the opportunity to manifest prosperity and pay down debt. If a new job is part of this cycle, you most likely found one that has a higher salary base and attractive benefits that nurture your security gene and stimulate your goal to be more competitive. That will happen before long when Jupiter moves into Gemini on May 25 and pulls you toward classes that focus on increasing your revenue and making it work productively through retirement and beyond. The other planet that occupies Taurus at this time is Uranus, which turns direct on January 27 and lives up to its reputation for creating upheavals, leaving you with upsetting situations to figure out quickly and solve. This planetary shakeup inducer will finally leave your solar first house in 2025 to wrap up its seven-year cycle in your sign. Be on the lookout for a variety of surprises.

Your solar eleventh house continues to host laid-back Saturn in Pisces, adding incentive to your desire to build new, less frenetic networks of compatible advocates who support charitable causes and offer relief to those who have suffered loss in the past few years. Also occupying your solar eleventh house is impressionable Neptune, on a mystical journey through the last few degrees of Pisces, where it adds insight to the compatibility of personal friendships and professional organizations.

The last of the outer planets to weigh in this year is Pluto, occupying your solar ninth house of the higher mind and distant locations. You can bet that Pluto is at work helping you clarify your outlook on education, relocation, writing, and foreign interests. With greater realization of the truth, you can more easily release blocks that have stood in the way of progress in these areas. This year Pluto spends a few months in its successor sign, Aquarius, giving you a preview of what life will be like when the planet of transformation enters your solar tenth house of career and ambition for good. In 2024, two eclipses occur in your solar sixth house and one each in your solar twelfth and eleventh houses. Elevate the quality of your life by launching successful new beginnings.

Jupiter

How much do you know about Jupiter? Most individuals are unaware that this lucky planet does much more than set you up for a lottery win or increase your riches. Taurus, you can usually count on a growth cycle when Jupiter visits your solar first house and ushers in a bevy of innovative options to consider for action during the year. Optimism soars as you expand the scope of your goals. Whether you're taking on work projects or a household renovation, planning the vacation of a lifetime, or preparing for the birth of a baby, your activity level increases and stretches your self-confidence. Invitations pour in from near and far, and the temptation to binge on the wide array of food offerings can easily expand your waistline if you indulge, one of the quirks of Jupiter passing through your first house. A key concept of the first house is image, and that ties in beautifully with the condition of your health. You will get clues about not eating so fast via gastric upsets that force you to keep antacids on hand. When your favorite clothes are too tight, Jupiter bellows that buying a new wardrobe is a strong yet expensive possibility unless you demonstrate the discipline to drop the unwanted pounds. Enjoy the burst of prosperity when Jupiter moves into Gemini and your solar second house of assets and income on May 25 and gives you insight into managing rising interest rates to fund housing and the spiraling cost of food, goods, and services. Learn techniques for negotiating a salary increase, competing for bonuses, and implementing cost-saving measures. In 2024, Jupiter's retrograde period begins on October 9 and ends on February 4, 2025, in Gemini, most affecting Tauruses born between April 3 and May 11.

Saturn

Known as a stern taskmaster, Saturn continues its cycle that began in March 2023 in Pisces and your solar eleventh house of goals, friendships, organizational affiliations, and work teams. Saturn is committed to making sure you keep your promise to carry out responsibilities you made to business leaders and members of professional groups, your personal goals for self and family, and your vision for improving conditions for humanitarian causes. When Saturn moves through this house, even in the less intense sign of Pisces, you are sure to be reminded if you are lax about attending important meetings or ignoring requests for input to shape the operating agenda and implement agreed-upon goals. Phoning it in could be a reason for termination. This planet, famous for nagging until action is evident, will help you manifest success when you expand powerful networks that show support for the planned accomplishments of the organization. When Saturn lands in this house for its two-and-a-half-year transit, your work takes a considerable analytical turn to meet demands, sometimes with little advance notice. What an asset your signature common sense becomes during this high-action period. Those of you born between April 23 and May 10 are most highlighted during this cycle. Saturn's retrograde period begins on June 29 and ends on November 15.

Uranus

When you have Uranus, the most unpredictable planet of all, occupying your Sun sign and taking up space in your solar first house of enterprise, individuality, and passion, you must be Taurus in 2024, hoping to make it through the final phase of this erratic seven-year transit. I believe you when you say that you are exhausted from the stormy behavior and blustery dustups that evolve from Uranus explosions. Not only are you edgier than ever, but people you encounter who are normally calm seem ready for a conflict without warning—just like the unique weather patterns worldwide that are shaking up the status quo. Thank goodness you prefer to display your even temperament and reasonable approach to solving differences. Those of you born between May 8 and 19 notice the impact of this Uranus passage the most in 2024. On September 1, Uranus turns retrograde and remains so until January 30, 2025. Many individuals report that when Uranus transits their first house, they are more nervous and jittery than usual. Assess what types of conditions make you feel that way, and use mind-calming methods and exercise to control runaway feelings. Build a balanced support network to sustain you during the remaining months of this transit.

Neptune

Keeping company with transiting Saturn in Pisces is dreamy Neptune, celebrating its thirteenth year in your solar eleventh house and setting precedents for how to manage plans, goals, dreams, and wishes as well as honor diverse associations and friendships. Longtime contacts may notice that you are taking more risks to improve the quality of professional and organizational settings, including the way you engage in collaborative work and assume leadership for humanitarian initiatives. You have lost the intensity but not your edge. The spiritual side of you is harmoniously awakening this year and blending well with your steady Taurus personality. Neptune goes retrograde on July 2 in the last degree of Pisces and resumes direct motion on December 7. Let's hear it for integrating your psychic gifts and visionary insight into the analytical approach you use in getting your work in outstanding form to meet deadlines and please your boss. Since April 2011, the compassionate planet has influenced your approach to work and awakened your sensitivity to your true calling. This year, the members of your sign who have the most contact with this energy are those born between May 17 and 20. Don't be surprised if you embark on a new career in the next two years.

Pluto

All the way back in January 2008, Pluto took up residence in Capricorn and your solar ninth house of advanced educational studies, the higher mind, foreign lands and cultures, publishing, religion, and long-distance travel. In January, Pluto moves out of its shell and shifts into early Aquarius and your solar tenth house, turning retrograde on May 2 in Aquarius and then going direct on October 11 in the last degree of Capricorn. Those with birthdays between April 20 and 22 will notice the presence of Pluto in hard aspect to their Sun during this period. You'll likely either feel a wake-up call or retreat from any push to act. Last year Pluto advanced to the first degree of Aquarius on March 23, then turned retrograde on May 1 and retreated back into Capricorn in mid-June. The time just wasn't quite right then to let go of the stubborn blocks that remain. What resonates with you in this final year of Pluto's transit of Capricorn, and what facets of your life are you ready to completely transform? Go ahead—let go of the secrets, guilt, and simmering angst.

How Will This Year's Eclipses Affect You?

This year's four eclipses, two lunar (Full Moon) and two solar (New Moon), are ready to generate intense periods that start to manifest a few months before their actual occurrence. The Libra/Aries cycle wraps up in March 2023 to make way for the Pisces/Virgo eclipses, the first of which makes its debut in September of 2024. Eclipses unfold in cycles involving all twelve signs of the zodiac and usually occur in pairs about two weeks apart. Never fear eclipses—just think of them as opportunities for growth that allow you to release old patterns. Expect surprises that elicit both positive and perplexing feelings and outcomes. The closer an eclipse is to a planet or point in your birth chart, the greater the importance it has in your life, especially if one of those planets is in the same degree as the eclipse.

The first Lunar Eclipse of 2024 falls on March 25 in Libra and your solar sixth house of daily routines, organizational skills, health, nutrition, pets, and colleagues. You could be bowled over by the facets of workplace efficiency that are in need of attention through streamlining. Add value to the operation by eliminating practices that constrain the flow of productivity and are the subject of complaints behind the scenes. Pay attention to medical ailments that you normally brush off, and be sure to schedule doctor visits and routine testing along with a visit to the dentist. This is a good year to modify the intensity of your work schedule and balance your life with quality work breaks.

The year's first Solar Eclipse occurs on April 8 in Aries and your solar twelfth house of charity, visiting the sick, healing from ailments and injuries, regrouping, taking a sabbatical, studying metaphysics, and keeping secrets. If the burden of keeping too much inside starts to affect your health or concentration, it may be time to relieve your mind and work on a strategy that helps you get a good night's sleep. Don't agree to anything that goes against your life philosophy. Improve your self-talk and find the courage to discuss issues with any individuals who may be involved. One of them could be your boss. Meditate on what would be the perfect job and then go find it.

The site of the second Lunar Eclipse of 2024, which occurs on September 17 in Pisces, is your solar eleventh house of goals, plans, groups, humanitarian projects, friendships, and diverse professional associations. This house is on energy overload, sharing the limelight with transiting Neptune and Saturn in Pisces. You'll be worn out from the competing vibrations you sense from peers, members of organizations, heads of associations, the management team, and your best friend. More individuals than you could ever imagine might be asking for a piece of your mind, a donation, a membership application, or your resume. Keep priority goals in front of you and you'll soon be saying that dreams really do come true.

Mark October 2 as the date of the final Solar Eclipse of 2024, which occurs in Libra and your solar sixth house of routines and schedules, the main thrust of your workday, task management, teammates, cooking and nutrition, your health, and care of animal companions. Since the middle of spring, you may have been exploring medical complaints with a variety of doctors, paid a healthy sum to your dentist, shed extra pounds to meet a weight goal, or enrolled in a fitness program. Some of you may have lost a cherished pet and are contemplating adopting a rescue animal. Congratulate yourself on your resilience.

Taurus | January

Overall Theme

Mercury in Sagittarius moves direct on the 1st and puts a winter get-away high on your new year agenda. The Capricorn New Moon on the 11th could reunite you with distant relatives and friends for a trip that promises fun and relaxation. Uranus in your sign turns direct on the 27th, giving you the green light to fund a special project that has ample rewards attached to a successful outcome.

Relationships

You and your partner are in a festive mood on the 6th, possibly excited about upcoming travel. Share feelings and grow closer through the 10th. Group members rally at a meeting on the 15th to support a high-visibility merger. Single Tauruses share a first date with a new love interest.

Success and Money

Spoil children with a high-tech game on the 29th if you have promised them a treat. You still have leftover holiday cash to spend on the home furnishings you've been waiting to buy at a post-holiday sale. Put more cash into your vacation fund.

Pitfalls and Potential Problems

Avoid conflict with your work team over project details on the 3rd, when you know half the group is split over strategies. Assign members to a work exercise to look at pros and cons of options. At the January 25th Full Moon in Leo, you may want to keep a low profile at home base when tensions run high.

Rewarding Days

6, 10, 15, 29

Challenging Days

3, 16, 21, 25

Taurus | February

Overall Theme

Celebrate the Lunar New Year of the Dragon on February 10 and watch your fortunes change as you put upcoming plans to work for you after the Aquarius New Moon on the 9th. Meet your friends at your favorite restaurant and wish them abundant prosperity as you hand them red envelopes filled with a cash gift.

Relationships

Snap up a travel bargain on the 7th and treat your spouse to a mini vacation on a romantic island as part of your Valentine's Day celebration. Riches come to you in the form of a loving relationship with your soulmate. Set aside Sunday, February 25, as a day dedicated to pleasing your children. Agree on an entertainment venue the whole family will enjoy and treat everyone to a memorable meal.

Success and Money

Give consideration to job announcements that are circulating in your workplace. If you are interested in making a change, engage your boss to state your interest. Show your motivation for taking on new responsibilities and increasing your salary. Venus, Mars, and Jupiter are compatible this month.

Pitfalls and Potential Problems

Stay away from squabbles over money on the 4th, when there is the potential for arguments about paying off credit card debt before buying new appliances. A date with a romantic prospect may not be what you bargained for on the 24th. Take this as a sign that you need greater compatibility.

Rewarding Days

3, 7, 10, 25

Challenging Days

4, 21, 24, 26

Taurus | March

Overall Theme

Pluto in Aquarius joins a lineup of fixed signs early this month, with Venus and Mars in Aquarius and Jupiter and Uranus in your sign. Romantic encounters offer many options. They could be passionate and pleasing or argumentative and negative. March 13 is a good day to just chill and schedule a little spa time and a mental health break.

Relationships

March 1–3 could be a memorable weekend for those getting engaged, starting a honeymoon, giving birth to a baby, or hosting a child's wedding. Invite favorite people for celebratory gatherings to honor these milestones. A romantic tone on the 5th could come from a long-distance connection.

Success and Money

The first few weeks of this month favor your financial picture. Study increases in earned interest on accounts with your partner. Talk over strategies for investing in outlets that build cash reserves. Discuss the possibility of moving with your spouse if you feel you have outgrown your home. Research desirable neighborhoods.

Pitfalls and Potential Problems

Your boss seems to be in a penny-pinching mood on the 8th that sets the tone for the rest of the month. Don't ask for a raise. The year's first Lunar Eclipse falls in Libra and your solar sixth house on the 25th and reignites the tension you've been sensing for the last three weeks, especially on the 19th, when communication seems strained.

Rewarding Days

2, 5, 13, 21

Challenging Days

1, 8, 19, 22

Taurus | April

Overall Theme

Prepare for the year's first Mercury retrograde on the 1st in Aries and your solar twelfth house and then its direct station on the 25th, freeing you to proceed with plans you put on hold. The Aries New Moon on the 8th marks the year's first Solar Eclipse and occurs in your solar twelfth house. If you are a single Taurus, give some thought to engaging with potential love interests who have come into your life.

Relationships

Family visitors arrive from out of town for a short visit around the 3rd and look for insight from you in solving a personal dilemma. You'll have to compose yourself on the 4th when your boss has a hot-button item that needs your personal attention. A member of a professional association invites you to lunch on the 6th and requests your help in facilitating a key meeting.

Success and Money

On the 11th you could learn that you have been nominated for a prestigious monetary award. Follow up with your boss and express gratitude for this honor. You receive written testimonials and learn that other authorities have also noticed your excellent performance record.

Pitfalls and Potential Problems

You butt heads with a key contact on the 9th and wrangle with this individual again on the 22nd. This connection calls you stubborn and a few other unflattering names. Get to the bottom of the conflict to avoid having the issue go to a higher authority.

Rewarding Days

3, 6, 8, 11

Challenging Days

4, 9, 16, 22

Taurus | May

Overall Theme

The New Moon in Taurus on the 7th puts you in the mood for beach travel, but your filled calendar tells you to stick to the workload and enjoy brief outings with friends. One of them pops up on the 3rd and you start the weekend with old pals who introduce you to individuals hiring people with your skill set. Get tasks out of the way so you can enjoy your anticipated vacation in July.

Relationships

Cousins call you around the 12th to save the date for a Memorial Day gathering. Check the schedule with family members to make sure the time is agreeable. Neighbors may ask you to help with a commemorative concert and picnic on the 25th that honors local heroes. Gladly participate.

Success and Money

The first two weeks of the month look promising for financial transactions, whether you sign a loan contract, purchase a home, or transfer money to a savings account. If you are expecting a bonus, it comes through after the 12th. Job offers are a possibility after the 17th.

Pitfalls and Potential Problems

Who is stringing you along in a business deal? Put it to rest before Pluto turns retrograde on the 2nd in Aquarius and your solar tenth house of career. Look closely at insurance policies related to home or business deals. Don't modify building plans on either the 15th or the 24th until you have answers regarding potential cost overruns.

Rewarding Days

9, 13, 18, 22

Challenging Days

3, 5, 11, 31

Taurus | June

Overall Theme

Look at the nice lineup of Gemini planets this month, starting with Mercury, Venus, and Jupiter, plus the New Moon on June 6. The energy feels hospitable, friendly, and energetic, the perfect time for an outdoor spring activity. Host a cookout around the time of the summer solstice and prepare your favorite recipes. Guests will love your delicious cooking.

Relationships

Conversation with family members is upbeat and everyone feels the support of a safe sounding board. Input regarding upcoming vacation fare nets a few welcome surprises that delight all members. Enjoy an excursion with your work group compliments of your manager on the 26th.

Success and Money

Collaboration among team members strengthens the goal to complete the current stage of project development this month. A meeting to review strategies could prove successful on the 4th. Travel and entertainment venues that mesh with current vacation plans offer satisfying options through the end of the year. Jupiter's recent entry into your solar second house of money adds a cash source to your purchasing power.

Pitfalls and Potential Problems

The tone at home base is volatile on the 11th after family members lay their cards on the table over dissatisfaction with house rules and nonexistent accountability. The array of planets on the 13th challenges a date option, so stay home. Saturn in Pisces turns retrograde on June 29 in your solar eleventh house of friendship, possibly affecting the likelihood of meeting a close friend for a scheduled visit.

Rewarding Days

2, 4, 10, 26

Challenging Days

3, 11, 13, 21

Taurus | July

Overall Theme

Jupiter in Gemini graces your solar second house of money now, making favorable connections with Mercury and Venus in Leo and triggering a number of unexpected sales, jewelry bargains, gifts, or bonuses. If staying home for the Fourth of July, plan a backyard buffet and invite the neighbors.

Relationships

Social networking is a priority for you this month, whether you are at home or traveling. Siblings, cousins, and neighbors accept your invitation to a festive gathering for the holiday. A coworker invites you to a party around the 12th that has you raving over the food and asking for recipes to supplement your gourmet collection.

Success and Money

Your support for a family charity supplies those in need with bedding, linens, and sundries for the bathroom. Giving to those in need is a sacred gift to you. When you suggest donating food to a well-known local food pantry, your work team enthusiastically responds and several volunteer to collect and deliver food.

Pitfalls and Potential Problems

Neptune in Pisces goes retrograde in your solar eleventh house on July 2, right ahead of the Fourth of July holiday. Make sure your home windows are closed securely, with no evident signs of leaks. Prepare yourself for a deluge of rain, thunder, and lightning if you are traveling. After a productive workday on the 12th, your boss discovers a key section of the project missing that necessitates calling staff to work on Saturday the 13th.

Rewarding Days

6, 12, 18, 20

Challenging Days

4, 13, 15, 24

Taurus | August

Overall Theme

With Mercury moving retrograde in Virgo and your solar fifth house on the 5th, travel works best for you after August 29, when the planet is again in direct motion in Leo. Short trips please your family, especially after Labor Day next month. Head to the beach once the crowds thin out after the 11th. Paint the fence or your mother's front porch on the 25th.

Relationships

The management staff may offer weekly team-building workshops on the premises to strengthen interaction and solve problems more efficiently. Invite a sibling to join you for a short getaway on the 29th to explore museums of interest. Outings with friends and neighbors are perfect vehicles to wrap up summer's fun. Be generous but cautious about picking up too much of the tab.

Success and Money

Decide on a new vehicle after assessing the cost of keeping it on the road and the price of fuel. Are you ready for an electric car yet, an option you have for spending hard-earned bonus money? What classes are you looking into for personal self-development? Enroll by August 2 for a guaranteed space.

Pitfalls and Potential Problems

The Full Moon in Aquarius on the 19th could start the workweek off on a cranky note, when several employees are late for work and admit they packed too much into their weekend. If you're in charge, let it go, cancel the morning meeting, and call the troops together for an early afternoon update.

Rewarding Days

9, 11, 25, 29

Challenging Days

5, 12, 19, 22

Taurus | September

Overall Theme

On September 17, the final Lunar Eclipse of the year falls in Pisces and your solar eleventh house of friends and affiliates, one of your busiest houses of the year, bringing attention to personal and professional goals, membership agreements, and revenue marked for funding new enterprises.

Relationships

The best bonding time with children and sports team members occurs on the 2nd. If you coach, treat the team to burgers and shakes to welcome them to a new season of friendly competition. Invite your boss and family to Sunday dinner on the 15th, engaging in friendly trivia games after the meal.

Success and Money

During the first week of September, line up a decorator to give you an estimate for sprucing up your home office. Bond with neighbors at a community meeting that addresses local priorities on the 26th. Ask for input from members to suggest a fundraising initiative for the fall giving season that supports one of the organizations in greatest need of help and take a vote.

Pitfalls and Potential Problems

Uranus goes retrograde in Taurus on the 1st and puts you on alert to compare prices for proposed contract work for home services. Business travel flights could be delayed on the 12th. Don't book another flight, as there is a good chance it will happen again. The Moon in Leo on the 27th in hard aspect to Venus could put an emotional chill on household harmony.

Rewarding Days

2, 15, 21, 26

Challenging Days

3, 12, 17, 27

Taurus | October

Overall Theme

Keep your eyes on your money when Jupiter, the planet of prosperity, goes retrograde in Gemini and your solar second house of income on the 9th. If you have ordered any big-ticket items, follow up closely to make sure the specs are accurate and no add-on costs have been applied. Take advantage of networking opportunities that cater to career moves on the 8th.

Relationships

Love blooms and cordial relationships skyrocket when plans for a romantic getaway materialize on October 5. Enjoy the quality of enduring friendships by attending a class reunion and bonding again with favorite people and faculty members. Thank a medical professional who made spot-on recommendations following a diagnosis.

Success and Money

The Solar Eclipse dawns favorably in Libra and your solar sixth house of daily routines on October 2, signaling excellent news and relief over findings in your comprehensive health tests. Your partner scores a windfall for joint savings when a generous bonus check clears the week of October 6. Celebrate a friend's promotion with a lunch date. Express your pleasure at your colleague's success.

Pitfalls and Potential Problems

After a long retrograde period, Pluto in Capricorn turns direct on October 11 and makes its way back into Aquarius on November 19, where it applies well-directed transformation to your solar tenth house of career. Financial advice needs closer scrutiny on the 2nd, suggesting you check numbers carefully. Watch sparks from temperamental managers on the 13th.

Rewarding Days

5, 8, 15, 23

Challenging Days

4, 13, 17, 25

Taurus | November

Overall Theme

November is another action-oriented month for planetary activity. On the 1st, the New Moon in Scorpio and your solar seventh house has you conferring with your partner about plans for the upcoming holidays. You love a big, beautiful feast on Thanksgiving and suggest hosting a formal meal to include a sumptuous multi-course menu. Get the invitations out early and take off most of the week to work on food preparation and décor.

Relationships

Siblings and their spouses and family join yours, along with parents who are living nearby. Accept a party invitation from dear friends on the 11th to exchange personal news. Invite neighbors for cocktails and appetizers on the 19th. Saturn in Pisces moves direct in your solar eleventh house on the 15th just as college-age children arrive home.

Success and Money

Welcome a holiday bonus from your employer around the 8th and put these riches toward holiday expenses and gifts for your family. You and your partner are the designated "it" couple based on all the charity work you have taken on to uplift holiday spirits, selflessly honoring those in need.

Pitfalls and Potential Problems

The Taurus Full Moon in your solar first house on the 15th could zap your energy, sending you to bed early. The cost of food and beverages escalates beyond your allocated budget when you pay for a catered luncheon for the staff on the 18th. Mercury in Sagittarius goes retrograde on the 25th just as guests begin to arrive for Thanksgiving, increasing the possibility of weather or flight delays.

Rewarding Days

1, 3, 11, 19

Challenging Days

5, 9, 18, 22

Taurus | December

Overall Theme

This last month of 2024 is full of activity and new beginnings, with two New Moons, a Full Moon, Neptune in Pisces moving direct on the 7th, and Mercury stationing to move direct on December 15 in Sagittarius. Many of you will start the month traveling for business and end the month traveling for pleasure. Wrap up holiday shopping before you hit the airport.

Relationships

Be mindful of the health of relatives living at a distance and share love and caring gestures toward them. Have a festive lunch with dear friends on the 9th, reminiscing over past holiday happenings. Plan holiday-themed entertainment with children on the 27th.

Success and Money

You have done wonders with your holiday budget purchasing gifts for family members and close friends that reflect your excellent taste and appreciation for quality. No doubt the gifts are wrapped and ready to send early in the month. By showing commitment to charities that count on your contributions to lift the spirits of those who need help, you enjoy much-deserved rewards.

Pitfalls and Potential Problems

Mars turns retrograde in Leo on December 6 in your solar fourth house, indicating the presence of unusually high and possibly erratic energy at home base. Temper outbursts or arguments are possible on the 12th and 21st. The passionate planet will move direct on February 23, 2025. This Mars transit increases the likelihood of delayed travel plans and the need to follow safety guidelines.

Rewarding Days

9, 14, 22, 27

Challenging Days

6, 8, 12, 21

Taurus Action Table

These dates reflect the best—but not the only—times for success and ease in these activities, according to your Sun sign.

	JAN	FEB	MAR	APR	MAY	JUN	JUL	AUG	SEP	OCT	NOV	DEC
Move	10		5				6			23		4
Romance	6	10						11	2		1	
Seek counseling/ coaching					18			29			11	
Ask for a raise				11		26			15			
Vacation		7		3			20					31
Get a loan			2		9					8		

Gemini

The Twins
May 21 to June 21

Ⅱ

Element: Air

Quality: Mutable

Polarity: Yang/masculine

Planetary Ruler: Mercury

Meditation: I explore my inner worlds

Gemstone: Tourmaline

Power Stones: Ametrine, citrine, emerald, spectrolite, agate

Key Phrase: I think

Glyph: Pillars of duality, the Twins

Anatomy: Shoulders, arms, hands, lungs, nervous system

Colors: Bright colors, orange, yellow, magenta

Animals: Monkeys, talking birds, flying insects

Myths/Legends: Peter Pan, Castor and Pollux

House: Third

Opposite Sign: Sagittarius

Flower: Lily of the valley

Keyword: Versatility

The Gemini Personality

Strengths, Talents, and the Creative Spark

Endowed with a quick yet changeable mind that misses little, you find ways to examine as many sides of a situation as possible. This gift comes to you compliments of your Gemini Sun sign, which governs the communication-oriented solar third house of cousins and other relatives (including siblings), your community, neighbors, local travel, the vehicles that get you where you want to go, and all forms of transportation. Your sign dominates education and media interests that connect others in distant places to meetings in every part of the world, including computers, faxes, the Internet, phones, social networks, and interface tools like Skype and Zoom. The third house describes your mind, especially how it works, your intellect, and how you converse with others or form creative relationships, and the impact it has on your mental outlook. Mercury is the planetary ruler of your sign, which is symbolized by the Twins. Gemini is both an air sign and a mutable sign, allowing you to fulfill your role as an analyst who questions relationships with authorities, gives goals a high priority, and assimilates ideas.

Where you find Gemini, you usually discover an excellent writer and grammarian who masters spelling with the best of them and knows how to put unique concepts into words. Your affiliation with Mercury makes you a compelling speaker who can deliver a message with fiery passion, rollicking humor, or a soft touch, depending on the audience. Most of you seldom shy away from the microphone and are terrific at delivering ad-libs, unless some criticism of your style early in life damaged your self-confidence and the stigma stuck. Intellectual versatility complements your need for constant stimuli and makes you a popular choice for emceeing events, running meetings, and teaching workshops.

Intimacy and Personal Relationships

If you are in the mood for having a conversation with a fascinating friend, phone a Gemini. They are full of ideas, love to pick your brain and exchange ideas, and will help you become popular on the social scene because they know a lot of people. Geminis receive numerous invitations and are always on the go, frequently fulfilling social obligations. Romantically, they play the field longer than most signs and may consider three dates with an individual a "long" relationship. Deep down they really want a relationship with a person who enjoys listening to their perspective on life and has a mind that matches their desire to make life a learning adventure. Geminis hope to capture the heart of a prospective mate through their intellect. Gemini, you may find this desirable connection through the other two air signs, Aquarius and Libra, who share your passion for electronic technology, games that stimulate your memory and pick your brain, or trips to the beach. For passion and true heart stimulation, choose an Aries or Sagittarius, who share your love of travel and could actually redirect your attention from working overtime to taking a road trip or playing in the great outdoors. Relationships with children usually involve a strong educational theme in how you spend time with them, which may include visits to museums, colleges, libraries, and UNESCO sites, as well as tours with manufacturers of educational toys and inventions to stimulate their curiosity.

Values and Resources

One of the characteristics you value most is having a fine mind that allows you access to an abundance of information that you quickly absorb and use to keep current on timely topics that benefit your competitiveness at work. Acquisition of educational credentials and advanced degrees, as well as certification programs that offer tools for changing operating practices in your work world, are your jam. People are important resources in your work, including those in specialized networks that are conduits for jobs, industry expertise, analyzing organizational strength, and offering training that ensures continuous improvement in the work environment. Solving problems appeals to you, and you generally take the time to examine pros and cons, polling participants for feedback and analyzing the data for accuracy before you apply the solutions. Many a Gemini enjoys teaching as a career and has a flair for developing courses, seminars, and workshops that stimulate learning of the unique facets of the material.

Blind Spots and Blockages

Known as a whirlwind in your field, you get in trouble when you overextend the time you spend on your work and finish assignments at the eleventh hour. Distractions from the assignment often get in the way in the form of too many Internet exchanges, learning about online programs that offer insight into timely material even when it doesn't relate to your tasks and shouldn't interrupt your schedule, and failing to record the project accomplishments on the timeline to be able to easily show the status of activity to team members. Many Geminis talk too much. No matter how interesting the information may be, it looks unprofessional to ignore the allotted time you have on the podium to deliver a talk that affects the flow of subsequent speakers. If you are a member of the management team, colleagues often complain that you forget to use "we" when describing accomplishments or don't mention the team by name to give them credit for the contributions they made on the project.

Goals and Success

You are one of the most gifted multitaskers in the zodiac and enthusiastically share information and swiftly get the message out in Mercury's signature way. You put an abundance of passion into assignments as a keynote speaker for a conference, when delivering reports or pep talks to the company staff, or as a coach of your children's sports team or the chair of the neighborhood homeowner association. A career in some form of communication suits you best. Geminis often succeed in more than one area of specialization. Your wit and lively personality are the perfect combination for working in the comedy field as a performer, a writer, or both. As a whiz in the recruitment department, you have an eye for making excellent matches in selecting talent for a variety of positions. Your fluency in foreign languages brings opportunities for assignments in the diplomatic corps, in a variety of foreign countries to foster goodwill for your company relationships, and in medical, military, or social services. Keep your point of view broad and you'll easily adapt to changing circumstances.

Gemini Keywords for 2024
Ideas, inquisitiveness, intelligence

The Year Ahead for Gemini

Anticipate celebrations, Gemini! This could be the year to break out the champagne and toast your successes with Jupiter moving into your sign on May 25, urging you to shine, travel, and accept the new career directions that are manifesting. Jupiter starts off the year in "get ready" mode in Taurus and your solar twelfth house, giving you the space to perfect your resume, refine your skills, and look over the employment offers that have come your way. If retirement is your goal after the turbulent increases in the cost of living and interest rates, as well as the scarcity of people, products, and services, you could begin to work independently as a contractor who offers diverse communication venues and presents material with humor and vivacity. Two of the four eclipses this year will fall in your solar fifth house of children, recreation, and romance, with a Lunar Eclipse starting the cycle there on March 25 and the last Solar Eclipse of 2024 in that house on October 2. The first Solar Eclipse occurs on April 8 in Aries and your solar eleventh house of friendships, groups, and goals, and the second Lunar Eclipse of the year falls in Pisces and your solar tenth house of career, authority, and status on September 17.

Expect changes in plans with Saturn in Pisces transiting your solar tenth house of career, which could indicate new leadership or work in a company that is changing its philosophy and altering its mission. Also present in this house is spiritually attuned Neptune in the last degrees of its long cycle through Pisces. And don't forget about Uranus, which is still hanging out in Taurus and your solar twelfth house of solitude. This havoc-oriented planet has no doubt sent more than a few shock waves through this house since 2018. Count on a few more from September 1 of this year through February 2025. The final outer planet of note is Pluto, which makes a transition into compatible Aquarius in January after occupying Capricorn since 2008. The planet of deep change will wrap up unfinished Capricorn business in your solar eighth house during a brief period from September 1 through November 19. Start planning your new course of action and welcome the freedom to blaze a new trail in local and long-distance markets.

Jupiter

With fast-paced Jupiter in Aries and your solar eleventh house back in 2023, you became a magnet for highly visible associations in need of your superior writing, project management, and presentation skills. Contacts from networks increased, with key players calling on you to chair programs, *ad hoc* committees, and special events. Certain organizations approached you about helping to recruit candidates with special skills. By the time Jupiter moved into Taurus and your solar twelfth house in mid-May of 2023, you were fielding requests to find highly qualified IT individuals. The shortage of workers continues in 2024, and you are likely to start out the year focusing on finding candidates with strong budgeting, forecasting, and reporting expertise.

On a personal level, you are no doubt elated to have Jupiter in Gemini and your solar first house starting on May 25 through the end of the year. How nice it is to feel like a money magnet when offers easily come your way. Get your wish list moving and go after the work, benefits, relationships, and travel you desire. Opportunities abound. The planet of expansion moves retrograde on October 9 and turns direct in Gemini on February 4, 2025. Those born in the first twenty-one degrees of your sign benefit most during this period. The remaining Gemini degrees wrap up this abundant Jupiter cycle by June 10, 2025.

Saturn

In some circles, Saturn has a reputation for being the meanie of all the planets, always placing a restriction or limitation on you that can be frustrating and depressing. Let's take a fresh look at the planet of accountability and authority as it transits your solar tenth house of career, achievements, management teams, and the status quo in laid-back Pisces and challenges you to put a little mellowness into your decision-making. You quick-thinking Geminis like to get to the point and don't like dragging your feet when there is a decision pending. That quality puts you in good standing with employers, who see you as a professional who cares about meeting deadlines and organizes work assignments efficiently. Saturn in Pisces might want you to operate a little differently, preferring that you take some time to ponder those important decisions a bit or maybe send them to a focus group for discussion, a trend you may see more of in 2024 while Saturn continues its two-and-a-half-year journey through this house.

Achievements, accomplishments, and career objectives are topics that come up for you in 2024. How happy are you in your work? Do you enjoy the compensation and benefits your organization offers? If not, are you considering applying for a new job or starting your own company? Saturn gives you something to think about regarding your boss and coworkers. If turnover has been high, it may not always be a comfortable environment for you, with all the changes in dynamic. With your people-oriented skills, you should be able to work out differences and offer workable solutions. In 2024, Saturn goes retrograde on June 29 and moves direct on November 15 in Pisces. Geminis most affected by the planet of consequences and earned rewards are those born between May 25 and June 11.

Uranus

During the past few years, your solar twelfth house has been a place of breakthroughs, healing, metaphysical experiences, unexpected events, private planning, sabbaticals, and secrets. Uranus in Taurus has been present there since May 2018, tempting you to make rash decisions about your future or random purchases with money targeted for planned acquisitions. In extreme cases, some of you could elope, carry on a secret tryst, or destroy someone's reputation by spreading untrue gossip. Uranus advances several degrees in Taurus this year as it makes its way through the last degrees of this sign. Although Uranus began 2024 in retrograde motion, it will go direct on January 27. The chaotic planet will station to go retrograde on September 1 and remain so until January 30, 2025. Chase away the blues by writing one of your comedic monologues for an emcee gig and enjoy the applause.

Neptune

One of the busiest houses for you in 2024 is your solar tenth house of authority, ambition, career, management priorities, organization matters, and the status quo related to you and your family. This year transiting Saturn in Pisces and the second Lunar Eclipse of 2024 on September 17 are both in this house. Neptune's properties are very different from those of your planetary ruler, Mercury. Although both planets are creatively intelligent, their operating styles are quite different. Neptune wants to hear everything you have to say and let it percolate until a clear vision comes at a later date and then maybe take some action if the risk isn't too high. The Neptune fog sets in and blocks out the interference. With Mercury as your ruler, Gemini, you are often talking so much that you tune out the basics of another's input in favor of showcasing your excellent ideas that come rapidly and clearly in your mind. Adapt and beautifully blend the ideas you have creatively structured and bring a new vision to your organization's energy. If you daydream more frequently than usual during this transit, you'll know that you have fallen under Neptune's spell. Use your disciplined mind and teaching tools to restructure key facets of current practices, presenting concepts with humor and compassion. If you were born between June 15 and 20, Neptune's transit will more meaningfully affect you, giving a good pull to your solar plexus and alerting you to impending change. This year Neptune turns retrograde on July 2 and stations to move direct on December 7. Value your higher mind and inner instincts.

Pluto

What were you doing in January of 2008 when dwarf planet Pluto entered Capricorn and your solar eighth house and had you questioning your financial security and sex appeal? Pluto in the eighth house relates to births, deaths, physical chemistry, wills, estates, joint money and debts, and matters that rest in your subconscious. That's a long time to be coping with unwanted fears, anxiety, and doubt about your strength and willpower. Over the years, you have no doubt unearthed some of the reasons for the tensions that have surfaced as power struggles and are now ready to leave the unwanted baggage behind. Nothing puts strain on a marriage more than unmanageable debt and rejection from your lover. Congratulate yourself, because you truly have made inroads in contacting the karma cleaners to come in and divest you of stress-inducing burdens, and your heart seems so much lighter. In January, Pluto moves out of rigid Capricorn and shifts into humanitarian Aquarius and your solar ninth house of foreign countries and culture, the higher mind, philosophy, publishing and writing, in-laws, and long-distance travel. Those with birthdays between May 21 and 24 experience harmonious vibes from this early Aquarius transit. While Pluto is in the last degree of Capricorn between September 1 and November 19, Geminis born between June 19 and 21 experience tension. Give yourself the gift of release and let go of any lingering emotional or financial guilt that you have carried around. Envision your life without the old problems and embrace the joy that is present in 2024.

How Will This Year's Eclipses Affect You?

This year's four eclipses, two lunar (Full Moon) and two solar (New Moon), are ready to generate intense periods that start to manifest a few months before their actual occurrence. The Libra/Aries cycle wraps up in March 2023 to make way for the Pisces/Virgo eclipses, the first of which makes its debut in September of 2024. Eclipses unfold in cycles involving all twelve signs of the zodiac and usually occur in pairs about two weeks apart. Never fear eclipses—just think of them as opportunities for growth that allow you to release old patterns. Expect surprises that elicit both positive and perplexing feelings and outcomes. The closer an eclipse is to a planet or point in your birth chart, the greater the importance it has in your life, especially if one of those planets is in the same degree as the eclipse.

Get ready for the appearance of 2024's first Lunar Eclipse on March 25 in Libra and your solar fifth house of amusements, children, fun, games, risk-taking, romance, sports, teaching, and vacations. Identify ways to strengthen bonds with children and lovers, schedule vacations and entertainment to keep promises to loved ones, take a break from too much work, and find solutions to coaching or educational challenges that beg for a fresh perspective.

On April 8, the first Solar Eclipse of the year arrives in Aries and your solar eleventh house of associates, dreams, goals, members of groups, friends, plans, and professional organizations. This is the second Solar Eclipse to occur in this house in the past year. No doubt you activated more than one membership in an important business or humanitarian enterprise that was looking for the creative leadership you are able to provide. You're focused now on recruiting members, anticipating funds to build interest in key initiatives, and looking to the future to bring stable conditions to the lives of deserving people. In 2024 you'll spend more time with cherished friends.

On September 17, you'll greet the second Lunar Eclipse of the year when your solar tenth house hosts the lunation in Pisces, giving vibrant attention to your ambitious mindset, career, interactions with authorities, management of prominent goals, and attention to responsibility and commitment. What you accomplish will come to the attention of the organizational hierarchy, becoming the catalyst for the prominence, awards, and bonuses that come your way as you are recognized for achievements in your field. Be sure to adapt your style to current workplace norms so that productivity succeeds and the team players understand the reasons behind the critical changes you're implementing. Celebrate unity.

The final Solar Eclipse of 2024 will occur on October 2 in Libra and your solar fifth house of children and their interests, fitness and sports, amusements and entertainment, gambling, romance, speculation, sports, and vacations. In the six months since the last Libra eclipse drew attention to this important house, you may have met that special someone or tied the knot, traveled with family and friends to a bucket-list vacation spot, started a business, or taken a random trip to Las Vegas and cleaned up playing the slots. Enjoy the successes you have achieved thus far and celebrate the benefit that listening brings to better understanding those in your circle.

Gemini | January

Overall Theme

With Jupiter in your sign most of the year, not only is 2024 a good year for improving your financial picture, but several dates this month suggest that windfalls or new income sources are available. Mercury goes direct in Sagittarius on the 1st, and Jupiter in Taurus trines Mars on the 12th. Work on your resume now and then put the final touches on it after Uranus in Taurus goes direct on the 27th.

Relationships

As the year begins, excitement thrills your partner over the way you two have bonded passionately. Close friends start calling on the 18th, checking available dates for bringing favorite people together. At midmonth you have new respect for your boss after watching them negotiate for leadership of a plum acquisition.

Success and Money

A cash infusion arrives around the 11th that covers credit card balances and holiday expenses, coinciding with Capricorn's New Moon that day in your solar eighth house. A short weekend trip refreshes your soul, giving you the energy to vigorously tackle a new assignment when you return on the 16th.

Pitfalls and Potential Problems

Settle a conflict between children on the 3rd over the use of media equipment. Your partner has the Monday morning blues on the 8th and wants to call in sick. Although you're sympathetic, don't support this form of bad judgment when it could kill chances of career advancement. Ask them, "What is at risk if you stay home?"

Rewarding Days

11, 14, 18, 24

Challenging Days

3, 8, 23, 30

Gemini | February

Overall Theme

Toast the Lunar New Year of the Dragon on February 10 by treating your loved ones to a festive meal. This month adds an extra day to 2024, with Leap Day falling on Tuesday, February 29, giving a dramatic aura to the day's events for the lucky Pisces who celebrate officially every four years.

Relationships

A new work colleague invites you and your spouse for a lovely dinner on the 3rd in gratitude for the quality time you have spent making sure orientation to the organization is thorough and answers outstanding questions. Your partner discusses potential plans for an early spring vacation with you around the 5th. This year Cupid offers up a dine-in Valentine's Day celebration due to a hectic work schedule.

Success and Money

Around the 7th, the executive team nominates you for a performance bonus to highlight the extra incentive you showed in finalizing the sequence of events necessary for implementing a reorganization plan. The New Moon in Aquarius and your solar ninth house on the 9th brings good news from a new alliance impressed with your presentation skills.

Pitfalls and Potential Problems

You register doubts about inconsistent information from a love interest on the 1st when stories change and dates don't happen. Neighborhood tension could escalate over vandalism issues. Engage your neighborhood watch group to make residents more aware of safety measures that are currently in place.

Rewarding Days

3, 5, 7, 20

Challenging Days

1, 4, 21, 23

Gemini | March

Overall Theme

March is yet another month where there is an emphasis on your increasing financial growth and the value of your assets. When the Pisces New Moon shows up on the 10th in your solar tenth house this month, your career-oriented department receives maximum attention based on a promotion opportunity that is coming your way that also raises the salary base for members of your team.

Relationships

If you are a single Gemini, the chance to meet new romantic prospects increases after the first week of March. Those of you already in a solid relationship are likely to rekindle your passion for each other, sharing intimate dinners, toasts, and tender affection. Attend a business-related affair on the night of the Pisces New Moon on the 10th, showing your charm and wit.

Success and Money

The financial insight this month focuses on salary increases, debt repayment, and extra interest earned on savings and investment accounts. Fund vacations or household projects with bonus money that arrives before mid-month. The year's first Lunar Eclipse occurs in Libra and your solar fifth house on the 25th, strengthening a personal relationship bond.

Pitfalls and Potential Problems

Public interests take over local topics in your community most of the month. At a meeting on the 20th, neighbors could oppose higher assessments in property values that are sure to raise taxes, and appalling road conditions might be another concern. Suggest identifying critical priorities and vote on a reasonable level of funding that will cover shortfalls.

Rewarding Days

5, 6, 10, 18

Challenging Days

3, 17, 20, 26

Gemini | April

Overall Theme

Don't hurry to sign important documents when Mercury goes retrograde in Aries on April 1. This is no April Fools' joke. Three weeks later, Mercury moves direct on the 25th, giving you a chance to resume tabled activities. Lunar activity includes a Solar Eclipse on the 8th in Aries and your solar eleventh house, suggesting the start of new directions related to membership in a growing organization.

Relationships

Intimacy comforts you on April 2, when you and your partner share deeply personal feelings. You may be discussing financial strategies with your banker or investment adviser. You realize that a day of quiet downtime is important to you to catch up on pending deadlines and opt to work from home on the 11th.

Success and Money

Financial planning is in the cards this month. Meet with key money experts on the 2nd or 6th but finalize deals after the 26th. Your neighborhood sports team needs equipment and uniforms. You decide to donate a substantial sum to aid their cause. When Jupiter makes a rewarding aspect to Mars on the 19th, attend a game when the team wears their spiffy new duds.

Pitfalls and Potential Problems

It's hard to read the energy in the room on the 9th when a business meeting falls apart. Key representatives fail to make their case in requesting funding and mission support. By the Full Moon in Scorpio and your solar sixth house on the 23rd, you learn that arguments lacked substance.

Rewarding Days

2, 6, 11, 26

Challenging Days

9, 12, 22, 23

Gemini | May

Overall Theme

The month you've been anticipating arrives when Jupiter moves into Gemini on the 25th and promises a new wave of prosperity for the rest of the year. May-born Geminis reap the benefits first through mid-July, enjoying positive vibes in their career sector. Pluto in early Aquarius makes a retrograde station on May 2 in your solar ninth house, urging you to look closely at studies you're pursuing or documents you're producing.

Relationships

Executives at your workplace, team members, and cooperators in joint projects fill your calendar this month, especially during the first week of May, setting up an intense schedule of meetings and collaborative work. Those of you in service industries get a pay boost. You'll be glad to have a day off on the 8th to work on personal chores and bond with family.

Success and Money

Funding for projects comes through, as does the go-ahead to hire additional staff to meet critical goals. You advise your boss that even with their excellent qualifications, new hires will need time for training and orientation, and make adjustments to the schedule. Your home garden design brings glowing praise from the neighbors.

Pitfalls and Potential Problems

Stay grounded in partnership matters on the May 23rd Full Moon in Sagittarius and your solar seventh house, when petty arguments and nagging over unfinished household tasks could put a dull sheen on the prospect of a weekend trip. Counsel a new employee who turns in a first report that misses the mark.

Rewarding Days

4, 8, 19, 31

Challenging Days

1, 5, 11, 23

Gemini | June

Overall Theme

With planets transiting your solar first house, romance is in the picture when the New Moon in Gemini on the 6th aligns with Jupiter in Gemini and Pluto in Aquarius, keeping good company with Venus in Gemini. If you take a few days to visit a favorite recreation spot, you'll be glad you did when the end of the month throws a curveball that could delay vacation plans.

Relationships

Join good friends for an enjoyable evening on the 1st. Mercury enters your sign on the 3rd, suggesting you stay close to home for a few days to attend children's end-of-school activities, ball games, and awards ceremonies. Plan an outing focused on children's interests on the 15th.

Success and Money

The week of the 10th brings praise and positive feedback to you and your work team. The hierarchy is impressed by the unified approach. Finances are up and down this month. Thanks to a pre-retrograde boost from Saturn to transiting Mercury and Venus in Cancer, transactions go smoothly late in the month.

Pitfalls and Potential Problems

The Capricorn Full Moon on the 21st opposes the Sun, Mercury, and Venus, putting a damper on date night for single Geminis. Wet blanket Saturn in Pisces moves into retrograde motion on the 29th and pushes back the start date of the vacation you booked for July. Look over plans carefully, rebooking rooms and checking dates and your credit card to avoid double charges.

Rewarding Days

1, 3, 15, 23

Challenging Days

7, 14, 21, 25

Gemini | July

Overall Theme

How delightful to have compatible planets like Jupiter in Gemini and Mercury in Leo close by as you anticipate the Fourth of July holiday. This combination is perfect for celebrating with family and friends, spending quality time in your local area. The Cancer New Moon on the 5th is a perfect day for finding bargains at outlets for items like outdoor furniture and gardening supplies.

Relationships

Invite visiting family and friends to celebrate the nation's birthday by staying close to home base this year. Participate in the local parade, watch the national Hot Dog Eating Contest, play some softball, feast on favorite goodies, and enjoy the fireworks at the end of this action-filled day.

Success and Money

From July 2nd on, the month proves to be a powerful one for your financial picture. Spend modestly and don't forget to negotiate on the price of luxury goods such as pools, home purchases, vehicles, and jewelry. Put your bonus or birthday money to good use if you're shopping for a car, and find good deals on the 5th and 30th. Donate to a local food bank to fund a holiday picnic.

Pitfalls and Potential Problems

As the month begins, transiting Neptune turns retrograde in the last degree of Pisces on July 2 in your solar tenth house. Don't sign any important documents that day, and when you return to work the following week, edit and look over pending papers to identify bloopers. Be very careful and thorough.

Rewarding Days

1, 4, 5, 30

Challenging Days

2, 9, 14, 24

Gemini | August

Overall Theme

Mercury is feeling organized in meticulous Virgo as the month begins, but quickly changes its tune when it goes retrograde on August 5, moves back into Leo, and then goes direct in Leo on the 28th. All the Mercury retrograde periods this year are in fire signs. The New Moon on the 4th in entertainment-loving Leo occurs in your solar third house, suggesting a newfound interest in taking acting lessons.

Relationships

Attend an event with neighbors on the 3rd and enjoy the festivities. A sibling and family visit on the 4th, a long-planned event that will bring them to town for a few days, giving you precious bonding time. Choose age-appropriate outings that all visitors can enjoy. Keep cooking to a minimum and order out instead. A professional group leader asks you to consider an alternative assignment on the 23rd.

Success and Money

Your lucky streak could pay off on the 2nd or 3rd when a scratcher lottery nets a nice win. Workplace compatibility is refreshing, and leaders compliment the enterprising team members for the outstanding rapport. Important announcements from your network could open competition for a long-awaited job announcement on the August 4th New Moon in Leo.

Pitfalls and Potential Problems

With retrograde Mercury in Leo forming a stressful inconjunct aspect to transiting Neptune in Pisces on the 15th, a planned monthly meeting might be postponed. The event planner might not have realized how many principals would be away on vacation. Household tranquility could be disrupted when important paperwork is missing on the 14th.

Rewarding Days

3, 4, 9, 23

Challenging Days

10, 14, 15, 31

Gemini | September

Overall Theme

The New Moon in Virgo on Labor Day, September 2, in your solar fourth house of home and family reminds you to treasure important memories of people in your domestic zone. Let's hear it for a comfortable haven and the coziness of your house! The final Lunar Eclipse of the year occurs on the 17th in Pisces in the opposite house, your solar tenth house of career and ambition, calling attention to important changes and work responsibilities.

Relationships

Your most intimate moments of the month may occur on the 13th, when you and your partner choose a weekend rendezvous for a romantic interlude. Abundant friendships and acquaintances add meaning to your life. You're likely to get together with a friend or two on the 18th. Enjoy a tantalizing dinner at a trendy restaurant.

Success and Money

Another excellent money cycle comes your way this month. There is something about the way you keep your wits together and churn out excellent products and services that makes you a frequent recipient of bonuses and awards. The last two Wednesdays of September (the 18th and the 25th) bring good news about raises or bonuses. Buying power soars and helps you find good sales.

Pitfalls and Potential Problems

Aspects for the Labor Day holiday are strained, potentially indicating illness or emotional tension with a difficult person. Uranus doesn't help when it goes retrograde in Taurus on the 1st and you feel edgy or sleepless. Steer clear of a potential partner who becomes agitated and angry on the 11th.

Rewarding Days

13, 18, 25, 30

Challenging Days

1, 11, 14, 20

Gemini | October

Overall Theme

Planetary activity becomes very personal in October when Jupiter in Gemini turns retrograde on the 9th in your solar first house in hard aspect to transiting Saturn and Neptune in Pisces in your solar tenth house. These two retrograde tenth-house planets remind you to be patient if you have transactions in the pipeline that come to a standstill.

Relationships

A Solar Eclipse occurs in Libra and your solar fifth house on October 2, highlighting romance and exciting local entertainment. Work crew collaboration on October 5 will lead to a strategy that addresses and solves a complex problem by the middle of November. Your significant other cherishes a surprise date with you on the 8th, noting how much time you have been spending on difficult challenges affecting your workplace.

Success and Money

Mars in Cancer this month piques your interest in learning about current trends designed to increase your assets. Investments look profitable around October 11, when Pluto turns direct in Capricorn and your solar eighth house. You give the go-ahead to move money on the advice of your broker. Your boss asks you to plan and facilitate a meeting regarding a start-up project targeted for 2025.

Pitfalls and Potential Problems

Scheduled staff meetings this month come with pitfalls indicated by planetary challenges that create action blocks, such as on October 10. The Full Moon in Aries and your solar eleventh house on October 17 has mixed aspects. Messages from leaders appear to send confusing signals over work assignments they are hoping to prioritize.

Rewarding Days

2, 5, 8, 11

Challenging Days

4, 9, 17, 25

Gemini | November

Overall Theme

An air of festivity presides over the workplace chatter, with colleagues eagerly sharing ideas for making plans, taking trips, and discussing favorite holiday traditions. How refreshing to see soaring spirits make the transition from enthusiasm over managing work responsibilities to creating enthusiasm for holiday celebrations for family and friends. Saturn turns direct in Pisces on the 15th in your solar tenth house of career, favoring releasing contracts on hold and issuing holiday bonuses.

Relationships

What a good time to donate to charities that offer meals to those in need. Issue invitations to relatives at a distance, coworkers, and local in-laws to share a place around your Thanksgiving dining table. Watch guests savor the tasty recipes you prepare and give thanks for the bountiful feast you've prepared. Treasure those you love with a grateful heart.

Success and Money

By month's end, you'll hear news about the expanding work agenda for 2025. New positions have been created and existing positions will have stepped-up salary bases. With citations lauding your professionalism and efficiency, you may be asked to apply for a leadership position. Update your resume.

Pitfalls and Potential Problems

The Thanksgiving Moon in Scorpio on the 28th clashes with Mars in Leo. Count on heated discussions over political conditions and citizen unrest. Steer conversations away from controversy to preserve a pleasant and peaceful atmosphere. Use music, games, and humor to please your guests and leave them smiling as you send them home with tantalizing leftovers.

Rewarding Days

1, 4, 15, 30

Challenging Days

3, 10, 18, 28

Gemini | December

Overall Theme

Geminis can't wait for the holiday events to begin. You'll be the first to accept party invitations or issue your own. First, let's talk about the Moon. You'll be treated to two New Moons this month, the first in Sagittarius on December 1 and the second in Capricorn on December 30. Party season starts early for you, with events scheduled from the 9th through the 23rd, after Neptune goes direct in Pisces on December 7.

Relationships

The weekend of the 6th, you'll visit family or close friends at distant locations who can't be with you for the upcoming holidays. Children melt your heart with their caring words for those in need. You're stoked to buy the young ones in your life their favorite toys. Have a holiday meal with good friends on December 10.

Success and Money

The management team may honor you with a performance award on the 9th for achievements in oral and written communication. You say goodbye to 2024 with a feeling of stability through experiencing personal growth, leadership recognition, and prosperity. Analytical expertise is your signature gift.

Pitfalls and Potential Problems

Planetary update: Neptune in Pisces turns direct on December 7. Mercury in Sagittarius stations to move direct on December 15, with the Full Moon in Gemini occurring at the same time, suggesting you avoid travel on that date. Mars moves retrograde in Leo and your solar third house on the 6th, possibly affecting transportation reservations later in the month.

Rewarding Days

7, 9, 10, 23

Challenging Days

6, 11, 15, 28

Gemini Action Table

These dates reflect the best—but not the only—times for success and ease in these activities, according to your Sun sign.

	JAN	FEB	MAR	APR	MAY	JUN	JUL	AUG	SEP	OCT	NOV	DEC
Move	11						5			2		
Romance			5	26				13		8	3	7
Seek counseling/coaching		3			4				18			10
Ask for a raise		20		2	31		30	25				
Vacation						1					4	
Get a loan	24		18			23			13			

Cancer

The Crab
June 21 to July 22

Element: Water

Quality: Cardinal

Polarity: Yin/feminine

Planetary Ruler: The Moon

Meditation: I have faith in the promptings of my heart

Gemstone: Pearl

Power Stones: Moonstone, Chrysocolla

Key Phrase: I feel

Glyph: Crab's claws

Anatomy: Stomach, breasts

Colors: Silver, pearl white

Animals: Crustaceans, cows, chickens

Myths/Legends: Hercules and the Crab, Asherah, Hecate

House: Fourth

Opposite Sign: Capricorn

Flower: Larkspur

Keyword: Receptivity

The Cancer Personality

Strengths, Talents, and the Creative Spark

With the Moon as the planetary ruler of your sign, you are driven by an instant radar that keeps you aware of most things taking place in your environment. You may not say anything, but you feel it and just know. Acquaintances often remark that when they look into your eyes, they simply must tell the truth. The Moon watches over the solar fourth house of home sweet home, your dear family members, foundations, base of operations, mother and sometimes father, your sixth sense, gardening and plants, your emotional temperament, your responsiveness to the plights of others, and household matters, including decorating, design, renovation, and real estate. This section of the chart represents parts of your life or personality that describe how you interact with family members, how you work through issues and solve related problems, what you like to do around the house, people you connect with or those with whom you share your home, how you equip your kitchen, and also your eating habits and cooking skills. Many of you are gourmet chefs.

Born under the sign of the Crab, you are both a water sign and the second of the four cardinal signs. You came here to explore and share the depth of your feelings, some of which may have been repressed in your shyer years. The Moon and its house and sign placements in your birth chart show how you display your personality. You push hard to meet your goals. If you aspire to wear a toque and run the kitchen of a fine restaurant as the chef de cuisine, you'll find a way to do it. With your entrepreneurial flair, it's not unusual for you to follow an unconventional career path and run your own business, allowing you to utilize multiple talents while using your well-developed sixth sense.

Intimacy and Personal Relationships

You want intimacy. Although you may know instantly that "this is the one," you need time to process the deep feelings that come over you. When the chemistry exchange takes place between the two of you, it is all but impossible to resist the urge to hug and kiss your partner every time you can from the pedestal of adoration you've built in your heart. On the quest to successful love, Cancers often choose their opposite sign, Capricorn, or resonate with one of the other water signs, Scorpio and Pisces. Other compatible signs include a grounded Taurus or Virgo, because your values are similar and you adore dear ones. Family and friends hold a high place of honor, allowing the ties of these relationships to give you the security you crave in an intimate circle you cherish forever. It's heartache for you when close relationships become severed and seem incapable of healing. Keep on sharing those loving feelings.

Values and Resources

With your incredible memory, you seldom forget those who have treated you with kindness and care and often share events with others from various times in your life when describing how individuals have shown respect and devotion to you or offered encouraging words when you needed to hear them. Likewise, you can be the thoughtful friend who never forgets a birthday with a card, note, or gift. You value all the people and traditions that reflect the fourth house of home and foundations—parents, partner, children, and relatives—and love to have them close at hand for holidays and special occasions. You have a special place in your heart for the role of parent, showing affection, encouragement, and patience to your children as you guide them in their goals on their chosen paths to success. Your must-have household appointments usually include a large dining room, a spacious kitchen with high-tech appliances, a food preparation center, and at least two refrigerators and a freezer to hold the quantity of food that you'll cook for family and friends. Keep hosting those parties, backyard barbecues, and celebrations using every tool in the pantry. Cancers usually enjoy working from home. Many of them excel at running successful catering or home baking businesses.

Blind Spots and Blockages

Being the sensitive Cancer you are, you dislike chastising others and let poor performers get away with inefficiency for much longer than necessary before letting them know you expect to see improvement. This excessive tolerance seems contradictory, since you are normally action-oriented and driven in the way you manage tasks at home or in the work arena. If the perpetrators feel safe when you remain silent or do some of their work instead of waiting for them to pitch in, they'll soon feel the claw of the crabby Cancer when you unleash your criticisms and issue a long-warranted ultimatum. Be sure the inevitable outburst is not a public one or your reputation could suffer over your impulsive deed. You don't take criticism well and dwell on any that is directed at you, even losing sleep over the tape that keeps playing in your head, wondering what you could have done to have prevented the tirade. Learn to recognize and value the lesson learned. Above all, let go and replace the incident with a positive example of a win. Use your intuitive gifts to recognize the truth.

Goals and Success

Specialization is your forte, and you have several key areas to explore to fulfill your employment and career dreams. Known for working more than one job at a time, you seldom give up your main paycheck until you identify the ideal match for your skills. Those of you with a teaching, instructor, or writing background may be able to incorporate your talents into developing training materials, blogs, or courses that support your perspective. Two types of Cancers operate in the work world. The first values security and makes it a point to stick with the local, state, federal, or military government organization that offers benefits during and after a long tour of duty as well as a generous pension that helps them maintain a comfortable lifestyle. They usually seek enjoyable work as supplemental income after retirement. The other type of Cancer starts working at a fairly young age, amassing a variety of work experiences in both government and private industry that they hope will give them the confidence to someday break free and start their own company. These Cancers have the energy, financial expertise, and talent to make a good income using their leadership skills to drive the goals that create opportunities for enjoying internal happiness. Logical choices for a business may include the specialties mentioned in preceding paragraphs. An alternative is the field of metaphysics, which includes astrology, energy healing, feng shui, meditation, and tarot, as well as teaching modalities affiliated with learning these subjects.

Cancer Keywords for 2024
Family, feelings, flow

The Year Ahead for Cancer

The year 2024 will find you incredibly busy with new life phases since the cardinal signs dominate three of the four eclipses that will occur this year in your solar fourth house (two eclipses in Libra, on March 25 and October 2) and your solar tenth house of ambition, authority, career, and responsibility (a Solar Eclipse in Aries on April 8). The third eclipse of the year occurs in Pisces on September 17, a Lunar Eclipse in your solar ninth house of the higher mind and travel. If any of these eclipses falls in a degree that directly aspects your Sun or other Cancer planets in your birth chart, you could be making major life changes.

If you have been waiting for relief from delays in important business, you'll get your wish quickly when Mercury in Sagittarius turns direct on January 1, giving the go-ahead to hire more staff, finalize project plans, and allocate resources to cover the cost of expansion in the work environment. Cancers who have been ill will enjoy a return to good health indicated by favorable Jupiter-in-Taurus aspects while the benevolent planet transits your solar eleventh house through May 25. Jupiter then moves into Gemini and occupies your solar twelfth house for the rest of 2024.

Another planet that occupies your solar eleventh house this year is Uranus in Taurus, which turns direct on January 27. Erratic energy is sure to pop up from this rebellious planet, which will finally leave Taurus in 2025, reducing the amount of conflict stemming from group activity. Occupying your solar ninth house along with the September Lunar Eclipse in Pisces are Saturn and Neptune also in Pisces. A number of factors could put the kibosh on travel plans this year or restrict them, including budget shortfalls, illness, transportation issues, or a job move.

Neptune occupies late degrees of Pisces this year, piquing your interest in studying new languages, cultures, or spiritual material. Certain Cancers may enroll in a degree program to support qualifications for a new position. Pluto in Capricorn has been stimulating relationships with personal and business partners in your solar seventh house since 2008. No doubt you have weighed in on how these relationships are working and what could be done to improve them. This year Pluto races to the finish line to reveal how love and other close partnerships are faring after this long testing period. You'll even get a short glimpse of how Pluto will behave when it moves into Aquarius on January 20 in your solar eighth house of financial holdings and debt and energizes those of your sign born between June 21 and 23. Pluto will turn retrograde in Aquarius on May 2, head back into Capricorn on September 1, station to move direct on October 11, then enter Aquarius for good on November 19. Celebrate the release of old relationship baggage.

Jupiter

This year starts out with Jupiter in Taurus moving through your solar eleventh house of associates, friendships, groups, humanitarian interests, and professional organizations. If you are interested in changing jobs or taking on a leadership role in an important group, it's time to consult your networks and lobby for the opportunity. The window is short, because Jupiter will embrace Gemini in your solar twelfth house on May 25, turning the focus for the rest of the year to healing, private matters, pursuing metaphysical subjects, taking a sabbatical, developing new plans, writing, or visiting the sick, including family and friends. Those options require adjustments to the status quo. Most Cancers will be affected by this Jupiter-in-Gemini transit in 2024, especially those of you born between June 21 and July 13. Jupiter's retrograde period begins on October 9 and ends on February 4, 2025. Take advantage of these fertile months to develop creative plans, turn options into an enterprise that is your perfect fit, and exude confidence, your true gift from Jupiter.

Saturn

As 2024 begins, Saturn in Pisces in early degrees of the sign finds a somewhat unsettled home in your solar ninth house in company with transiting Neptune and the second Solar Eclipse of the year on September 17. Although planets in Pisces are usually compatible with your sign, Saturn may want to hold your feet to the fire, insisting that you travel discreetly by planning well and keeping costs down through purchasing discount fares and lodgings. Saturn's reputation for throwing a few restrictions into the mix is highly likely, so be sure to check reservations and departures periodically after you book a long-distance trip. Those of you enrolling in college, language courses, or law or nursing programs will need to be mindful of rising educational costs, the need to register early, and the pressure to earn good grades to keep up with the competition. Studies or work abroad may be very demanding and challenging. If a job change occurred in the aftermath of the long pandemic period of the previous few years, adapt to the new environmental norms by adding skills to your portfolio through formal or online coursework. Cancers most affected by Saturn's exacting schedule this year are those born between June 24 and July 11. Saturn's retrograde period begins on June 29 and ends on November 15.

Uranus

How are your important friendships and professional relationships with members of key organizations faring in 2024? Are they on an even keel or tossing about as Uranus in Taurus transits your solar eleventh house of best friends, dreams and goals, and important networks? Uranus starts the year in retrograde motion, going direct on January 27 and soon keeping a brisk, action-oriented pace through September 1, when it turns retrograde again and remains so until January 30, 2025. When an erratic planet like Uranus travels through this house, you're likely to experience unpredictable encounters with those you work with over shared responsibilities, tasks critical to humanitarian initiatives, and money to operate projects. With unpredictable economic forces affecting your financial bottom line, competition for resources and coveted jobs may become scarce, including special interest appointments to committees, advisory boards, and homeowner associations. During favorable Uranus transits, you could receive a job offer out of the blue. Think through the details before responding. Keep in mind that breaches in old friendships sometimes occur when political or social disagreements get in the way. Those of you born with planets in the eleventh house may see more activity in 2024, especially if your birthday falls between July 10 and 21.

Neptune

Spiritually oriented Neptune continues its dreamy adventure through compatible Pisces and your solar ninth house, a transit that began in April 2011. Undoubtedly you have learned a few lessons since then regarding the illusions that Neptune artfully generates to tempt you to engage in decisions that may not be in your best interest. You know better, Cancer. The message of this watery planet is to remind you that not everything is what it appears to be. Pay attention to the opportunities that are coming your way and complete old business as this insightful planet weaves its way to the finish line after spending thirteen years in your solar ninth house of mind expansion, higher education, newly framed thinking patterns, in-laws, travel, foreign countries and cultures, and spiritual insight. If you are a writer and have material to finish, now is the time to use your psychic insight to create the rest of your vision. Those of you who chose a gap year to postpone university studies are probably ready to resume attendance and finish your degree. Clear up any confusion you have about planning your future and increase the flow of activity that helps you meet your goals. Cancers born between July 16 and 22 will experience the pleasant trine aspect from Neptune this year. Enjoy the uplifting vibes and consider new opportunities that come your way that call for expert use of your insightful gifts.

Pluto

Pluto first entered Capricorn and your solar seventh house of personal and business partners all the way back in 2008, and during this period the slow-moving dwarf planet has reminded you of the benefits and shortfalls of your relationships. Intimate partnerships have needed a clear and open path to communicating feelings and expressing love. Where that has not been possible, your sensitive Cancer heart has suffered repression, dealt with emotional angst, and contended with illness that potentially led to cardiac issues (such as hypertension), ulcers, or stomach disorders, including overeating. It's time to let go of the baggage, and that includes toxic people in your life if long-standing problems still exist. Similar conditions may be present in business relationships, calling for you to examine ongoing conflicts and resolve them through peaceful means or by severing the agreements or business partnerships once and for all. The karma cleaners hope you realize that time is up. On January 20, Pluto slides into Aquarius and your solar eighth house before turning retrograde on May 2 and then moving back into the last degree of Capricorn. Pluto resumes its inquisitive journey in Aquarius on November 20. Enjoy the relief and the inner peace that warms your soul.

How Will This Year's Eclipses Affect You?

This year's four eclipses, two lunar (Full Moon) and two solar (New Moon), are ready to generate intense periods that start to manifest a few months before their actual occurrence. The Libra/Aries cycle wraps up in March 2023 to make way for the Pisces/Virgo eclipses, the first of which makes its debut in September of 2024. Eclipses unfold in cycles involving all twelve signs of the zodiac and usually occur in pairs about two weeks apart. Never fear eclipses—just think of them as opportunities for growth that allow you to release old patterns. Expect surprises that elicit both positive and perplexing feelings and outcomes. The closer an eclipse is to a planet or point in your birth chart, the greater the importance it has in your life, especially if one of those planets is in the same degree as the eclipse.

Welcome 2024's first Lunar Eclipse on March 25 in Libra and your solar fourth house of home, family, foundation, conditions related to your home's structure, and the pulse and temperament at home base. Expect to learn considerable information related to residents of your home or family members close to your heart. Heal differences, repair or remodel your home, or plant a garden. Maintain an aura of goodwill that welcomes harmonious dialogue with all who cross your threshold.

On April 8, the first Solar Eclipse of the year arrives in Aries and your solar tenth house of career, ambition, authority, recognition for performance, and the status quo. An eclipse in this house often reflects a new beginning in some part of your work environment. Your attitude toward the way you earn your living may either bring you rewards or challenge you in some manner, depending on how the economy is affecting your workplace and how well you are able to honor commitments that are in place. You may have a new CEO, for example, and are adapting to a new style. This time period is important to review your personal goals, assess how well your career path fits with any new direction, and what the leadership changes could mean to the level of commitment you can provide. Conversely, you may decide to look for another position.

When your solar ninth house hosts the second Lunar Eclipse of the year on September 17, you'll welcome the lunation in Pisces and your solar ninth house, giving critical attention to higher learning degrees, love of education, interest in spirituality, the desire to travel or relocate, and interactions with publishers, foreign cultures, in-laws, and legal specialists. With Neptune also here near the eclipse degree, you could experience major breakthroughs in psychic insight and find yourself processing discoveries that appear in your dreams. Transiting Saturn in Pisces adds stability to the overall analysis.

The final Solar Eclipse of 2024 occurs on October 2 in Libra and your solar fourth house of family, home, life foundation, and attitudes and behavior at home base. Your intuition about home-related issues has been spot-on, and you may have solved trouble spots or done damage control to avert further conflicts. Changes among residents may have occurred since you experienced the March 25th eclipse in this same house. A child may have returned to live with you temporarily and will be moving to a new space shortly. Check your home's foundation and plumbing for possible leaks. Share more affection with family members and comfort those who need a hug.

Cancer | January

Overall Theme

Energy seems to abound for you at the start of the year when Mercury turns direct on the 1st and joins Venus and Mars in Sagittarius and your solar sixth house. What an incentive to continue the celebratory mood and feel the bonds of connection with your work team. Take socializing and entertainment seriously the first week of the month before settling into your demanding work routine.

Relationships

Visits from siblings and neighbors monopolize your time early in the month. Children take center stage on the 6th, when a holiday gift includes dinner out and then a special event creates a memorable experience for them. You and your partner have special plans around the 10th and rekindle the love connection. Warm hearts and caring gestures strengthen relationships.

Success and Money

The Moon in your sign on the 24th could indicate the start of a short trip to a nearby resort, the perfect way to spend holiday gift cash and enjoy some much-deserved playtime. A new assignment could await you when you return on the 29th ready to develop a strategy for getting an important project off the ground.

Pitfalls and Potential Problems

Several coworkers could call in sick on the 8th, leaving the team scrambling to meet requests for information and assistance. Uranus in Taurus turns direct on the 27th, creating a bit of confusion over planned activities for the weekend. Are you double-booked for a Saturday dinner?

Rewarding Days
1, 6, 10, 24

Challenging Days
4, 8, 16, 21

Cancer | February

Overall Theme

Think compassionately about humanitarian plights that have been in the local news. If any affect your neighborhood, find out what you can do and contact local groups to see about collecting food and clothing. Offer to organize a drive and ask for help from volunteers.

Relationships

Game night and a sleepover for the kids and their friends is likely on February 3. A romantic prospect invites you to celebrate the Lunar New Year of the Dragon on February 10. Accept, especially if you have never before participated. In light of possible business travel on February 14, have dinner with your spouse to celebrate Valentine's Day early.

Success and Money

A long-distance business trip excites you over the potential for career growth on the 11th. Make reservations and phone contacts at the site to learn more about management needs. Your boss is thrilled with the direction you're taking in organizing the daily operation. Privately you learn on the 13th that a promotion is in the works. The New Moon on the 9th in Aquarius and your solar eighth house brings excellent financial news regarding business funding.

Pitfalls and Potential Problems

Costly repairs to a household appliance are possible on February 8. You and your partner discussed spotty performance on the 1st, when signs of equipment failure first showed up. Cut your losses by replacing this older appliance. Discussions with siblings on the 24th do not lead to the agreement you were expecting. Revisit on February 27.

Rewarding Days

3, 7, 11, 13

Challenging Days

1, 4, 8, 24

Cancer | March

Overall Theme
Spring gardening calls out to your itchy green thumb, tempting you to plant the seeds you ordered last month. Welcome the vernal equinox on March 19, followed by the first Lunar Eclipse of 2024 in Libra on March 25. With a Venus-Mars conjunction in Aquarius and your solar eighth house of intimacy early in the month, single Cancers feel strong romantic vibes.

Relationships
Enjoy productive rapport with coworkers on the 2nd by announcing details of new procedures scheduled for implementation by mid-month. Spend time with your significant other on the 5th to discuss affordability of travel plans and pending household expenditures. Contact relatives at a distance on March 9 to learn more about upcoming family wedding plans.

Success and Money
Meet with your boss to verify allocation of staffing resources prior to beginning new operating procedures. A raise is likely by the third week of the month. Money is available for banking transactions to fund a home remodeling project at excellent rates. Begin it by March 21.

Pitfalls and Potential Problems
Get to the bottom of a child's sulky behavior on March 1. Have you noticed a buildup of anger or a bout of jealousy with siblings? Discuss what you've observed with your child. Weather patterns that include snow and ice lead to delays or cancellations of flights. Consider traveling after the equinox on the 19th.

Rewarding Days
2, 5, 9, 21

Challenging Days
1, 8, 20, 25

Cancer | April

Overall Theme

Mercury goes retrograde in Aries on April 1 and turns direct on the 25th. Take precautions not to sign important documents near these station dates without double-checking facts and figures. Limit travel plans and go with the flow when scheduling meetings that may have sparser than usual attendance.

Relationships

The Sun, Venus, and Mercury spend most of April in Aries and your solar tenth house of career and responsibility. Sometimes this connection draws you closer to your boss for collaborative reasons, or you could develop a huge crush. Caution! The Solar Eclipse in this same house on the 8th makes you particularly vulnerable. Bond with your partner on April 2 and 5.

Success and Money

Most of this month favors recognition of your performance in light of innovation and creative problem-solving. Your career sector shines with center-stage attention, and you have more cash in your pockets. Consider booking a trip in early May to take a break from the intense work pattern that allowed you to meet every deadline with room to spare.

Pitfalls and Potential Problems

You could feel exhausted on the 12th, ready to turn in early to rest and recover over the weekend. On the 21st, entertainment fare in the household results in a debate. Opt out and play games. By the 23rd you're back in the rat race, with deadlines hitting almost every day. Buy dinner for any teammates who have to work late.

Rewarding Days

2, 5, 8, 10

Challenging Days

9, 12, 21, 23

Cancer | May

Overall Theme

Pluto in Aquarius stations to move retrograde on May 2 in your solar eighth house of joint income and debt. If you're feeling frustrated with the status quo, work on eliminating the revolving debt that keeps you juggling bills and saving little to improve finances. Pluto's presence here foreshadows an invitation to release what you no longer desire from your fiscal responsibilities.

Relationships

The Moon is in Cancer on Mother's Day, May 12, with perfect aspects for enjoying the celebration with a light and loving touch as you embrace the special women in your life. Shower them with love and fond tributes for the loving memories you have of their presence.

Success and Money

A close friend shares a collaborative idea for a project when you meet to discuss it on May 8. Kick off the workweek of May 27 with an invitation from a business partner that has promising prospects for advancement in a field that interests you. Extra money is available from savings on a home project, enough to fund a short getaway next month.

Pitfalls and Potential Problems

A project contact seems unfocused on May 3, discouraging you from negotiating any solid deal. On May 7 your energy is high, but a reworked proposition lacks substance. Put your wallet away on the 15th or a business lunch could be outrageously expensive. Ditto for shopping on that day, when sales enticements could be disappointing.

Rewarding Days

8, 12, 22, 27

Challenging Days

2, 10, 15, 24

Cancer | June

Overall Theme

You have a case of wanderlust this month, Cancer. You and a friend may travel after the 4th for a short work break after completing an intense assignment. You seek privacy with the New Moon on the 6th in Gemini and your solar twelfth house while dealing with emerging business decisions and making final plans for a pleasure trip late in the month.

Relationships

Your significant other enjoys your company on a planned outing on the 23rd and shares excitement and expectations over a long-distance trip that begins on the 27th. Contact friends or relatives in advance to determine whether you will be able to link up with them during this hiatus. Look for suggestions for venues that will accommodate your plans and dates.

Success and Money

Schedule time with your boss around June 1 to further discuss prospects for making an internal job change. You'll be pleased with a discussion about salary, especially if the change in responsibilities appeals to your desired goals. Early in the month, enjoy harmonious vibes from Mercury, Venus, and Jupiter in Gemini that bring humor, recreation, and anticipation your way.

Pitfalls and Potential Problems

Refrain from overloading a meeting agenda on June 12 or you run the risk of not getting to hear all the speakers. Although Saturn turns retrograde on June 29 in Pisces and your solar ninth house of long-distance travel, you'll be able to make your anticipated trip if you keep to the planned schedule.

Rewarding Days

1, 4, 23, 27

Challenging Days

3, 7, 12, 22

Cancer | July

Overall Theme
Join the festivities at summer venues starting on the 1st, when the Moon in Taurus favors the Sun, Mars, Venus, and Saturn. Enthusiasm is high to celebrate the holiday and maybe your birthday if you are born in early July. The New Moon on the 5th in Cancer and your solar first house attracts favorite friends and relatives.

Relationships
Close friends pop in and out of your life starting on the 1st and again toward the end of the month when you take an amusement-filled vacation with a favorite person whose tastes reflect your own. No one knows more than you how to accommodate unexpected visitors and an abundance of invited guests to enjoy your sumptuous Fourth of July fare.

Success and Money
A favorable transit from Jupiter in Gemini benefits you in the form of discounts on goods and services, including lodging and airfare for planned travel. There's nothing like getting bumped to first class over a scheduling mix-up by the airline! By the 30th, you modify work plans that give you approved leverage over staffing coverage when the Moon lands on Jupiter in Gemini.

Pitfalls and Potential Problems
Check the quality of food you order on the 2nd to make sure it has been properly stored and prepared. Avoid spending money on July 9-10 for a workshop run by developers who have provided scant information about content expectations. Your workday on the 19th could be extended when you discover a work document has missing components.

Rewarding Days
1, 5, 28, 30

Challenging Days
3, 9, 13, 19

Cancer | August

Overall Theme

Your money and social life look good this month. Buoyancy and energy prevail with Mars and Jupiter in Gemini working to help you balance your schedule to include invitations for favorite venues. Your partner will sing your praises if you devote at least one of your favorable days, like August 4, to complete household chores.

Relationships

The Leo New Moon on the 4th promises a positive shopping outcome with your partner to price materials and supplies for a home project. Designs dazzle! Select favorite options for imminent purchase. Later, enjoy a night of light entertainment with your family. Enjoy romantic lunar aspects between Venus and the Moon on the 11th.

Success and Money

Say yes to an invitation for brunch from a member of your business network on the 25th and ask plenty of questions regarding a lead on emerging business opportunities. Follow up early in October and find out how many principals you can meet with to discuss details. Tread softly, yet show your interest if you like what you hear.

Pitfalls and Potential Problems

Tempting summer clearance sales lure shoppers. Avoid purchasing jewelry or luxury items on the 5th, when Mercury turns retrograde in Virgo, then moves back into Leo on the 14th and turns direct on August 28. Maintain home-based harmony on August 10, when feelings are fragile and family members seem too distracted for serious talks.

Rewarding Days

4, 9, 11, 25

Challenging Days

5, 10, 14, 19

Cancer | September

Overall Theme
The New Moon on Labor Day, September 2, in Virgo and your solar third house could make your home the perfect site to host a holiday cookout with relatives and neighbors on the guest list. Plan the menu and get out the games to treat young and adult guests to magical moments and new experiences in competition.

Relationships
Affection, intimacy, and entertainment fill your timecard this month. You and your partner enjoy intimate moments together the weekend of the 13th, bonding joyfully through the 18th. Out-of-town relatives may visit when the second Lunar Eclipse of the year occurs on September 17 in Pisces and your solar ninth house.

Success and Money
Mercury moves into Virgo on the 9th, putting contract negotiations or leases in the limelight. Propose the most favorable terms for your enterprise. The combined resources of you and your partner allow you to make a deposit on a home or new vehicle around the 15th. You're pumped when the appraiser tells you how much your current home has increased in value.

Pitfalls and Potential Problems
Uranus, the planet of upheavals, starts off the month going retrograde on the 1st in Taurus and your solar eleventh house of group endeavors, plans, and friendships. Let the Lunar Eclipse in Pisces on the 17th pass before you take off on a business trip. Check your credit standing after the 27th in response to multiple text or email messages. It's probably spam, but be proactive to avoid misunderstandings.

Rewarding Days
2, 13, 15, 18

Challenging Days
1, 6, 20, 27

Cancer | October

Overall Theme

The final Solar Eclipse of 2024 falls on October 2 in Libra and your solar fourth house, highlighting family business and relationships and how you interact with members. The planet of prosperity, Jupiter, makes a retrograde station on October 9 in Gemini and your solar twelfth house, suggesting you reconsider making a large purchase.

Relationships

Family members near and far take top billing this month, with some needing TLC and others asking for advice on how to manage problem areas. You and a child bond over mutual interests and enjoy a nice day together around the 5th. Work team relationships gel on the 8th and lead to productive dialogue on the value of new procedures that add to efficiency.

Success and Money

Look to mid-month to learn more about new projects that are about to begin and add excitement to assignments. You may be tapped to take on a new position or additional duties when the dust settles. Be sure to give credit to coworkers for their contributions and success in meeting current goals.

Pitfalls and Potential Problems

Write it off as the Monday blues on the 7th when you return to work feeling down. Pluto, the slow-moving planet of internal change, moves direct on October 11 in Capricorn and your solar seventh house of personal and business partners. Allow time to process remaining baggage you have worked to discard, giving your psyche the sought-after release you desire.

Rewarding Days

2, 5, 8, 15

Challenging Days

7, 10, 14, 20

Cancer | November

Overall Theme

The holidays are on your mind this month, along with all the required prep work. You're prompt at extending a dinner invitation to the big feast on November 28 and expect a large number of guests. Your social life picks up this month and you'll be accepting invitations from other hosts throughout November, savoring the spirit of the season.

Relationships

November 1 is perfect for wining and dining a new love interest. Work colleagues meet for a celebratory gathering around the 3rd, enjoying a friendly rapport and sharing holiday plans. Cherished relatives, friends, and a few workmates celebrate Thanksgiving with you in awe of your Cancer gift to prepare a chef-worthy meal that seems to capture the preferences of every guest.

Success and Money

Donate a generous gift to a local food pantry by the 8th to cover holiday foods. Start shopping for holiday treats and presents for loved ones using your bonus cash. Let children participate in decorating cookies and baking pies. Honor those at a distance who can't be with you for Thanksgiving with a video chat after the 15th.

Pitfalls and Potential Problems

Avoid showdowns with stubborn workmates on the 5th, when task management draws criticism. Saturn in Pisces stations to move direct on the 15th, eliminating a frustrating delay in executing personal plans to travel. Mercury turns retrograde in Sagittarius on the 25th, possibly delaying travel plans for arriving Thanksgiving guests.

Rewarding Days

1, 3, 8, 11

Challenging Days

5, 7, 17, 25

Cancer | December

Overall Theme

December is no ordinary month. We will celebrate two New Moons, the first in Sagittarius on December 1 and the second in Capricorn on December 30. If you're ready for some pre-holiday R&R, the week of the 9th should net you airfare and lodging bargains in a relaxing locale. With ongoing erratic planetary movement, be sure to stay flexible with plans.

Relationships

Enjoy spontaneous moments with your significant other on a date night on the 7th, sharing heartfelt feelings. Strengthen family ties on the 23rd, when relatives gather for the seasonal festivities and remind you of how completely family love expresses the true meaning of the holiday spirit.

Success and Money

Add a new motivational word to your personal mantra and then use it to reframe your business work plan. Work authorities are pleased with your performance and reward you with a holiday bonus. Finalize shopping for remaining gifts and complete holiday meal planning by the 9th. Purchase festive party favors for your holiday dinner service.

Pitfalls and Potential Problems

Mars in Leo moves into retrograde motion on December 6. Then Neptune in Pisces stations to move direct on the 7th, followed by Mercury turning direct in Sagittarius opposite the Full Moon in Gemini on the 15th, a good day to avoid travel. Tempers may flare in the executive circle on the 11th, so stay calm and centered.

Rewarding Days

3, 7, 23, 27

Challenging Days

11, 12, 15, 28

Cancer Action Table

These dates reflect the best–but not the only–times for success and ease in these activities, according to your Sun sign.

	JAN	FEB	MAR	APR	MAY	JUN	JUL	AUG	SEP	OCT	NOV	DEC
Move		11									11	
Romance	10		9	2		23		11		5		7
Seek counseling/coaching					8		28		2			
Ask for a raise		13		8		1						
Vacation	6				12		30		18			27
Get a loan			21					4			8	

Leo

The Lion
July 22 to August 23

♌

Element: Fire

Quality: Fixed

Polarity: Yang/masculine

Planetary Ruler: The Sun

Meditation: I trust in the strength of my soul

Gemstone: Ruby

Power Stones: Topaz, sardonyx

Key Phrase: I will

Glyph: Lion's tail

Anatomy: Heart, upper back

Colors: Gold, scarlet

Animals: Lions, large cats

Myths/Legends: Apollo, Isis, Helios

House: Fifth

Opposite Sign: Aquarius

Flowers: Marigold, sunflower

Keyword: Magnetic

The Leo Personality

Strengths, Talents, and the Creative Spark

Leos are known for daring to be different in the face of unexpected occurrences that call for a firm decision. Your sign is the second fixed sign and the second fire sign in the zodiac. Known for having a take-charge attitude, creativity, and a flair for entrepreneurial activity, you shine as a leader, adoring the role of boss. With drama and panache, you usually bring good cheer to your many friends and fans. Your affiliation with royalty could mean that purple tones, jade, and rich blues are part of your color scheme. Your famous gift of generosity attracts many friends and colleagues charmed by your display of enthusiasm. Leo rules the back, blood, circulatory system, heart, spine, and metabolism. Illness can result when your emotions are blocked and you don't know how to release your anger. If someone rejects you or manages to bash your ego, you retreat, licking your wounds, pretending it didn't matter, or finding new interests to pursue. If you are a parent, you are enthusiastic and enjoy getting involved in your children's activities, often taking the liberty of sharing their accomplishments with others.

The Sun rules your sign and the exciting, adventure-oriented fifth house of games, social life, children, lovers, dating experiences, sports, exercise, freelancing, romance, and speculative undertakings. Whatever talent you express is bound to highlight your magnetic personality, displaying the qualities most affiliated with Leo. The list is long and is bound to include pride of accomplishment, entertaining, socializing finesse, adoring your love interests, recreational pursuits, and all things romantic. When planets appear in the fifth house of your birth chart, they describe the complexity of emotions and the range of creative, recreational, and social interests you possess. A number of you are sports fans, either active participants or dedicated spectators. Other Leos might excel in pursuing entertainment, performance venues, or showmanship and seldom miss an offering of a favorite play or musical show. I fondly recall a client who saw *Jersey Boys* five times, and that number may have doubled by now. Whether you are a roaring "Lion" type of Leo or a more reserved "Cat," you feel powerful and enjoy basking in the limelight.

Intimacy and Personal Relationships

You are happiest, Leo, when you are in love and have an engaging romantic partner, whom you'll work hard to keep happy. Some say you wrote the book of love, with your appealing gestures that include wine, music, gifts, and divine food. You pay attention to every like and dislike your partner displays and make sure to fulfill your loved one's dreams and fantasies with gifts, entertainment, cuddling, and endearing words. If the relationship ever ends, you'll be a difficult lover to replace. An expert at spontaneous gift giving, you know a treasure when you spot it and scoop it up to present to the object of your affection for no particular reason except to please. Among the best matches for you are the other two fire signs, Aries and Sagittarius, as well as the air signs Gemini and Libra and even your opposite sign, Aquarius, unless you find one who is too aloof to appeal to your warm heart. Children get special treatment and pampering, too, especially regarding their school activities and talent in sports, music, and art. You encourage the development of skills, attendance at a reputable university, or a career in entrepreneurial ventures. Friends love you for your loyalty, generosity, and remembrance of them throughout the year.

Values and Resources

What you value most is the opportunity to engage in activities and roles that highlight your magnetic Leo qualities. The development of plans, pride of accomplishment, autonomy in carrying out your assignments, and especially a chance to shine as a leader in your field appeal to you most. You prefer a pristine, well-organized work environment with up-to-date equipment and elegant decor. Employee or teammate loyalty means the world to you. You love a stage to give you the comfort of being in charge, whether it is as a teacher commanding a classroom, a coach shaping the talents of the athletes, a manager running the grocery market, or the chief executive officer of a corporation. Generous compensation for your work is high on your list. You want to be paid well and feel secure knowing that you will receive incremental raises for accomplishments. True to your fifth-house roots (Leo rules the fifth house), you love the feel of a win and often put lottery tickets in the family holiday stockings, hoping your winning streaks rub off on others.

Blind Spots and Blockages

Sometimes the fixed-sign attribute of stubbornness emerges when you face opposition to your goals in personal and professional arenas. You struggle if you perceive rejection of your ideas or feel like your way is best and don't want to entertain further options. Love is sublime when it works well and you beam with joy, yet love is complex and it takes time to master the intricacies of forming permanent, loving relationships. Your actions can be perceived as alienating to others, and arguments can occur. Observers think you are being overly confident in your decisions when you cut others out of the action. More importantly, your health suffers if you bottle your feelings and let anger build up instead of addressing the elephant in the room. You might hold grudges way too long before you decide to break the ice and work on healing the rifts that occur in either your work or your romantic life. Patience is a must in working on goals to move up the career ladder and is a quality that will prove valuable if you take the time to develop it. Likewise, let love blossom as you demonstrate deep, immovable devotion.

Goals and Success

You work hard to achieve the multitude of goals that you consciously develop in favorite areas of life. No one has to prod you to keep on top of them since you are adept at managing them and keeping tabs on progress. Success means celebrating what you achieve. In your personal life, you gather loved ones to share progress and plan parties, getaways, and fancy dinners to express your happiness, which may also include purchasing cherished gifts to pamper the family members who have ardently supported you in your quest. As a Leo, you are very happy when you are able to coach your work team to perform at high levels. No matter what your job entails, you value an environment that offers a path to build self-confidence and an opportunity to play a starring role in the enterprise. You're known for taking a gamble on the unknown and turning it into a win. You enjoy delegating work to others for a growth opportunity while allowing you to take a nice vacation or a break instead of maintaining a workaholic schedule. Leos excel in a wide variety of positions, such as athletes, educators, government workers, manufacturers, park rangers, sales personnel, and entertainers. By sharing information routinely with your team, you gain admiration and respect in your profession.

Leo Keywords for 2024
Heart, honor, humor

The Year Ahead For Leo

As you enter 2024, communication-driven Mercury turns direct on the 1st in your solar fifth house of romance and humor. Could it be that you pop the question to your sweetheart and start off the year making plans to unite permanently? Uranus in Taurus in your solar tenth house of career and authority stations to move direct on January 27, supporting plans for implementing new initiatives that had been put on hold. Expect a shakeup or two in this house after the highs and lows of the last seven years. Jupiter in Taurus in your solar tenth house ignites career options for you as well through May 25, when the lucky planet dignifies your reputation by manifesting prosperity in the form of promotions or raises before moving into Gemini and your solar eleventh house for the remainder of 2024. Then you'll have an opportunity to work on manifesting your fondest dreams and wishes with friends or trusted members of professional organizations whose analytical minds you greatly admire.

Two planets occupy Pisces and your solar eighth house this year. Saturn starts out in early degrees of Pisces in its two-and-a-half-year cycle in your solar eighth house of partnership income, assets, and debt, giving you a chance to stabilize financial management in important areas. Glamorous Neptune in Pisces covers the last few degrees of the sign and makes sexy overtures to confuse you about intimate relationships or to cloud issues connected with the analysis of what you actually owe to creditors. Pluto, the remaining outer planet, is transiting the last degree of Capricorn and your solar sixth house of daily activity, work conditions, and health, helping you organize priorities and let go of ineffective habits that prevent you from performing efficiently. Aquarius, the next sign Pluto will occupy, is waiting in the wings to interest you in strategic ways to treat personal and professional relationships when this planet moves into your solar seventh house on January 20. Eclipses in 2024 occur in your solar third house (a Lunar Eclipse and a Solar Eclipse), your solar ninth house (Solar Eclipse), and your solar eighth house (Lunar Eclipse). Get ready to learn powerful new information and to fulfill your desire to travel.

Jupiter

Benefic Jupiter moved into Taurus in May of 2023 and continues to bring attention to your solar tenth house of ambition, career, authorities in charge, and the status quo until May 25, when it enters Gemini and your solar eleventh house of goals and friendships. The economy could be affecting the overall budget and expenditures for your company and the number of planned purchases and hires. Astute management allows you to develop alternatives to keep your goals on track. You might also consider retirement, if eligible, or a job change, if restless. Those of you born between July 27 and August 22 are most affected by this transit. Leos born between July 23 and August 14 benefit most from networking, special memberships and associations, group endeavors, humanitarian pursuits, and friendships during this cycle. During Jupiter's retrograde period, which runs from October 9 through February 4, 2025, spend time refining details in proposals, editing books and manuscripts, deciding what organizations you would like to support, or determining how best to use employer's resources for maximum benefit to all.

Saturn

In the sign of quiet reflection, intuitive mental capacity, and deep sensitivities, Saturn in Pisces is cycling through your solar eighth house of partnership assets involving joint earnings, savings, loans, estates, wills, and debts. Saturn puts pressure on you to develop a plan to save more of your earnings, start a retirement fund, and economize to limit the use of credit cards while inflation is high and refinancing rates may not be as favorable as you prefer. Neptune also transits Pisces and your solar eighth house in 2024 and could tempt you to take a chance if you are caught off guard by a sudden offer. A reasonable approach to debt management works best, with no need to focus on the worst-case scenarios, which could be job loss or bankruptcy. An eclipse here on September 17 could bring you an unexpected windfall that boosts your spirits. Saturn's transit in Pisces this year most affects Leos born between July 26 and August 12. Saturn's retrograde phase begins on June 29 and ends on November 15. For greatest success, involve your partner in strategies that meet your needs and solve problems with honor and compatibility.

Uranus

When Uranus pops in for a visit, the affected department of your life can feel like you've entered a maze of unexpected glitches that have you constantly rethinking goals and using your best problem-solving skills. That is what you have this year with Uranus in your solar tenth house of career and ambition. The planet of surprises goes direct on January 27, keeping urgent pressure on you through September 1, when it turns retrograde and remains so until January 30, 2025. Leos born between August 11 and 18 feel the most impact from this transit. Uranus has been here since May 2018, serving up a wide range of disruptions that may include a change in leadership at your organization, moving the location of your workplace, conflicts with personnel over philosophical differences in the work plan, firings and layoffs, retirements, and mergers. While salaries are likely to increase due to inflation, the pot of money usually reserved for performance awards and bonuses may be leaner. Use creativity to develop alternative ways to reward employees.

Neptune

Somewhere in every chart in 2024, Neptune in Pisces is going to link up with Saturn in Pisces to offer options for resolving differences. Your opportunity affects the way you handle other people's money, including what you and your partner have amassed during your union, the debt you have incurred, and how you pay it back. Your playground is your solar eighth house of financial holdings and resources, where these two powerhouse planets are holding court and expecting to see miracles in the form of more money in your accounts despite a financially challenging world economy. Neptune is probably going to tell Saturn that it is not only about the money, but also involves showing compassion for when one of you overspends impulsively, ignoring your goal to reduce debt. If Saturn plays the stickler, Neptune may say that the stern taskmaster planet has no heart and has lessons to learn about the psychological meaning of money. Neptune's retrograde period starts on July 2 in Pisces and resumes direct motion on December 7. You'll have the most contact with Neptune in 2024 if you were born between August 18 and 22. Enjoy the greatest success by investing your best assets in work you love surrounded by people you cherish.

Pluto

This year is truly a reflective one for you, Leo, taking you all the way back to 2008, when Pluto first entered Capricorn and your solar sixth house of daily living and working patterns. You started paying attention to your health and nutrition, what you ate and how you prepared it, and how well you were getting along with coworkers and colleagues. On January 20 this year, Pluto emerges from its cautious shelter and moves into Aquarius and your solar seventh house of partnerships. It then turns retrograde on May 2 in Aquarius, moves back into Capricorn on September 1, and goes direct on October 11 in the last degree of Capricorn. Only those of you born between July 23 and 26 are likely to feel the impact of the Pluto opposition to your Sun, and you'll learn greater detail after November 19, when Pluto enters Aquarius and your solar seventh house of partners for good. In the meantime, assess the quality of your personal and professional partnerships. What has manifested in recent months that troubles you or leaves you searching for answers? Do anger issues come to mind? Slowly but surely, the Pluto transit pushes these concerns into the spotlight, reminding you to clear the air.

How Will This Year's Eclipses Affect You?

This year's four eclipses, two lunar (Full Moon) and two solar (New Moon), are ready to generate intense periods that start to manifest a few months before their actual occurrence. The Libra/Aries cycle wraps up in March 2023 to make way for the Pisces/Virgo eclipses, the first of which makes its debut in September of 2024. Eclipses unfold in cycles involving all twelve signs of the zodiac and usually occur in pairs about two weeks apart. Never fear eclipses—just think of them as opportunities for growth that allow you to release old patterns. Expect surprises that elicit both positive and perplexing feelings and outcomes. The closer an eclipse is to a planet or point in your birth chart, the greater the importance it has in your life, especially if one of those planets is in the same degree as the eclipse.

When the first Lunar Eclipse of 2024 falls on March 25 in Libra and your solar third house of communication, your mind, education, local travel, your neighborhood, siblings, and various forms of transportation, you'll have your hands full with issues that demand your attention, so keep your humor handy. Make solid plans to purchase a new vehicle or plan a trip with siblings. Look over contracts related to business and personal acquisitions carefully to make sure the terms clearly represent want you want. Welcome new neighbors to the area, and mend fences with any neighbors with whom you have strained relationships. If you are a writer, this is a good period to develop inspiring articles, books, or plays.

The year's first Solar Eclipse occurs on April 8 in Aries and your solar ninth house of the higher mind, advanced education, your in-laws near and far, long-distance travel, philosophy, religion, publishing, relocation, and foreign countries, languages, and cultures. Distant business centers and satellite offices could draw Leos to spend time in temporary quarters this year, possibly to set up the organization, help with the hiring, or conduct program reviews. Some of you may move for a multi-year or permanent assignment. Be sure your credentials are well documented in case an offer comes to you with little notice. Other Leos book their dream vacation and bring the family along for adventure.

The site of the second Lunar Eclipse this year is your solar eighth house of joint finances, savings, and debt; wills and estate matters; and psychological depth, regeneration, sex, birth, and death. This eclipse falls on September 17 in Pisces, encouraging you to fully address any money issues that need attention, with the intention of paying off bills and credit cards, adhering to a workable budget, and noting the fiscal trends that affect financial conditions globally. Get more than one quote if funding a mortgage or refinancing a loan. Shop competitively when making large purchases. Be on the lookout for unexpected wins or cash in your pocket.

The year's final Solar Eclipse occurs on October 2 in Libra and your solar third house of your neighborhood, local travel, communication, technology purchases, your state of mind, vehicles, siblings, cousins, and agreements. Do all you can to maintain a healthy outlook, and sharpen your focus on areas that matter most. Find ways to spread cheer and uplift the morale of those around you. Organize your home and work site to facilitate efficient operation and remove chaos from routines. Develop affirmations that speak to your goals and watch how the shift in energy changes your body, mind, and spirit.

Leo | January

Overall Theme

Key planets shift motion this month, with Mercury in Sagittarius moving direct on the 1st, giving you a thumbs-up for a winter vacation. The Capricorn New Moon on the 11th shines on a new work project, creating interest and excitement with the team. Uranus in Taurus turns direct on the 27th in your solar tenth house, ending a holding pattern for funding special initiatives.

Relationships

Take a vacation with your partner around January 13 for a rewarding respite from intensive work assignments. Both of you are in a festive mood and eager to celebrate an extended happy new year. Share intimate moments with your significant other on the 15th, enjoying the deep feelings you have for each other. Single Leos mix and mingle with new love prospects.

Success and Money

Lucrative savings help you start out 2024 on a high note for buying household goods and planning home renovations. Family members prosper with the addition to college funds or savings accounts you set up. The work environment buzzes with enthusiasm after hearing news of the successful implementation of multi-year contracts.

Pitfalls and Potential Problems

Aspects are mixed on the 3rd, when you split hairs at a work meeting over prioritizing assignments to meet timeline deadlines. Several employees may express concern over the rising costs of doing business and suggest cutting expenses. The January 25th Full Moon in your sign indicates high tension and exhaustion. Turn in early to recharge and get a good night's sleep.

Rewarding Days

1, 6, 11, 15

Challenging Days

3, 8, 16, 25

Leo | February

Overall Theme

The planets are reasonably quiet this month, giving you time to plan a celebration of the Lunar New Year of the Dragon on February 10. You enjoy rituals designed to increase prosperity and good fortune. Plan a meal around your favorite cuisine, placing plants in a golden bowl as the centerpiece while toasting your guests with favorite drinks in anticipation of a change in fortune.

Relationships

February 3 is all about family. Plan entertainment and a meal around the availability of multiple generations who join you for the day. Enjoy a romantic outing on the 13th to celebrate Valentine's Day early and put a big smile on your partner's face. Dedicate the last Sunday of the month, February 25, to a favorite sports event to please your children.

Success and Money

Organizational changes in your workplace favor a new assignment you have been anticipating. Apply after the 7th and have your resume ready for management review. If you shop or attend an auction on February 25, you could discover an outstanding item that surprises you and adds greater value to your net worth.

Pitfalls and Potential Problems

Be prepared for arguments over the content of mixed messages or squabbles on the 4th. If you discover that prices have increased considerably at a favorite restaurant around February 6, suggest a venue with more modestly priced cuisine. Entertainment plans with your partner on the February 9th New Moon in Aquarius won't materialize if inclement weather scuttles transportation options.

Rewarding Days

3, 7, 13, 25

Challenging Days

4, 6, 9, 22

Leo | March

Overall Theme

Planets in several fixed signs line up early in the month and challenge you to join the activity, which is not an easy feat since Venus and Mars in Aquarius oppose your Sun starting on March 1 just as Pluto in early Aquarius joins forces. Jupiter and Uranus in Taurus add tension to the mix. Love vibrations between you and your sweetheart are romantic during the first two weeks of the month.

Relationships

Work colleagues gather around the 5th to discuss new practices and policies in the implementation process. Offer to facilitate the discussion, allowing all to have their voices heard. March 16 looks ideal for making plans with friends for dinner or entertainment venues. One of the hot topics may be wedding plans for a mutual friend.

Success and Money

The Lunar Eclipse in Libra on March 25 ignites your solar third house. With your love of community and fondness for seniors, why not spearhead a project to install a pickleball court in a general-use area in your neighborhood. Look for positive feedback from your boss around the 13th, with discussion of a raise or bonus.

Pitfalls and Potential Problems

March 3 ruffles the feathers of a would-be love interest new to your life. If you are already in a relationship, be careful not to communicate the wrong vibes to your existing partner or a jealous streak could escalate by the time the Lunar Eclipse arrives on the 25th.

Rewarding Days

5, 13, 16, 21

Challenging Days

3, 7, 19, 25

Leo | April

Overall Theme

Expect confusing communication from distant contacts when Mercury in Aries turns retrograde in your solar ninth house on the 1st. The messenger planet resumes direct motion on April 25, encouraging you to activate plans you put on hold. The Aries New Moon on the 8th is 2024's first Solar Eclipse, occurring in your solar ninth house. Expect to make travel plans and reconnect with individuals who have been out of touch in recent years.

Relationships

Your work environment takes center stage from the 2nd through the 12th. Review key timelines, identifying tasks that call for extra human resources. Date night works well on April 6, so schedule romantic plans with your partner. Cherish the time you spend with that special someone on April 28 and make it memorable for the growth of this relationship.

Success and Money

On April 10 a conversation with your superiors reveals that their confidence in you is growing and much of the success of program implementation will fall in your lap. Enjoy the praise and honor you receive and acknowledge the salary increase that has made a difference in the financial security you've earned.

Pitfalls and Potential Problems

The April 23rd Scorpio Full Moon in your solar fourth house highlights tension at home base when family members demonstrate petty annoyances involving the dinner menu, upcoming plans, and entertainment choices. Expect challenges over the cost of venues. Don't play into the hands of one member who seems to have the biggest ax to grind.

Rewarding Days

2, 6, 10, 28

Challenging Days

4, 9, 22, 23

Leo | May

Overall Theme

When the New Moon in Taurus falls in your solar tenth house of career on the 7th, you feel a rush of excitement as well as an inner pang of angst that suggests the workload is going to intensify. Travel plans will have to wait until management clarifies assignments. Then organize tasks that are doable, showcase your efficiency, and clear your calendar for time off at the end of the month.

Relationships

Enjoy private time with your partner on May 3 and 28. Plan activities you have never experienced before and embrace adventure. Celebrate veterans on Memorial Day by assisting with neighborhood events in their honor.

Success and Money

Company executives meet to discuss the status of the working budget around the 8th to ensure that all anticipated expenses are covered for ongoing work. A networking lunch on the 9th proves productive when you get vital leads on two highly skilled specialists who would be a real coup for the organization. Shop for loan rates related to refinancing on May 3.

Pitfalls and Potential Problems

On May 2 Pluto turns retrograde in Aquarius and your solar seventh house of partners. What partnership issues have been on your mind lately? If you think important information is missing, start asking questions. The Full Moon on the 23rd in Sagittarius and your solar fifth house could indicate disappointment in a child's decision or in a potential partner you recently met. Question them carefully for best results.

Rewarding Days

3, 8, 9, 28

Challenging Days

2, 11, 16, 23

Leo | June

Overall Theme

Special remembrance dates populate the calendar this month on the 14th (Flag Day), the 16th (Father's Day), and the 19th (Juneteenth). With an engaging lineup of compatible Gemini planets in the first half of the month, including Mercury, Venus, Jupiter, and the June 6th New Moon, waves of patriotism, remembrance, and compassion fill the air, honoring special people and events that hold personal meaning.

Relationships

If you scheduled a vacation for June 1, pack your bags and take off joyfully to spend time with family near and far. Leos traveling for business take a short trip to gather information for an administrative status report. Accept a dinner invitation from a good friend and share catch-up news on June 6. Enjoy bonding time with your significant other on June 26.

Success and Money

Meet with your boss on June 4 to discuss findings related to recent business travel or program reviews. Suggest collaboration with key staff to take measures that correct performance shortfalls or streamline procedures. Recognize staff who are adept at keeping goals on target. Jupiter's recent entry into Gemini and your solar eleventh house highlights important personal goals.

Pitfalls and Potential Problems

Political differences with professional affiliates surface during a funding meeting on June 3, leaving talks in an unsatisfactory state. Mending the dispute falls in the hands of the chair. Saturn in Pisces turns retrograde on June 29 in your solar eighth house, discouraging you from tapping savings to fund a vehicle purchase.

Rewarding Days

1, 4, 6, 26

Challenging Days

3, 7, 13, 29

Leo | July

Overall Theme

Jupiter in Gemini favors vacation time with friends, accentuating enjoyable summer venues while Mercury and Venus in Leo make favorable connections. While touring, you may discover unexpected bargains at a local sale, including bucket-list items that you'll purchase with some of your bonus money.

Relationships

Social aspects this month bring a variety of invitations your way. Make them a priority and let go of workaholic tendencies for a few days. Be sure to plan a gathering with siblings and their children, treating them to a favorite amusement park for a day of fun and games around July 12. A mid-month gathering of neighbors features a cookout, enjoyable games, and contests designed to entertain guests of all ages.

Success and Money

Feedback from the company hierarchy around the 1st brings outstanding news for star performers on the team whose output has exceeded goals. Expect an invitation mid-month to a festive evening celebration that includes spouses or partners to present awards and acknowledge dedicated commitment to meeting goals. Be proud.

Pitfalls and Potential Problems

On July 2 Neptune in Pisces goes retrograde in your solar eighth house just before the Fourth of July holiday. Rainy weather often accompanies this transit, and household plumbing could spring an unexpected leak. Be sure sinks and toilets are in good shape if you plan to travel. Schedule an extra day off on the 5th to recover or make repairs if necessary.

Rewarding Days
1, 5, 12, 20

Challenging Days
2, 9, 14, 23

Leo | August

Overall Theme

Mercury, the messenger planet, goes retrograde on the 5th in Virgo and your solar second house and then resumes direct motion on the 28th in Leo and your solar first house. Be on top of schedule changes, missing information, or confusing messages. Postpone signing important documents if possible.

Relationships

August 9 is one of the best days for bonding with individuals in your local area. You could hear from siblings, cousins, neighborhood residents, and your children's teachers. Accept an invitation to a Sunday brunch on the 11th hosted by parents or another close relative. Get ready for a visit from relatives living in a long-distance location around August 23.

Success and Money

Be sure to pay tuition bills before mid-August for children attending private school or college with the money set aside in education accounts. The last week in August indicates a flurry of activity from the management team looking at dates to schedule key meetings once most employees have returned from vacation. Wrap-up dates for a project are a possibility.

Pitfalls and Potential Problems

The Full Moon on the 19th in Aquarius and your solar seventh house reveals tension with your partner just as you are leaving for work. Suggest discussing the problem later on, letting no distractions keep you from exploring the source of the angst and creating an open-minded environment for sharing dialogue objectively.

Rewarding Days

9, 11, 23, 25

Challenging Days

5, 10, 19, 26

Leo | September

Overall Theme

Check out all the activity taking place in your solar eighth house this month as you welcome the final Lunar Eclipse of the year in Pisces on September 17. You have been rearranging finances, paying down debt, and creating savings options with insistent Saturn in Pisces in residence in this same house while contending with late-degree Neptune in Pisces tempting you with attractive investment options.

Relationships

Work with loan officers after September 2 to explore competitive rates. On the 13th, rapport with colleagues extends into the dinner period when most members agree to attend a happy hour and celebrate the strengths of the group before heading home for the weekend. Bond with your mate on the 15th, enjoying a sports event and a festive fall-themed dinner.

Success and Money

Recent storm activities that took a toll on the local community inspire you to initiate a fund drive to buy food, supplies, and maintenance services to repair damage. Your boss likes the idea, gives you a generous check to seed the cause, and gives you permission to ask employees for help. Visualize the pot of gold growing for a worthy cause.

Pitfalls and Potential Problems

I hope you're ready for Uranus to turn retrograde on September 1 in Taurus and your solar tenth house of career, creating sudden shifts in direction and alerting you to stay flexible to reworking parts of a current project.

Rewarding Days

2, 13, 15, 21

Challenging Days

3, 11, 12, 17

Leo | October

Overall Theme

After securing a refinancing loan and identifying a contractor to make household renovations, you could learn that the terms of the original agreement have shifted, meaning you have to renegotiate the loan. Options include shopping for a new lender and canceling the contract. Jupiter goes retrograde on October 9 in Gemini and your solar eleventh house of goals and dreams, greatly influencing the direction of these plans. Keep shopping.

Relationships

The year's final Solar Eclipse falls on October 2 in Libra and your solar third house, highlighting rapport with neighbors. Why not prepare a pot of chili and invite nearby football lovers over to share this savory dish while watching the Sunday afternoon game on October 18. You and your partner strengthen your relationship by sharing many romantic moments this month.

Success and Money

Looks like the work environment that houses your team is in line for remodeling and/or upgraded equipment, another perk tied to valuable mental processes that crank out important solutions for everyday operation. Your partner is likely to receive a promotion or bonus this month. Acknowledge the show of excellence.

Pitfalls and Potential Problems

Pluto resumes direct motion in Capricorn on October 11 after being retrograde in both Aquarius and Capricorn since May 2. This transformative planet will enter Aquarius and your solar seventh house of partners for good on November 19, prodding you to examine what is working in close relationships and what needs enrichment.

Rewarding Days

2, 5, 8, 15

Challenging Days

4, 14, 17, 25

Leo | November

Overall Theme

Everything seems to be falling in place for you when the New Moon in Scorpio shines in your solar fourth house on November 1. Home renovations are scheduled for completion ahead of the holiday. Activity centers around family gatherings, visits, and multiple phone calls and text messages. Plans take a successful turn when Saturn in Pisces goes direct on November 15 and you finish shopping for upcoming holiday meals.

Relationships

Set a big table for the Thanksgiving feast. Get help with party favors and flowers. Guests could include not only immediate family and nearby parents and kin but also your boss and a few coworkers who may be unable to travel home. Invite friends for cocktails and appetizers on the 22nd for a pre-holiday toast.

Success and Money

Feeing prosperous, you and your partner may opt to visit a local shelter to make donations of cash and supplies for those who have struggled through recent hardships. Mars in your sign for most of November gives you added energy to complete shopping for holiday gifts for friends and family. Donate food to your favorite charity.

Pitfalls and Potential Problems

Watch financial transactions on the 10th, especially if you are ordering goods online. Check receipts carefully. Long-distance communication is poor on the 13th, necessitating additional phone calls or messages to clarify details. Mercury in Sagittarius turns retrograde on the 25th just as arriving guests gather for Thanksgiving, indicating possible delays.

Rewarding Days

1, 8, 15, 22

Challenging Days

4, 10, 13, 25

Leo | December

Overall Theme

High activity and new beginnings prevail this month, with two New Moons in Sagittarius (on the 1st) and Capricorn (on the 30th), a Full Moon in Gemini on the 15th, Neptune in Pisces moving direct on the 7th, and Mercury stationing to move direct on December 15 in Sagittarius. Attend a holiday lunch with your work team the week of December 9. Wrap up business travel by December 3.

Relationships

Children are center stage this month, beginning on December 1 when you plan a special outing and photo op to see Santa at his local workshop. Siblings arrive around December 23 for a holiday visit in a week filled with festive events. If you live in a cold climate, make reservations around December 27 to enjoy snow-related winter sports such as ice skating, skiing, and hockey with visitors.

Success and Money

You return from your final holiday shopping spree loaded with bargains on the 9th, when pre-holiday sales offer slashed prices on popular toys and hot ticket items the younger set enjoys. Buying power soars with discounts. Write that final check of the year for your favorite charity.

Pitfalls and Potential Problems

Mars turns retrograde on December 6 in Leo and your solar first house, so it might be wise to stay close to home and away from any erratic energy created by this feisty planet. Mars won't go direct until February 23, 2025. Bide your time wrapping presents, baking, and gathering ornaments to trim an elegant tree. Finalize your holiday menu. Avoid arguments at work on the 12th.

Rewarding Days

1, 9, 23, 27

Challenging Days

6, 12, 15, 21

Leo Action Table

These dates reflect the best—but not the only—times for success and ease in these activities, according to your Sun sign.

	JAN	FEB	MAR	APR	MAY	JUN	JUL	AUG	SEP	OCT	NOV	DEC
Move		13				1				8		
Romance			16		28				15		22	1
Seek counseling/ coaching	11		13		9		12	9			1	
Ask for a raise		25		10			1		21			
Vacation				28				23		2		
Get a loan	15					26						9

Virgo

The Virgin
August 23 to September 22

♍

Element: Earth	Glyph: Greek symbol for containment
Quality: Mutable	Anatomy: Abdomen, gallbladder, intestines
Polarity: Yin/feminine	Colors: Taupe, gray, navy blue
Planetary Ruler: Mercury	Animals: Domesticated animals
Meditation: I can allow time for myself	Myths/Legends: Demeter, Astraea, Hygeia
Gemstone: Sapphire	House: Sixth
Power Stones: Peridot, amazonite, rhodochrosite	Opposite Sign: Pisces
	Flower: Pansy
Key Phrase: I analyze	Keyword: Discriminating

The Virgo Personality

Strengths, Talents, and the Creative Spark

Virgo, your sign exudes intelligence and discernment. Mercury, your planetary ruler, takes extraordinary pride in shaping your mentally driven, analytical nature. The sixth house, which is associated with your sign, has a foothold in overseeing work you perform and keeping an eye on colleagues, daily environments, routines, and schedules. You love your pets, too, especially smaller ones no larger than dogs. Virgos are fascinated by certain medications, vitamins, health practitioners, fitness, bodyworkers, massage, and exercise, including yoga. You may even explore alternative medicine to learn new techniques. Nutrition is important to you and draws you to using and possibly growing health-enhancing herbs and spices while assessing your kitchen's utility and upgrading appliances for maximum efficiency. Virgos often run the office, taking a hands-on approach to organizing the space, problem solving, and assuming an administrative role. Those of you who have studied feng shui might make excellent space organizers, giving consideration to the placement of furniture and equipment that maximizes employee comfort and concentration.

Many of you seek employment in communication-oriented careers, fact-finding, libraries, patient advocacy, publications, editing, and writing. Virgos find their way into a variety of healing fields, such as nursing, pediatrics, and veterinary medicine. The two distinct types of Virgos view the kitchen as either a place of domestic punishment or a culinary paradise, complete with state-of-the-art equipment and food knowledge in the form of gourmet-like presentation of visually beautiful dishes. Many top chefs are Virgos or have planets in this sign. You move through processes and do it well. This sign rules the bowels and intestines, and Virgos often have problems with digestion and are germophobes, exhibit hypochondria, go through phases where they overdose on vitamins to keep disease away, or go from being a neat freak to the outer spectrum of messiness.

Intimacy and Personal Relationships

Your preference in a partner is someone with an independent spirit, who is self-sufficient, financially stable, and emotionally grounded. You may have a tendency to attract a person who is needy and lacks money, self-esteem, or focus. When you spot these traits, you move into full fixer mode. You take out the tool kit and get ready to repair the individual's psyche, teaching them how to set priorities and connecting them with a headhunter if they are looking for a job. You normally feel at home with your fellow earth signs, Taurus and Capricorn or other Virgos. In 2024 you might be drawn to a Gemini who loves to talk and has Jupiter transiting their sign in your solar eleventh house of contacts. Be aware, Virgo, that you can be a bit critical of others who may not understand why you're complaining. A Gemini may enjoy competition and intellectual exchanges with you but will walk away if your desire to remake personal tendencies goes overboard. Then you'll probably set your sights on a serious Scorpio or a home-loving Cancer. Children in your life benefit from your keen interest in their education, teachers, and after-school activities. To their delight, you budget time to help with projects, fundraising drives, and sports activities. Friends usually have many common interests with you, and you socialize regularly.

Values and Resources

A calendar and your cell phone are among your favorite tools. You're seldom without them since you place a high priority on tracking appointments, schedules, and the timeline on work assignments. You show passion for meeting work-related challenges and are often at the center of workplace relationships with clients, coworkers, collaborators, colleagues, and customers. Not surprisingly, you're often at the center of managing the daily routine in the organization, making recommendations for implementing more efficient performance options, evaluating processes and procedures, and replacing equipment with updated models. Your ability to settle differences among staff and solve problems adds a dimension of responsibility to your work that makes you valuable to executives. You're adept at working compatibly in organizations that are diverse in size and complexity, yet you often prefer small companies or practices, where you build loyal rapport and bond with the team.

Blind Spots and Blockages

Virgos have a tendency to internalize stress and easily fall into worrywart patterns, even if they don't show it on the surface. If something occurs that you don't like, you can engage in excessive nagging or complaining, often to people other than the person you hold accountable. You have been known to report incidents with a one-sided view that can give the other party an undeserved bad reputation. Learn to accept people for who they really are. Holding a grudge can take a toll on your body, affecting digestion and leading to ulcers, stomach disorders, and problems with the bowels. Critics say you spend too much time focusing on details, reediting your work, or sending work back to staff for corrections multiple times when you are the one initiating excessive minor tweaks. Acquaintances complain about your frugal nature and reluctance to make donations to charities or buy gifts for family and friends.

Goals and Success

Dedication to your work, along with the passion to perform it, makes you a conscientious role model focused on monitoring the integrity and quality of the final product. People in your circle acknowledge the high work standards that you proudly display even when you seem to do everything that lands in your lap instead of delegating a portion to others. You could write the book on how to succeed in service-oriented professions. Once you are happily employed in a job you love, you assess the function of daily routines, enjoying harmonious relationships with staff. Nirvana for you is acknowledging that you have landed a position that offers a great deal of leverage to run the operation and witness the positive effects that your role plays on producing satisfied administrators, clients, customers, patients, and support staff. Management strategies you offer and how you implement them have a strong impact on the success of the organization thanks to your eye for detail, troubleshooting, and focus on the goals.

Virgo Keywords for 2024
Analysis, assignment, assimilation

The Year Ahead for Virgo

In 2024 your solar seventh house of romantic and business partners could very well be your chart's most active zone. That's because Saturn in Pisces is there to remind you of the status of commitments you've made to those in your personal or professional circles. Simultaneously, transiting Neptune in Pisces is present there as well and continues to bring you admirers, baffle you with out-of-the-blue comments, and cast a dreamy spell over you. Also in your solar seventh house is the second Lunar Eclipse of the year in Pisces, which occurs on September 17. Wrapping up a cycle of travel, reunions, attention to higher education, and foreign affairs is Jupiter in Taurus, completing a run in your solar ninth house on May 24. Don't pause too long before looking to networks and friends for benefits and windfalls this year when transiting Jupiter enters Gemini and your solar tenth house on May 25 and the focus turns to your career aspirations, responsibilities, and organizational advancement. The ever-feisty Uranus in Taurus continues the final phase of its seven-year cycle in your solar ninth house, indicating a few more shakeups to your vacation plans, a new perspective on foreign interests, or a long-distance job offer you'd be reluctant to refuse.

Take a good look at your solar fifth house of romance, children and their interests, your social life, and sports and entertainment venues for signs that Pluto in Capricorn is ready to make its final exit after debuting here in 2008. No doubt you've learned how to have more fun by paying attention to the needs of your lover, your offspring, or children you coach, and taking a sabbatical from excessive work habits to kick back and enjoy life. Pluto escapes into Aquarius and your solar sixth house of daily living and working patterns on January 20 before inching back into Capricorn on September 1 and completing that important letting-go cycle that made you hang on far too long to what you didn't need. Besides the Pisces eclipse in September, three other eclipses pay visits this year. First, your solar second house of income and assets greets a Lunar Eclipse in Libra on March 25, then your solar eighth house hosts the first Solar Eclipse of the year on April 8, which lands in Aries and calls attention to the state of your finances. The final Solar Eclipse of 2024 appears in Libra and your solar second house of money and salary on October 2, providing clues about security, employment, and tempting avenues of self-development that lie ahead.

Jupiter

When Jupiter flew through Aries in 2003 and you managed both personal and corporate money, so much recovery and regrouping of finances took place in your solar eighth house that you thought working overtime was the new norm. Then Jupiter headed for Taurus on May 16, 2023, and your solar ninth house and you managed to take a nice, long vacation, reunite with family living at a distance, and sign up for a few career-enhancing courses. Now you have until May 24, 2024, to take another vacation before Jupiter transitions into Gemini and your solar tenth house of career and a new set of demands claims your time. Once Jupiter settles into this house, you'll discover plans that the manage-

ment team has for your future in the form of a new assignment, a promotion, a leadership position, or a transfer to another location. So nice
to have options! Jupiter here provides opportunities to expand your
interests and increase stability and security in the face of shaky financial
markets. The planet of prosperity goes retrograde on October 9 and
turns direct on February 4, 2025. Those of you born between August
23 and September 15 see the most action during this cycle. Explore the
variety of interesting work that is available to you and choose what satisfies your creative mind.

Saturn

As you begin the first full year with Saturn in Pisces and your solar
seventh house of partners, what are you looking forward to the most?
What qualities describe your most important relationships? Are your
relationships open and agreeable, or are you dealing with constraints?
The seventh house expands partnerships to cover advisers, collaborators, consultants, medical and legal professionals, and the public. A
Saturn transit like this opposition aspect to your Sun can open old
wounds or create new ones that need attention to ensure the relationship survives. Saturn transiting the seventh house can bring coldness
or indifference to the behavior of formerly loving couples. Arguments
can arise in the dealings of business partners, creating a growing rift
when parties have vastly different opinions on how to manage professional affairs. Mediation or critical advice from subject matter specialists opens discussion and presents the feelings of both sides objectively
so that solutions aid in healing differences. This year, both transiting
Neptune and a Lunar Eclipse on September 17 are in Pisces and your
solar seventh house of close partnerships, adding a triple layer of
complications to sort through—all doable if parties are sincere about
resolving differences. Virgos born between August 25 and September
13 relate the most to this year's transit.

Uranus

Since 2018, your solar ninth house of the higher mind, advanced education, foreign countries and cultures, in-laws, philosophy, religion, the
publishing and writing fields, and long-distance travel has been home to
unexpected events, erratic behavior, delays, or disruption while Uranus
has occupied Taurus, an earth sign that is compatible with Virgo. Communication and travel have been major sources of conflict that added

tension to daily routines and work plans, calling for analysis of conditions to get back on track. Multiple business or pleasure trips, scheduled training, job transfers, or visits from in-laws may have had to be canceled or postponed. Some were due to unexpected illness or shifting economic conditions. Thankfully those aspects are gone. Uranus starts off 2024 in retrograde motion, turning direct on January 27. The chaotic planet will station to move retrograde on September 1 and remain so until January 30, 2025. If your birthday falls between September 11 and 21, you are likely to experience notable activity from transiting Uranus this year. Tackle assignments, assimilate new information to aid productivity, and stay optimistic during this phase.

Neptune

The major sphere of operation for you this year, Virgo, is your solar seventh house, where Neptune in Pisces continues to influence the action involving personal and business partners, including advisers, cooperators, consultants, dreamers, love interests, open enemies, psychics, the public, and legal and medical professionals. You have had to shake your head more than once since 2011, when Neptune landed in this house and seemed to mask the truth or distort the facts that your logical Virgo mind was processing in favor of showing you fairy-tale endings, easy outs, glamour with no pain, and people who were very different from what you thought they were. You may be tempted to daydream or ignore those feelings coming from your gut that are telling you all is not stable in relationship paradise. Tap into Neptune's soft spot by using compassion and understanding to draw important people into serious discussions and sort out the sources of angst. With both transiting Saturn and the September 17th Lunar Eclipse in Pisces, you could be dealing with more than one hazy situation. Take advantage of Neptune's psychic side. Be alert to those who display negative energy, and protect yourself from manipulation. Those of you born between September 17 and 22 see the most activity this year as Neptune moves closer to completing this long cycle in Pisces. Neptune goes retrograde on July 2 and stations move direct on December 7. Use discipline and a fair mind to ferret out the truth. You have the tools and the resources, Virgo. What a powerhouse you'll be when you put it all together and use your intuitive gifts to assimilate the truth.

Pluto

You're probably watching the calendar, Virgo, to make sure that Pluto in Capricorn is not stalling for any more time in your solar fifth house, where it has been since January 2008. You are naturally inquisitive and enjoy asking questions. You just don't want anyone probing for more than you want to divulge. Pluto enjoys going on a mining expedition to find out where you have hidden the blocks that keep you from letting go of hurts. This planet's lengthy residence in your solar fifth house has been instrumental in your dealings with children, competitive events, your social and romantic life, outdoor activities, risk-taking, speculation, and vacation destinations. You should be experiencing satisfying freedom from pain associated with many of these areas.

On January 20, Pluto enters Aquarius and your solar sixth house of daily routines and schedules, health, nutrition, pets, and those you interact with in the workplace. Your service-oriented nature knows this territory all too well, and it won't be long before Pluto starts reminding you that you don't have to tolerate unresolved issues connected to your mental and physical body, workplace relationships, fears about compatibility with the organization's management style, and balancing work with leisure time. Pluto goes retrograde on May 2 in Aquarius, moves back into Capricorn on September 1, and goes direct on October 11 in the last degree of Capricorn in your solar fifth house. Virgos born between August 23 and 26 experience a few stressful shifts during Pluto's transit of the early degrees of Aquarius, while those of you born between September 21 and 23 breathe easier when Pluto completes its transit of Capricorn on November 19 and hands the responsibility for probing the subconscious over to impersonal Aquarius.

How Will This Year's Eclipses Affect You?

This year's four eclipses, two lunar (Full Moon) and two solar (New Moon), are ready to generate intense periods that start to manifest a few months before their actual occurrence. The Libra/Aries cycle wraps up in March 2023 to make way for the Pisces/Virgo eclipses, the first of which makes its debut in September of 2024. Eclipses unfold in cycles involving all twelve signs of the zodiac and usually occur in pairs about two weeks apart. Never fear eclipses—just think of them as opportunities for growth that allow you to release old patterns. Expect surprises that elicit both positive and perplexing feelings and outcomes. The closer an eclipse is to a planet or point in your birth chart, the greater the importance it has in your life, especially if one of those planets is in the same degree as the eclipse.

The first Lunar Eclipse of the year occurs on March 25 in Libra and your solar second house of assets, money, personal income, planned purchases, valued material goods, and self-development. You're likely to come into contact with bankers and financial experts and learn more about credit scores, loan terms, and purchasing power, as well as the outlook on the economy and incremental raises that reflect how others see your career potential. Make appointments with fiscal experts to review your portfolio, and manage savings and debt wisely.

On April 8, the first Solar Eclipse of the year arrives in Aries and your solar eighth house of joint holdings, investments, estates, wills, sex, birth, death, taxes, and mortgages. With the economy in a state of flux, you'll profit from doing a complete review of your budget to analyze what accounts could benefit from proportional adjustments, how you can be sure you are saving enough for taxes and insurance, and how to save more for retirement. If you need assistance, consider consolidating debt by consulting qualified experts.

A sign change accompanies the second Lunar Eclipse of 2024 on September 17, when the lunation appears in Pisces and your solar seventh house. This department of life covers personal and business partners, including spouses, roommates, common-law partners, and individuals with whom you have legal dealings. This eclipse could put pressure on you to address romantic relationships if you are contemplating an engagement, a marriage, or a separation (if discord has been an issue). This romantic Pisces eclipse could lead to a surprise proposal or elopement. Examine business relationships as well to make sure partners or investors are on the same page. Take steps to settle any misunderstandings or differences that keep you from enjoying what you cherish.

Two weeks later, on October 2, the final Solar Eclipse of 2024 occurs in Libra and your solar second house of earning power, assets, and planned purchases. Since the March 25th Lunar Eclipse in Libra occurred, you have most likely assessed the strength of your holdings and made changes to increase savings, limited use of credit cards, or paid down debt. You may have received a promotion as well, since eclipses in this money house are known to produce windfalls, sometimes when you least expect them. Your increased knowledge of money management leads you to success.

Virgo | January

Overall Theme

You have a good feeling about career and financial prospects as the new year dawns. This month Mercury goes direct in Sagittarius on the 1st and gives a thumbs-up to further discussion of a household project. Work on your resume if you are looking for a new job and send it to a headhunter after Uranus in Taurus goes direct on the 27th.

Relationships

Siblings gather on the 6th for sports or entertainment that includes games for the children. Share your favorite dish with your hungry guests. Single Virgos are ready to meet a new prospect on the 11th, when the Moon and Pluto send sexy vibes your way. Follow up when Jupiter in Taurus trines Mars in Capricorn on the 12th.

Success and Money

Plan spring travel to a favorite resort while Jupiter in Taurus finishes a cycle in your solar ninth house. Holiday cash funds a sale on winter clothing around the 11th, and you have enough left over to splurge on dinner with a friend when the New Moon rises in Capricorn that same day.

Pitfalls and Potential Problems

Watch out for credit card fraud in your neighborhood while making purchases around the 19th. Too many people may be present and not enough help. Don't listen to a rumor on January 21 related to workplace management. The facts are unsupported, so it is best not to discuss what you overhear.

Rewarding Days

1, 6, 11, 12

Challenging Days

8, 16, 19, 21

Virgo | February

Overall Theme

Spend time this month assessing the details of your financial accounts. Discuss ways to order in bulk to save money on groceries and goods with your partner without wasting anything. Look for free shipping on often-used products to save money on gasoline. Honor Leap Day on February 29 by ordering pizza and watching an enjoyable film.

Relationships

Agree to meet a cousin for lunch on the 3rd to catch up on family news. Expressions of love from dear ones fill your heart with happiness, motivating you to set up a surprise date with your significant other around the 11th to celebrate Valentine's Day early.

Success and Money

A budget meeting around the 8th outlines the quality and types of incentives your company plans to distribute this year. Look for a bonus based on the skillful way you performed your job and covered for a coworker out on extended leave. The New Moon on the 9th falls in Aquarius and your solar sixth house of daily living and working patterns, giving you a perfect time to gather staff for lunch with a menu that honors the Lunar New Year of the Dragon on the 10th.

Pitfalls and Potential Problems

You're more tired than usual when the Full Moon in Virgo on February 24 keeps you from tackling planned household chores after a particularly exhausting workweek. A good night's sleep helps. Don't react if messages are confusing on the 17th and communication shows strain.

Rewarding Days

3, 9, 10, 13

Challenging Days

1, 4, 17, 24

Virgo | March

Overall Theme

Start off the month donating time to a neighborhood project on March 2. The neighborhood association might free up funds to rework the common areas and could use your organizing and design skills. Figure out what popular new attraction would bring enjoyment to users and make the perfect addition to the local scene.

Relationships

Agree to attend a happy hour with coworkers on March 5. If single, you have the love vibes to meet a potential partner through mutual acquaintances. At the prompting of a friend, you could agree to join a sports team or enroll in an exercise class. When the Pisces New Moon shows up in your solar seventh house on the 10th, your love partner might monopolize your time and insist on a short vacation.

Success and Money

The year's first Lunar Eclipse occurs on March 25 in Libra and your solar second house, strengthening your resolve to compare credit card perks and consider opening a new account. If you are in the market, offers are abundant.

Pitfalls and Potential Problems

Household relationships are prone to misunderstandings on the 3rd when two family members clash over priorities, and both seem determined to get a neutral party to settle it. Don't volunteer. Electronic equipment may fail on the 7th, necessitating an unplanned repair that won't be completed until early the following week.

Rewarding Days

2, 5, 13, 18

Challenging Days

1, 3, 7, 25

Virgo | April

Overall Theme

Take April 1 seriously this year by noting that Mercury is turning retrograde in Aries on this day, so it won't be to your advantage to start new projects, sign contracts, or purchase a new car. As you wait out the three-week period until Mercury moves direct on the 25th, rework assignments in progress or edit written material before resuming your timeline.

Relationships

Get to know more about a new romantic prospect on April 2, when your interest grows fonder. Discover their favorite haunts and make a date to invest quality time in this person. Virgos already in solid relationships share deeply personal feelings on the 6th, when both of you feel the need to bond.

Success and Money

Vacation planning dominates priorities this month as you eagerly pore over brochures, resort sites, and travel videos selling once-in-a-lifetime experiences. Your biggest dilemma lies in whether to book domestic travel or go out of the country to satisfy your quest for adventure. A Solar Eclipse on the 8th in Aries and your solar eighth house highlights funds you have set aside for travel.

Pitfalls and Potential Problems

People at your workplace keep a low profile on the 12th. You may sense exhaustion over having to rework a proposal or a key assignment component. Limit discussion with your boss. A nice Moon-Jupiter aspect on the 14th turns momentum around, reviving the collaborative energy.

Rewarding Days

2, 6, 10, 14

Challenging Days

9, 12, 22, 23

Virgo | May

Overall Theme

Spontaneity drives the connection between you and your partner on the 3rd when you book a room for a quick getaway. You'll end the month on a romantic high, renewing bonds of affection.

Relationships

Both your love connection and your relationship with your boss claim major attention this month. The CEO tempts you with an attractive opportunity for a promising new position. Work demands fill your calendar during the first half of May. Give collaborators up-to-date reports before going on vacation.

Success and Money

The prospect is good for a raise or bonus during the first ten days of the month. If you work on commission, look for good news mid-month when greater-than-anticipated sales numbers show a successful first quarter. Look for improvements in your workplace when your CFO authorizes funds for renovation.

Pitfalls and Potential Problems

Pluto in early Aquarius makes a retrograde station on May 2 in your solar sixth house, urging you to simplify and organize work documents for easy access to data. Make medical appointments a priority. Disagreements among board members in a professional organization you work with could lead to the suspension of a vote and delay funding after May 11.

Rewarding Days

3, 8, 9, 31

Challenging Days

2, 10, 11, 23

Virgo | June

Overall Theme

With Jupiter in Gemini transiting your solar tenth house, career matters are the focus of activity, especially when the New Moon in Gemini on the 6th aligns with Jupiter in Gemini and Pluto in Aquarius. Venus in Gemini joins these planets, along with the Sun, giving you opportunities to experience positive money and career advancement and enjoy a rewarding vacation. Business travel is a possibility.

Relationships

Relatives or good friends travel from distant locations to spend time with you and the family around June 4. Could it be time for an in-law visit? Provide children with several games to keep them amused. The executive staff hosts an event on the 6th promising an enjoyable evening of fine dining and entertainment. Recognition for accomplishment brings inner joy.

Success and Money

There is so much to celebrate the first week of June that is praiseworthy and positive regarding the accomplishments of you and your workmates. This helps you all withstand worrying economic news that could affect staffing later in the year.

Pitfalls and Potential Problems

Saturn in Pisces goes retrograde on June 29 in aspect to transiting Mercury and Venus in Cancer, giving a little slack to unfolding events late in the month. Check departure dates and reservations for changes if you're traveling in late June. Neptune in Pisces is in the mix as well. The Capricorn Full Moon on the 21st opposes the Sun, Mercury, and Venus, which could put a crimp in date-night plans for couples.

Rewarding Days

1, 4, 6, 26

Challenging Days

3, 7, 21, 29

Virgo | July

Overall Theme

Early in the month you're in the company of planets in compatible signs, like Venus in Cancer and Mars and Uranus in Taurus, suggesting you get out to enjoy the Fourth of July holiday and the local attractions. Celebrate the nation's birthday by taking part in parades or other events.

Relationships

Welcome traveling guests arriving on July 2 to share the festivities with you. The Cancer New Moon on the 5th favors a meeting's success for approving new initiatives in a group project. Enjoy an outing with a close friend on July 6, the perfect day for attending an outdoor concert or watching a dance troupe perform.

Success and Money

Money matters work compatibly with your budget now thanks to your astute savings management. Summer sales yield clearance bargains for items like patio furniture, deck chairs, and barbecue equipment. Meet with your boss around July 30 to review deadlines and funding needs that cover fall projects.

Pitfalls and Potential Problems

Watch for a shift in dynamics when transiting Neptune turns retrograde in the last degree of Pisces on July 2 in your solar seventh house of partnerships, which could affect both intimate and business matters in coming months. Don't make waves with your partner if you see signs of tension related to the influx of holiday visitors that could throw scheduled events off course.

Rewarding Days

5, 6, 10, 30

Challenging Days

2, 13, 19, 24

Virgo | August

Overall Theme

Venus occupies Virgo for most of the month, adding lightness to your heart as you tackle your workload to clear the backlog of tasks accumulating after employment disruptions. Mercury goes retrograde on the 5th in your sign, then quickly moves back into Leo on the 14th before going direct on August 28. The Leo New Moon on August 4 fills your intuitive mind with insight on how to present new guidelines to staff when you schedule a briefing session on the 9th.

Relationships

You and some neighbors shop for supplies for a community event scheduled for August 11. Make this a festive gathering for families and children of all ages by adding ball games, spelling contests, or board games to the entertainment venue. If you are a single Virgo, a new neighbor could find you attractive and eager to exchange contact information.

Success and Money

Workplace communication flows smoothly and reflects an abundance of team spirit. Acknowledge the outstanding efforts of all to pick up the pace and pool talent to cover human resources shortfalls when attrition occurs. Accept the request to interview candidates for vacant positions.

Pitfalls and Potential Problems

Your love partner has an emotional setback when retrograde Mercury in Leo forms a stressful inconjunct aspect to transiting Neptune in Pisces on the 15th, possibly affecting weekend getaway plans. Explore the reasons why this loved one is feeling so fragile by seeking therapeutic advice.

Rewarding Days

4, 9, 11, 23

Challenging Days

10, 15, 19, 22

Virgo | September

Overall Theme

With the New Moon in Virgo on Labor Day, September 2 is a good day to shop for furnishings and dress up your lovely home. The final Lunar Eclipse of the year occurs on the 17th in Pisces and your solar seventh house of personal and business partners and focuses on the quality and continuity of important relationships. Pay attention to changes in attitude.

Relationships

September 2 brings an invitation to a get-together with favorite neighbors that makes you thankful for living in a community with a welcoming vibe. Single Virgos agree to spend an enjoyable weekend with a new love interest at a fancy resort on September 13. Married Virgos seek intimacy with their partner in a favorite getaway spot. Friends gather for a leisurely dinner around the 26th to choose musical entertainment options and lock in dates for the coming holiday season.

Success and Money

Another excellent career cycle focuses on the role you play in encouraging team cohesiveness. Positive aspects show your interest in providing quality time to assist coworkers, especially those new to the job, to improve their effectiveness. Going the extra mile to support others could lead to a raise or promotion when the management team notices results.

Pitfalls and Potential Problems

Uranus in Taurus goes retrograde on September 1, affecting Labor Day plans for many. Planetary aspects indicate tension in diverse circles. Don't get caught up in personal disagreements or argue about politics with these edgy vibes around. Get a good night's sleep after activities die down.

Rewarding Days

2, 13, 15, 26

Challenging Days

11, 17, 20, 27

Virgo | October

Overall Theme

Planetary movement heats up in October, beginning with Jupiter in Gemini's shift into retrograde motion on the 9th, creating tension with your Sun and any planets present at 21 degrees of the mutable signs (Gemini, Virgo, Sagittarius, and Pisces). Challenging aspects highlight any unresolved relationship issues. Be patient and talk them out.

Relationships

Spend quality time with your family on the 8th, enjoying a favorite comfort food meal and playing games. Treat your partner to an enjoyable evening out on October 15. Plan a visit with a friend to a trendy restaurant around the 23rd.

Success and Money

The second Solar Eclipse of the year occurs on October 2 in Libra and your solar second house of income, highlighting the money you and your partner have saved by cutting back on overstocking supplies and food—a nice sum that will go far in helping to fund vacations or holiday purchases. Assess your stock portfolio after October 11, when Pluto turns direct in Capricorn and your solar eighth house of investments.

Pitfalls and Potential Problems

You may learn that a child's school behavior is anything but admirable on October 10 and make arrangements to meet with the teacher to discuss details. The executive staff could be at odds around the 20th over how to handle extra assignments after they receive an assessment of needs from a major partner in a project.

Rewarding Days

2, 8, 11, 15

Challenging Days

9, 10, 14, 20

Virgo | November

Overall Theme

Lofty, insightful Jupiter in Gemini continues to preside over your solar tenth house of career and authority, exuding a festive air and prompting your CEO to gift generous bonuses to employees. Assimilate the holiday spirit as you cheerfully wrap up loose ends on your task list and begin planning your holiday celebrations.

Relationships

Make a donation to a local organization that offers a holiday meal to individuals short on funds. Start baking favorite treats with family members around November 3. Hold a place around your Thanksgiving table for cherished friends, then serve their favorite dishes. Toast those you love with sincere gratitude for their presence in your life.

Success and Money

Buy holiday gifts before Mercury in Sagittarius turns retrograde on November 25, giving you plenty of time to get them wrapped and sent. Use your earned bonus to fund holiday events and shop for decorations. Enjoy good news related to anticipated salary increases after the start of the new year.

Pitfalls and Potential Problems

The Thanksgiving Moon in Scorpio on the 28th in your communication-oriented solar third house clashes with retrograde Mars in Leo and your solar twelfth house of seclusion. Avoid participating in controversial discussions and watch for signs of guests imbibing too much alcohol. Cut off the supply graciously. A delicious meal and peaceful celebration is your jam.

Rewarding Days

1, 3, 11, 19

Challenging Days

7, 10, 17, 25

Virgo | December

Overall Theme
This month there are two New Moons, the first in Sagittarius on December 1 and the second in Capricorn on December 30. You're eager to get the holiday festivities rolling and probably sent out invitations to events the day after Thanksgiving. Consider participating in a service project with your children to help those in need.

Relationships
Neptune in Pisces goes direct on December 7 and party season begins, with early invitations from neighbors. You're likely to hear from family members at distant locations regarding holiday plans on this day. Bond with your love partner on December 9. Finish shopping by December 10 and purchase entertainment tickets as a final surprise for family members. The 10th is also a good day to have a holiday meal with good friends.

Success and Money
Projections for funding contract work with your input are spot-on. A performance award could be in the works after January 1. Embrace gratitude for meaningful work as the year ends while anticipating opportunities for career growth in 2025.

Pitfalls and Potential Problems
Mercury in Sagittarius stations to move direct on December 15 as it opposes the Full Moon in Gemini, suggesting you avoid travel on that date. Mars moves retrograde in Leo and your solar twelfth house on the 6th, reinforcing the advice to revise your itinerary.

Rewarding Days
7, 9, 10, 23

Challenging Days
6, 11, 15, 28

Virgo Action Table

These dates reflect the best—but not the only—times for success and ease in these activities, according to your Sun sign.

	JAN	FEB	MAR	APR	MAY	JUN	JUL	AUG	SEP	OCT	NOV	DEC
Move	11		13			4					1	
Romance		10		2					13		11	9
Seek counseling/coaching			18		31		6	11		15		
Ask for a raise					9		30					
Vacation	6			10					2			
Get a loan		13				1		23		2		10

Libra

The Scales
September 23 to October 23

♎

Element: Air	Glyph: Scales of justice, setting sun
Quality: Cardinal	Anatomy: Kidneys, lower back, appendix
Polarity: Yang/masculine	Colors: Blue, pink
Planetary Ruler: Venus	Animals: Brightly plumed birds
Meditation: I balance conflicting desires	Myths/Legends: Venus, Cinderella, Hera
Gemstone: Opal	House: Seventh
Power Stones: Tourmaline, kunzite, blue lace agate	Opposite Sign: Aries
	Flower: Rose
Key Phrase: I balance	Keyword: Harmony

The Libra Personality

Strengths, Talents, and the Creative Spark

The significance of your partnership-oriented Sun sign is that it rules the seventh house of romantic, business, and professional relationships, roommates, the public in general, advisers, counselors, diplomats, legal and medical practitioners, and your shadow self. You attract an abundance of relationships during your lifetime. Your claim to fame is that you take great pride in spending quality time with friends and associates and staying in touch with them frequently. Yours is the second of the air sign triplicity, which includes Gemini and Aquarius. Libra rules the kidneys, pancreas, lower back, and urethra. With Venus ruling your sign, many of you find yourselves occupied in careers where you exude charm and tact in your communication style, provide service to clients and customers, and show a flair for social organization. Most of you are big Internet or Web communicators, social networkers, and Facebook, Twitter, Instagram, or Snapchat fans, and you utilize Zoom conferences and are LinkedIn subscribers. If you aren't, you probably talk on the phone frequently or use Skype to connect with contacts in distant places. At any rate, you likely spend considerable time on your sophisticated phones, using the data-sharing features, sending photos, and staying in touch with contacts in both family and business. Some of you are eager sharers and may forget to listen.

Many Libras show creativity in the arts, crafts, and decorating, compete in sports or politics, or take up dancing. Others say your hands are magic in terms of what you develop or what you touch. You crave order rather than chaos and like routines that keep you on track, preferring a predictable work schedule. Indecisiveness and procrastination may get in the way of your plans, and you frequently comment that you wonder where the time goes. Don't worry, though, you're probably having fun. If you have a healthy earth presence (like Virgo or Taurus) in the planetary lineup of your birth chart, this distraction may not be an issue for you.

Intimacy and Personal Relationships

Libra is the universal sign of partnerships, and very few among you feel complete without a partner. You enjoy memberships in organizations and often play a leading role in their success, attracting many friends in your networks. You may marry young and eventually divorce, but it won't be long before you venture out into the dating world to find your next mate. Those of you with children often create blended families when you marry again. You are strongly drawn to individuals who share your desire for mental support and frequent communication. Clams who live in their own shell need not apply. You are very sociable and enjoy sharing dates with friends or members of groups with similar interests. Sometimes Libras become infatuated with a potential partner, which can lead to premature commitment before you know enough about the person to make a serious decision. Ask questions and spend time in a variety of settings so you see the individual displaying their attractive qualities as well as their flaws, temperament fluctuations, and anger management skills. You could be drawn to a member of your opposite sign, Aries, or the other air signs, Gemini and Aquarius. Leo and Sagittarius often make terrific travel and adventure companions. A more difficult union is with a Cancer or Capricorn, unless you have a compatible Moon or Ascendant to add a level of understanding to the relationship. You are very good about looking in on elderly or ill relatives and friends and thoughtfully stay in touch. Children cherish the special bonds you share.

Values and Resources

Peace and harmony appeal to your cooperative nature as the sign most affiliated with personal and business partners. You are out of your comfort zone when your love relationship suffers due to misunderstandings and tension permeates the home environment. You have a strong desire to talk it out and get to the bottom of issues, whether they exist at home base or dominate your daily routine at work. You look for ways to compromise when balance is missing and set your sights on reconciling differences of opinion or ideology. You prefer to create collaborative environments and restore harmony and goodwill when conditions unravel. Communication is one of your most valued assets. When the occasion calls for it, you put your diplomatic skills to work to resolve problems and appreciate dealing with parties who are willing to listen to key points intended to create receptive conditions for change.

Blind Spots and Blockages

You don't care for tense situations that make you feel hyper or lead to impulsive outbursts. Be sure to exercise to help you relax and work out internal stress. Creative avoidance, indecisiveness, and procrastination are potential downfalls, yet may be minimized with the presence of a practical Moon or strong Mercury in your natal chart. Be sure to discuss problems to avoid getting stuck in anger. If you are too close to the source of angst to be effective, consider using a mediator, a role that often suits your Libra personality. Those who interact with you frequently are known to declare they don't know where you stand on issues. Some label you wishy-washy because you won't take a position out of fear that someone might criticize you or show disappointment in your stance. Listen carefully to what others have to say and then negotiate a win for the greater good of the affected parties.

Goals and Success

Most contacts trust you and appreciate that you share information freely and keep everyone in the loop. Partnership enterprises appeal to you and often include working with your spouse in your own business. You're a sign who does well by having a sounding board for a partner. Just be careful not to say too much prematurely and risk damaging the fine rapport you have with your colleagues if you work in the corporate or government world. Many Libras show considerable flair when working with the public in a variety of fields such as the real estate industry, which can include the building and designing side of the enterprise, the sales end, or the banking side. You make excellent negotiators and mediators if the situation calls for better understanding of tense situations or resolving associated problems. You often have impeccable manners and the gift of diplomacy, which helps you assess other people's work fairly and recognize a job well done, adding to your desire to build a cohesive team. Additionally, you can succeed in a satisfying career in either the legal or the medical field, among the many suitable outlets that highlight your desire to help others achieve balance.

Libra Keywords for 2024
Clarity, compatibility, contact

The Year Ahead for Libra

In a year when two eclipses visit your sign and your solar first house, you could receive abundant attention from those in your circle who have a personal interest in your activity, appearance, and welfare. The first of these lunations occurs on March 25, a Lunar Eclipse that makes you consciously aware of your surroundings, body image, the fit of your clothing, your personality quirks, and your health. The second Libra eclipse occurs on October 2, a Solar Eclipse that highlights changes you have made in response to concerns you had earlier in the year. Your solar seventh house also hosts the year's first Solar Eclipse on April 8 in Aries, stirring up activity in your personal and business partnership sector. Two planets turn direct in January: Mercury in Sagittarius and your solar third house of communication, neighbors, and siblings on January 1, and Uranus in Taurus and your solar eighth house of obligations and joint funds and debts on January 27. What a relief to be able to resume the plans you had on the back burner and rejuvenate your sense of direction.

Pluto in Capricorn has occupied your solar fourth house of home and family since 2008 and has made you aware of what truths you have ignored and how to eliminate the baggage. On January 20, Pluto will make a move into Aquarius and your solar fifth house for several months before returning to Capricorn to finally finish its long cycle in your solar fourth house. Jupiter in Taurus will complete its rapid journey through your solar eighth house, leaving you with a better grasp of your financial picture and some surprise payoffs. On May 25, fortunate Jupiter will move into Gemini and your solar ninth house of higher education and long-distance travel. Will there be a dream vacation in your future, or will you opt to enroll in an advanced education curriculum? In the early months of 2024, transiting Uranus in Taurus will keep company with Jupiter in your solar eighth house as you watch the condition of your finances in this recovery-oriented year. Saturn in Pisces is guarding your solar sixth house of health, well-being, and daily routines, giving you a chance to heal your mind and body and clean out your inbox. Neptune in Pisces is hanging out at your workplace, too, reminding you to double-check important materials for accuracy and clarity. Create a cheerful space and be proud of all you accomplish this year.

Jupiter

Since your Libra Sun sign is ruled by Venus, you can appreciate the security bestowed on you as the year begins with Jupiter in Taurus, another Venus-ruled sign. You have instant rapport with the benevolent planet, as it alerts you to conditions that affect joint income, interest rates, mortgage and insurance payments, and the effort you and your partner are making to consolidate and pay off debt. You're probably grateful that you saw the writing on the wall in mid-2022 and refinanced your mortgage before interest rates skyrocketed and ate into your ability to pay down the loan balance. If you are still on the fence about the best strategy for eliminating debt, go slowly and concentrate on saving money, investing in government bonds, and earning a higher income. Look for the best interest rates on credit cards, too. Issuers will come looking for you if you have a stellar credit rating, something that appeals to your desire for balance. Libras born between September 28 and October 22 are most active while Jupiter is in Taurus. When Jupiter moves into Gemini, those of you born between September 23 and October 14 will benefit from the harmonious trine aspect to your Sun. Take action when opportunity knocks. Jupiter's retrograde period in 2024 runs from October 9 through February 4, 2025, in Gemini.

Saturn

Most likely you are not shocked that Saturn's entry into Pisces and your solar sixth house of work in spring of 2023 brought extra responsibilities to your workload, making you aware of the intensity of the changes taking place in your employment arena. Some of you may have been pushed to find a new job or left because you wanted better working conditions and wanted to feel appreciated. Transiting Neptune in Pisces is transiting here, too, and you may have been contending with mixed messages. On September 17 a Lunar Eclipse will land here and possibly bring to light any areas of business that need attention. If you have been in charge of managing staff or overseeing assignment distribution, you know how important it is to hire a cohesive group that works well together and has the talent to perform the work. While ideally the team gets along well, it is possible to encounter disagreements over core components, methods of accomplishing the work, and personality differences. It may be your job to head off enmity and motivate the crew to put aside differences to meet goals and timelines. Those of you born between September 25 and October 13 see the most action from this year's Saturn transit. Saturn's retrograde phase begins on June 29 and ends on November 15. Keep a clear head and enjoy success in the work environment.

Uranus

Electricity fills the air when Uranus, the planet of sudden occurrences, receives a charge and surges into action, as you are accustomed to seeing ever since this giant gas planet began its transit of Taurus and your solar eighth house of joint resources and debt back in May 2018. Although Uranus in Taurus turns direct on January 27 and you thoughtfully resume activities connected with financial affairs that you had put on hold, it will turn retrograde again on September 1 and remain so until January 30, 2025. The eighth house is one of your busy sectors in 2025 with Jupiter present for the first five months, urging you to take action to repair credit, find better loan terms, sell a property, settle a relative's estate, or select the best investments for you and your personal or business partners. Review your budget before spending hard-earned money. Be confident of positive money vibes. This transit is powerful for those of you born between October 11 and 21. You could also feel especially psychic during this period and receive impressions of all that is going on around you slightly ahead of when they actually occur. Enjoy that gift and explore opportunities that come to you in the form of job offers, raises, promotions, and lottery wins.

Neptune

Dreamy, impressionable Neptune is hanging out in your daily environment space called your solar sixth house of fitness, health, nutrition, pets, coworkers, and organizational abilities. Since Neptune has Saturn's company this year and a visit from the first eclipse in the Pisces series, you won't have much time for idle dreams and your spot-on analysis of conditions at the workplace will be put to the test. Fortify yourself with a strong cup of coffee or mug of tea and get ready to take a fresh look at your management style and the hot spots in your daily operations. The compassion you share with others will come in handy in light of shifting staff assignments, sudden job losses, health setbacks for some colleagues, or the high prices many are paying due to inflation. Think about restructuring the pay scale, providing training, reengineering key positions, and rewarding those who go the extra mile to meet timelines. Neptune is crawling to the finish line in this cycle, which most affects Libras born between October 17 and 22. The planet's retrograde period starts on July 2 in the last degree of Pisces and resumes direct motion on December 7. Treat yourself to a few good metaphysical books, meditate to stay focused, and enjoy a day at the spa when your spirit calls you to relax and chill.

Pluto

Phenomenal, transformative Pluto made its debut in Capricorn and your solar fourth house of home, family, foundations, and the end of matters back in 2008. Most of the energy work intended for this lengthy cleansing tour has been accomplished, leaving emotional and practical conditions in your household on higher ground while you experience relief that you no longer have to deal with old, troubling issues. You probably anticipated the clashes that occurred, since Libra and Capricorn have a testy relationship at times, and each degree of your sign experienced angst when Pluto came close enough to make a hard aspect to your Sun. How do you feel now: emptier if some family members have moved, quieter if you no longer have to contend with needy individuals who drain your energy, or less cluttered because you no longer store excess baggage related to guilt stemming from stressful encounters with housemates? Just breathe that refreshing air as you catch your breath and realize how courageous you have become saying no to intolerable conditions.

On January 20, resilient Pluto enters Aquarius and your solar fifth house, introducing a whole new set of dynamics to the art of releasing karma. You'll be dealing with the wide world of relationships involving children, lovers, friends, fellow entrepreneurs, individuals you teach or coach, and travel companions. Those of you born during the first three days of Libra will experience pleasant effects, even pleasant surprises, from this early Pluto transit in a compatible air sign. Pluto's retrograde movement starts on May 2 in early Aquarius and ends on October 11 in the last degree of Capricorn, affecting Libras born between October 21 and 23. Think pleasant thoughts and activate your sense of adventure for the positive changes that lie ahead.

How Will This Year's Eclipses Affect You?

This year the pressure is squarely on you, with two eclipses in your sign and one in Aries, your opposite sign. This year's four eclipses, two lunar (Full Moon) and two solar (New Moon), are ready to generate intense periods that start to manifest a few months before their actual occurrence. Eclipses unfold in cycles involving all twelve signs of the zodiac and usually occur in pairs about two weeks apart. Never fear eclipses—just think of them as opportunities for growth that allow you to release old patterns. Expect surprises that elicit both positive and perplexing feelings and outcomes. The closer an eclipse is to a planet or point in your birth chart, the greater the importance it has in your life, especially if one of those planets is in the same degree as the eclipse.

The first Lunar Eclipse of 2024 falls on March 25 in Libra and your solar first house of action, assertiveness, drive, health, image, innovation, and self-interest. If your birthday is between September 25 and 29, get ready for action and make changes you have been considering related to a fitness program, wardrobe makeover, medical procedure, or risk-taking venture. Eclipses often provide the impetus you need to take yourself out of the rat race and start your own business.

The year's first Solar Eclipse occurs on April 8 in Aries and your solar seventh house of personal and business partners, spouses, roommates, collaborators, medical and legal professionals, advisers, therapists, and public critics. Over the past year you have gained greater insight into those you cherish, admire, and work with, and who contribute to your future happiness. If your eyes have opened to conditions that need remedial work, discuss changes you would like to make and seek input from these key players. Be open to change and listen to what partners have to say. If you are engaged, 2024 could be the year you marry.

The year's first sign-change eclipse occurs in Pisces on September 17, a Lunar Eclipse in your solar sixth house of daily routines, the status of your health, work collaborators, pets, your approach to organizing personal space, work responsibilities, and operational conditions that facilitate efficiency. This eclipse may uncover any areas that have been loosely managed and need restructuring, along with performance shortfalls among staff. Sensitivity toward team members and recognition of their contributions will unify efforts. Your solar sixth house has been the site of much upheaval due to transits of Saturn and Neptune in Pisces. Busy is the word for the next two years.

October 2 is the date of the final Solar Eclipse of 2024, which occurs in Libra and your solar first house of action, adventure, passion, personal appearance, and fitness. No doubt you have had an opportunity to evaluate the personal choices you made earlier in the year to improve your health and image, undertake new ventures, travel, and take the lead in ensuring the fulfillment of your goals and cherished wishes. If a job change was part of the landscape for seeking professional satisfaction, you are on your way to a rewarding cycle that will unfold in the next few years. Make each step of the way count.

Libra | January

Overall Theme

The year's first New Moon falls on January 11 in Capricorn and your solar fourth house, giving you a feeling of pride as you reflect on family stability and your role as an anchor in the household. Retrograde Mercury goes direct on January 1 in Sagittarius and your solar third house, opening up options for refining goals you want to accomplish in 2024.

Relationships

Mercury, Venus, and Mars in Sagittarius do a happy dance in your solar third house early in the month, encouraging social activity with local dating prospects before the 8th. After the 15th, collaboration with workmates intensifies when team members return from holiday leave and dive into lucrative new projects. Invite your boss to dinner on the 24th, when the Moon is in family-oriented Cancer.

Success and Money

You'll be depositing large gift checks around January 6, putting funds away for anticipated purchases. Your boss reassigns challenging tasks that pique your interest and suggests you pick a few team members to help you get the job done. Select those whose analytical skills reflect exceptional compatibility with yours.

Pitfalls and Potential Problems

A meeting with a professional group could takes a tense turn when key funding matters come up for a vote on the January 25th Leo Full Moon. Suggest that members spend more time fleshing out the pros and cons before making a decision. Watch financial transactions on the 27th, when Uranus in Taurus goes direct in your solar eighth house of joint income and debt.

Rewarding Days

6, 11, 15, 24

Challenging Days

8, 16, 21, 26

Libra | February

Overall Theme

You should be feeling a harmonious vibe from Pluto in early Aquarius and your solar fifth house when the planet of transformation joins transiting Venus and Mars for a little romance. Enjoy the attraction that is growing between you and a partner and take your time getting to know what you love and admire about this person. Be responsive.

Relationships

You could be celebrating special events several times with loved ones this month. Maybe the first event is an early Valentine's Day party near the February 9th New Moon. Perhaps you'll celebrate the Lunar New Year of the Dragon on February 10 with a delicious family meal. Early on Valentine's Day, the Moon is in Aries and your solar seventh house of partnerships, perfect for expressing love and adoration for your romantic partner.

Success and Money

The leadership team at your worksite acknowledges the quality of your collaborative effort to meet important deadlines. Your compatibility keeps both external and internal customers happy, bringing compliments from the executive staff with public recognition around February 20 that could lead to a significant raise. Share praise with team members to build goodwill.

Pitfalls and Potential Problems

Local plans scheduled for February 4 may be tabled due to a weather-related delay or unexpected news from family or a neighbor. Be prepared for an encounter on the 22nd with a friend who seems overwhelmed by stress connected with a job change. Enjoy a quiet lunch and offer to listen.

Rewarding Days

3, 7, 13, 20

Challenging Days

4, 9, 22, 24

Libra | March

Overall Theme

Shower personal attention on yourself this month to alleviate the winter blues—a spa visit, a manicure, a new hairstyle, a tattoo, or a stylish wardrobe. Playtime for you and your partner works on the 5th. The Vernal Equinox welcomes spring on March 19, followed by the first Lunar Eclipse of 2024 on March 25 in Libra and your solar first house of personal activity.

Relationships

Early March works for a weekend trip while Venus and Mars are conjunct in Aquarius in your solar fifth house of romance. If work prevents you from traveling, save a few days around March 16 for a harmonious getaway that strengthens loving relationships. Schedule meetings with bosses on the 18th, when lunar aspects favor productive communication concerning staffing for the current workload.

Success and Money

Business enterprises thrive this month from March 2 to 5, when aspects are conducive to negotiating on prices, comparing products, and feeling positive about fiscal integrity. Keep an eye on your budget when shopping for big-ticket items or you could overspend on a product with more bells and whistles than you need.

Pitfalls and Potential Problems

Use diplomacy to let a child know that a proposed family outing on the 7th is triple the amount set aside for weekend entertainment. Provide more affordable options. If you scheduled a long-distance teleconference on the 19th, postpone it until the 27th to avoid a futile argument.

Rewarding Days

2, 5, 16, 18

Challenging Days

3, 7, 19, 25

Libra | April

Overall Theme

The major focus of the month is on communication with key people in your life—family, work team, partners, and siblings or neighbors. When Mercury launches a retrograde period on April 1 in Aries and your solar seventh house of partnerships, it's no joke when a number of mix-ups unfold through March 25, at which time the messenger planet moves direct again.

Relationships

Venus spends most of April in Aries and your solar seventh house of partnerships, giving you that loving feeling and providing opportunities for scheduling intimate time with your significant other beginning with April 8, the date of the first Solar Eclipse of 2024. Parents could join you for a family dinner on the 2nd, a coworker might invite you to a gathering on April 6, and siblings could propose a night out on the 26th.

Success and Money

Load up on self-confidence to take advantage of compatible career options that lead to discussions about raises and new assignments that you find attractive. By the end of the month, you'll probably hear news that your boss is hoping to fill positions and wants you to respond to the job announcements. Have lunch with a neighbor on April 26.

Pitfalls and Potential Problems

Those of you who coach children may have to deal with a disappointed player on the 4th who is upset over a position assignment. Make sure you discuss the issue in private to avoid involving team members. Address actual performance rather than personal traits.

Rewarding Days

2, 6, 8, 26

Challenging Days

4, 9, 12, 16

Libra | May

Overall Theme

People, partners, and Pluto occupy your mind this month in your romantic solar fifth house. The Moon in Aquarius begins the month near Pluto, which turns retrograde in Aquarius on May 2, creating an intense mood between you and a partner. Jealousy is a poison that kills romance and deters meaningful social interaction. Get to the bottom of what caused the discord.

Relationships

Whether or not you are a parent, the planetary aspects for Mother's Day on May 12 are promising for a reunion with children, grandparents, and caregivers. The Moon in Cancer is the perfect vehicle to honor them for showing love and stability unconditionally. Cherish loving memories and pay tribute to dear ones in ways that show others you care.

Success and Money

Money status shows an excellent management strategy, with steady increases in assets. Respect for your professional contributions tops the list of positive feedback from your boss during the week of May 12. Shop for travel bargains on May 8.

Pitfalls and Potential Problems

Organizational conflict is possible on the 10th, when assignments show gaps in accountability for a major facet of contracted work. Examine skill sets of the team and make suggestions on who is best qualified to accomplish related tasks. Poll team members for feedback if you are in charge, asking critical questions before making the decision.

Rewarding Days

3, 8, 12, 27

Challenging Days

1, 10, 15, 25

Libra | June

Overall Theme

This month's New Moon on the 6th falls on the anniversary of D-Day in Gemini and your solar ninth house, stirring the sentiments of military veterans in your family. You may be traveling at that time, responding to an invitation from relatives living abroad. A compatible lineup of Mercury, Venus, and Jupiter in Gemini promises a pleasant trip.

Relationships

You and your partner collaborate over the first weekend of the month, tackling a list of errands and keeping a loose agenda—no cooking, no rushing, just chilling and making progress on chores. Accept a sibling's invitation for a Father's Day meal to honor your father and the other fathers in the family on June 16.

Success and Money

By month's end, your home is buzzing with activity when a long-awaited remodeling project gets underway on the 23rd. The contracting crew lays out the guidelines and schedule for the work. Aren't you glad you put that bonus money away and have bonds you can liquidate in case of cost overruns?

Pitfalls and Potential Problems

Don't withdraw targeted savings funds impulsively on June 3 or you may face a shortfall late in the month when you need the money to cover planned expenses. Saturn turns retrograde on June 29 in Pisces and your solar sixth house of health. Within hours you could be reminded of the dental appointment you forgot to make.

Rewarding Days

1, 6, 10, 23

Challenging Days

3, 7, 21, 29

Libra | July

Overall Theme

The New Moon in Cancer on the 5th enhances your scheduled plans with weekend visitors. Mars in Taurus travels through your solar eighth house of joint funds through July 20, along with unpredictable Uranus in Taurus, giving this pair a feisty signature that reminds you to avoid sudden splurges while surfing the Internet.

Relationships

You'll see relatives from both sides of the family during this busy month, starting on July 3 with gatherings to celebrate the long Fourth of July weekend. Festivities include local celebrations, parades, contests, and fireworks to honor our nation. You may entertain visitors around July 20 who prefer amusement and water parks for keeping young relatives engaged.

Success and Money

Your summer vacation gets off to a lively start on July 30 when the Moon meets up with Jupiter in Gemini and your solar ninth house. Your itinerary promises fun and games at a lovely resort offering a wide variety of entertainment venues. Jupiter in Gemini raises the anticipation for adventure that creates memorable experiences for you and your family.

Pitfalls and Potential Problems

A holiday visitor could become high maintenance on the 4th by asking for foods, condiments, or entertainment you're not prepared to provide. Offer a compromise. A business group clashes over proposal details on July 9, putting a damper on a work lunch that was scheduled to finalize details. Use diplomacy to identify serious objections.

Rewarding Days

2, 5, 20, 30

Challenging Days

4, 9, 19, 24

Libra | August

Overall Theme

The Leo New Moon on the 4th sets the tone for expanding the scope of humanitarian projects through cooperation with other professionals who are deeply invested in the outcome that is likely to help a significant number of people looking for medical breakthroughs. Take a breather from an intense work schedule over the weekend.

Relationships

The Leo New Moon on the 4th in your solar eleventh house presents a perfect opportunity to meet up with friends for adventure and entertainment. Mars and Jupiter in Gemini contribute to humorous moments and lively conversation. Bond with your significant other on August 23 when the Moon in Aries occupies your solar seventh house of partnerships, creating space for loving moments and a night out for fun.

Success and Money

Meet with lenders if you are interested in securing a home loan around August 11, when financial aspects favor serious discussions. Shop rates and check your credit, which should be impeccable thanks to the work you've done to reduce debt.

Pitfalls and Potential Problems

Mercury's third retrograde period of the year starts in Virgo on August 5, a date you may have picked for a short vacation. Look on the bright side, because Mercury moves into Leo on the 14th and then turns direct in Leo on August 28. Work on details of a current project through research and editing. Postpone business travel scheduled for the 14th until after Labor Day.

Rewarding Days

3, 4, 11, 23

Challenging Days

5, 12, 14, 26

Libra | September

Overall Theme

September's first half favors spending time with family and social contacts, including those you date or spend time with on vacation. Venus in your socially oriented sign forms a positive aspect to transiting Jupiter in Gemini, allowing you to expand your network. The second Lunar Eclipse of the year occurs on September 17 in Pisces and your solar sixth house of work, indicating a demand for your services.

Relationships

From the 15th through the end of the month, the workload calls for strong collaboration with your team to set priorities, manage deadlines, solve problems, and satisfy management. Strategies you employ do the trick. By the end of the month, your employer applauds you for cutting the time it takes to accomplish tasks. Could a promotion be in your future?

Success and Money

Celebrate quietly when the New Moon occupies Virgo and your solar twelfth house on Labor Day, September 2. Relax and spend quality time on personal interests before returning to a demanding work space. Mercury moves into Virgo on the 9th, indicating that you may be working from home while you research innovative strategies to implement in your project. Schedule important medical appointments.

Pitfalls and Potential Problems

Uranus, the planet of chaos, starts off the month going retrograde on the 1st in Taurus and your solar eighth house of joint income. Remain objective regarding purchases and avoid impulse spending. Lunar aspects on the 27th affect lunch plans with a friend due to unexpected work demands. Set a makeup date and treat your friend.

Rewarding Days

13, 15, 18, 26

Challenging Days

3, 11, 20, 27

Libra | October

Overall Theme

Attention is on your solar first house with the last Solar Eclipse of 2024 occurring in Libra on October 2. Expansive Jupiter in Gemini turns retrograde on October 9 in your solar ninth house, forcing you to reconsider travel plans. Then Pluto, the change agent, moves direct on October 11 in Capricorn and your solar fourth house of home and family, racing through the final degrees of this sign.

Relationships

Relationships take center stage in October, especially those revolving around cousins and siblings, neighbors, and instructors. Your social calendar fills up quickly from the 8th to the 25th. Accept a lunch invitation from your boss around the 23rd and savor the good news about company expansion and adding new hires.

Success and Money

Interactions with financial experts dominate the early days of the month as you shop for deals on vehicles, household goods, and travel. You could be signing a contract or legal document by October 8. Collaboration on the 15th puts a smile on your face as you exceed both output and due date expectations for an important phase of a work project.

Pitfalls and Potential Problems

Family plans get the ax on the 10th when exhaustion sets in and you go to bed early. You'll welcome an intimate liaison on the Aries Full Moon of October 17, but you won't get much sleep. A long-distance business call on the 20th necessitates setting up a work trip to implement new procedures.

Rewarding Days

5, 8, 15, 23

Challenging Days

4, 10, 17, 20

Libra | November

Overall Theme

Plans for the holidays during the next two months include invitations to dinners, parties, and concerts. Accept a dinner invitation from a neighbor on November 3. Develop your Thanksgiving menu and start shopping early for supplies. Celebrate "Friendsgiving" with your network a week before the holiday, showing gratitude for these valuable relationships.

Relationships

If you are hosting this year's Thanksgiving dinner, contact invitees by November 1. Conversation turns lively when parents, siblings, and neighbors get together to talk sports, upcoming holiday plans, and the delicious food for the holiday feast. Donate items for meals prepared by local food pantries, sharing the bounty of the season with those in need.

Success and Money

The November 1st New Moon in Scorpio falls in your solar second house of earned income, indicating excellent cash flow in your accounts to cover holiday treats and extra supplies. Begin shopping for holiday gifts to satisfy the requests of loved ones. Exchanges with your boss on November 19 lift your spirits and motivate your passion for turning out excellent work.

Pitfalls and Potential Problems

Once you get past a flurry of confusion when Saturn goes direct on the 15th in Pisces and solar sixth house of daily routines, the flow of work becomes more productive. A family member may seem down on November 7. Give the individual some space to work out the source of angst. Due to transportation snafus, returning from a long-distance business trip could be inconvenient on November 18.

Rewarding Days

1, 3, 11, 19

Challenging Days

4, 7, 18, 22

Libra | December

Overall Theme

December is a rare month celebrating two New Moons, the first in Sagittarius on December 1 and the second on December 30 in Capricorn. Satisfy your craving for some pre-holiday R&R by taking a short trip to a favorite beach or other destination after December 15. After a day of holiday shopping on the 4th, order takeout and relax to watch seasonal programs.

Relationships

Several December dates favor spending time with family, neighbors, and friends. Bond with family and your partner on December 4 and 10, expressing gratitude for the love and warmth they bring to your home. Help a neighbor on December 2 with tree or outdoor decorating. Connections with family at a distance on December 14 confirm the arrival date for a holiday visit.

Success and Money

Use a holiday bonus to treat your partner to a lovely meal and entertainment around December 6. Finalize your gift list and make plans to complete the rest of your shopping by December 10. Join professional colleagues on the 14th to offer holiday toasts and well wishes for the coming year at a get-together. Express gratitude for the camaraderie you share.

Pitfalls and Potential Problems

Mars stations to move retrograde in Leo on December 6, while Neptune in Pisces turns direct on the 7th. The Full Moon in Gemini on the 15th occurs opposite Mercury going direct in Sagittarius. With this planetary lineup, you may wish to curtail travel. Stay calm on the 11th instead of arguing with your partner over a minor incident.

Rewarding Days

4, 7, 10, 14

Challenging Days

2, 6, 11, 12

Libra Action Table

These dates reflect the best—but not the only—times for success and ease in these activities, according to your Sun sign.

	JAN	FEB	MAR	APR	MAY	JUN	JUL	AUG	SEP	OCT	NOV	DEC
Move			16			6				8		
Romance		13		8			2		15			7
Seek counseling/coaching	15				3			3			11	
Ask for a raise	24		18		12				26		19	
Vacation				26			30					14
Get a loan		3						11		5		

Scorpio

The Scorpion
October 23 to November 22

♏

Element: Water

Quality: Fixed

Polarity: Yin/feminine

Planetary Ruler: Pluto (Mars)

Meditation: I let go of the need to control

Gemstone: Topaz

Power Stones: Obsidian, garnet

Key Phrase: I create

Glyph: Scorpion's tail

Anatomy: Reproductive system

Colors: Burgundy, black

Animals: Reptiles, scorpions, birds of prey

Myths/Legends: The Phoenix, Hades and Persephone, Shiva

House: Eighth

Opposite Sign: Taurus

Flower: Chrysanthemum

Keyword: Intensity

The Scorpio Personality

Strengths, Talents, and the Creative Spark

Let's hear it for powerhouse Scorpio, the eighth sign of the zodiac, a fixed water sign member and ruler of the deep space–oriented eighth house of money from partnerships and unusual sources, psychological matters, sex, death, birth, rebirth, estate matters, mortgage loans, goods of the dead, consumer debt, crimes, joint assets and investments as well as liabilities, mysteries, the subconscious, and complex human needs. Pluto rules your sign with its old ruler, Mars, as partner, planetary proof that you have a passionate spirit and take obligations seriously. You believe in rising above the fray when life produces lemons. You're one who seeks rejuvenation to get back on track after setbacks or situations that call for new directions. Colors you prefer include dark reds, maroon, magenta, oxblood, dark browns, and black. Members of your sign desire private time and go inward to recharge their batteries and regain focus. Your sign has dominion over the private parts of the body.

Scorpios often undergo more than one rebirth in a lifetime for diverse reasons when the going gets tough, such as the death of a partner, loss of a home, divorce, or financial bankruptcy. Like the Phoenix, you regenerate your mental outlook and material goods, rising again after eradicating what you no longer need in life. Born with a very developed sixth sense, you don't quit until you have solved any mysteries or perplexing conditions that exist around issues in your world. Determination surfaces as you manage obligations with your style of questioning and follow up with thorough analysis to get to the heart of the way another's mind works. You are never afraid to ask why, and others sometimes ask you if you are psychic when they meet your all-knowing eyes and hear your summary of what you have discovered. You thrive on knowing what makes people tick and expertly put your excellent observation skills to work. Perceptions you detect make you a great candidate for the field of criminal law or a career as an attorney, as an expert at jury selection for matters that go to trial, and for various facets of police work. Research fields are excellent choices. Many Scorpios have skilled hands and become excellent surgeons.

Intimacy and Personal Relationships

You are known for your loyalty. Your circle of friends goes way back, with many individuals confiding in you because they trust you with their secrets. You become a repository of these sacred confidences without revealing much about your own inner feelings. You truly are very romantic. You want to find your soulmate and live in the security of a sacred, loving embrace for the rest of your life. Often reluctant to declare your love until you are sure the feelings are mutual, you retreat and watch for signs that love is blooming. Once you know, you just *know* that you have found the perfect partner. Beneath your calm demeanor lies a very sensitive heart that can also show considerable possessiveness and jealousy with little warning. As with your friendships, you want a love relationship built on trust. Earth signs such as Virgo and Capricorn are particularly compatible with you, yet you'll find Taurus, your opposite sign, especially attractive in a magnetic way that captures your heart and soul. Water signs, like Cancer and Pisces and also members of your own sign, are fun and friendly and revere family traditions. The fixed signs Leo and Aquarius may seem too controlling for you. Many Scorpios marry young and often more than once. As a parent, you are protective to offspring yet encourage independence and creative expression.

Values and Resources

With a Sun sign that governs the eighth house of security and shared assets, you desire a career that pays well and allows you to acquire resources for the proverbial rainy day. The financial package must include the bricks and mortar that a lovely home provides to create a safe haven, a welcome environment for your children to entertain their friends, and a place for you to chill when you want to relax and tune out the drama of the day. Not only does your chosen career have to deliver a generous salary, but it also must provide the emotional satisfaction that your deep psyche craves. You don't like to leave any loose ends at the close of the day and are on the earth plane to offer service to others who seek help with financial, emotional, or physical burdens. Ideally you and your partner are on the same page regarding spending and saving habits. If one splurges, the other goes into orbit fretting over the possibility of diminishing resources, and that provides grounds for rehabilitating the couple's financial outlook.

Blind Spots and Blockages

Intimacy issues are frequently the source of friction between you and your partner and become the basis for a painful life lesson. You may not want to acknowledge flaws in the relationship and instead choose to ignore the angst, keeping it not only from family but from friends and work colleagues as well. That only works for so long and could lead to an affair or occupying separate bedrooms until one of you demands new rules. As a fixed sign, you don't like change and may run away from seeking a consultation with a marriage therapist. When talk of divorce surfaces, it is often the intervention that grabs your attention and brings you back to reality. Face the truth and admit that you often stay far too long in a relationship, whether an intimate one, a friendship, or a work situation. Be willing to remove psychological blocks that keep you in stagnant situations. Observers say you keep too much inside and would be much happier if you lightened your load and removed the baggage.

Goals and Success

As the second water sign in the zodiac (along with Cancer and Pisces), you thrive on keeping your word when you make a promise to a business associate or a partner. Some of you are content to stay in the same position for life if the qualities you look for are there. You have deep insight into a career path that suits your skills and allows you to passionately pursue the job of your dreams. Many of you excel at problem-solving, investigative work, medical specialties, or research in legal, political, or social science. Dentists, radiologists, surgeons, and lab associates are common positions, and the emergency or operating room nursing field is a good fit as well. Government work also appeals to you, allowing you to enjoy a lucrative salary and excellent benefits. While a fine earner, many a Scorpio binges on a spending streak and then has to grapple with paying the bills. Work on this streak of impulsiveness and you'll have the formula for fiscal stability and the ideal job, a much desired quest that satisfies your soul.

Scorpio Keywords for 2024
Faith, familiarity, filter

The Year Ahead for Scorpio

One of the key solar houses that comes to life in 2024 is your solar seventh house of personal and business partners, with Taurus on the cusp. The year starts out with Jupiter in Taurus in residence through May 25, putting the spotlight on the quality of close relationships and examining your joint goals. Combustible Uranus turns direct on January 27 in Taurus and your solar seventh house, throwing a few curveballs your way and offering your investigative mind a chance to solve the puzzle. No doubt this important house has been the site of unplanned shake-ups for several years. Your solar fifth house of romance, children, entrepreneurial adventures, and vacations hosts order-loving Saturn in Pisces all year, enabling you to keep an eye on both personal relationships and the status of business ventures. In this important house you'll also find transiting Neptune in Pisces adding a dreamy note to blossoming love relationships and a chance to dance, attend concerts, or take in stage shows and musicals.

Pluto in Capricorn weighs in by finishing a long cycle in your solar third house of the mind, contracts, education, neighbors, and siblings. On January 20 the regenerative planet moves into Aquarius and your solar fourth house, helping you identify blocks to family harmony and providing insight into how residents under your roof act on a daily basis. Eclipses in Libra and your solar twelfth house occur this year in March and October, while the first Solar Eclipse of the year occupies your solar sixth house of work and routines in Aries on April 8. A new cycle of eclipses begins on September 17 when a Lunar Eclipse in Pisces joins other planets in your solar fifth house of romance. Look forward to new ventures in 2024 by creating pathways that fulfill your dreams.

Jupiter

When Jupiter, the planet of expansion and personal growth, occupies your solar seventh house of business and personal partners for the first five months of 2024, you'll experience optimism and prosperity regarding matters connected with relationships. This Jupiter-in-Taurus transit started in May 2023. Collaborations may be lucrative, adding substantial amounts of cash or dividends to partnership arrangements via savvy investments or mergers. Engaged couples plan a wedding and honeymoon and could tie the knot during this cycle, fulfilling a dream and making future plans as a couple. Each degree of your sign received some attention during the occupation of Taurus in your solar seventh house. By May 25, Jupiter moves into Gemini and your solar eighth house of partnership income and debt, creating an opportunity to execute plans you started when Jupiter transited your solar seventh house. An air of celebration is in the air. Possibilities include weddings, business partnerships, the start of a new enterprise involving self-employment, a business partnership with your significant other, and opportunities for receiving a windfall that helps you eradicate debt via a win, an inheritance, or the sale of property at a considerable profit. Make use of your savvy negotiating skills this year. Scorpios born between October 23 and November 13 benefit most noticeably when Jupiter moves into Gemini. In 2024, Jupiter goes retrograde on October 9 and resumes direct motion in Gemini on February 4, 2025.

Saturn

You've been keeping your eye on Saturn in Pisces since it moved into your solar fifth house on March 7, 2023. Since Saturn dominates the concept of responsibility, you have paid close attention to the status of children's interests, romantic relationships, your social life, students you coach or teach, vacations and entertainment, and the progress of entrepreneurial business investments. Relationships may be very demanding of your time this year and could call for a higher degree of monitoring to assess strengths and areas in need of solid change. With Saturn, Neptune, and a September 17th Lunar Eclipse in residence, the fifth house is a place of intense activity now. You will be juggling priorities that call for your close scrutiny to make sure all the bases are covered for decisions involving your children, where to take an evolving love relationship, going on the vacation you've been postponing, making decisions about sports participation, and checking the returns on business investments. Those of you born between October 25 and November 9 experience the most prominent activity while Saturn is in a compatible sign to your Sun. This taskmaster planet will be retrograde this year from June 29 through November 15. Stay true to your commitments.

Uranus

Relationships are an area of unpredictability when Uranus in Taurus, your opposite sign, occupies your solar seventh house of personal and business partnerships, advisers, astrologers, consultants, roommates, public opponents, and individuals connected to the law and medical professions. No doubt you have noticed an edge that was not apparent before among those you have known for years. This year you may have run-ins with individuals whose political views clash with yours. Be cautious that feelings don't erupt to the point of violence and stay away from incendiary gatherings. At the very least, expect schedule fluctuations and unanticipated delays in implementing plans. What behavior has changed among those in your circle that has you concerned? Talk over differences amicably on one of your most receptive dates to initiate a solution and make sure each party's perspective surfaces. Ask for input on what would heal the rift or make the situation palatable. It is not unusual for individuals experiencing this type of transit to suddenly announce an elopement, a divorce, a separation, or a move. A clear head makes a difference in arriving at a viable solution. Those of you born between November 10 and 21 experience the most noticeable impact from these disruptions, which have been happening since 2018. On September 1, Uranus turns retrograde and remains so until January 30, 2025. Cultivate healthy relationships with balanced individuals and build trust with those whose attitude reflects calm intelligence.

Neptune

Inspiring, glamorous Neptune in Pisces keeps company with transiting Saturn this year in your solar fifth house of love, romance, children and their interests, adventures and vacations, the entertainment world, sports, your social life, and reasoned risk-taking. Lately you have developed a more personable outward style and seem less concerned about others exposing your vulnerabilities. That is part of Neptune's charm when it rolls through your solar fifth house and tempts you with a bit of playtime, allowing you to let go of the driven work pattern that keeps you relentlessly on deadline. Enjoy the spiritual allure that Neptune brings to attracting new relationships or adding a mystic aura to ongoing ones. You could truly find someone who keeps your heart beating to the rhythm of love. With Saturn present in this house this year, you could also make a serious decision to marry if you are single. Remember to integrate your critical psychic filter into daily analytical work for greater success. Look for Neptune to turn retrograde on July 2 in the last degree of Pisces and move direct on December 7. Members of your sign born between November 16 and 21 experience the most planetary activity from the planet of mystery, which has been present here since 2011.

Pluto

Self-talk must be breaking records since Pluto arrived in Capricorn and your solar third house sixteen years ago and activated the probing mechanism of your mind. You identify the mental baggage that has kept you busy culling out the important parts and deciding what to table for further examination while you juggle priorities that call for immediate action. Fears, threats, and a lack of confidence have kept you busy doubting your power for far too long. You are still keeping secrets, yet the idea of exposing them is less of an issue than having to confront them. You'd rather eliminate clutter to free up valuable time to explore current, more pleasant topics. Your wishes are about to come true. Pluto is leaving Capricorn and your solar third house for most of 2024 and moving into your solar fourth house of home and family with a new identity in Aquarius. More humanitarian angels emerge to show the way to greater household harmony by helping you identify family members who may be stuck in the fear of not embracing talents or taking on the responsibility of finding a new place to call home. Think about priorities you have for managing your life in 2024. What is the biggest freedom you desire? Pluto covers the first two degrees of Aquarius between January 20 and September 2. It turns retrograde on May 2 in Aquarius and goes direct on October 11 in the last degree of Capricorn, finishing up the tail end of pending transformations before settling back into Aquarius on November 19 for a multi-year tour in the sign that offers different possibilities and an impersonal attitude in relationships. Take a deep breath and release the old angst!

How Will This Year's Eclipses Affect You?

This year's four eclipses, two lunar (Full Moon) and two solar (New Moon), are ready to generate intense periods that start to manifest a few months before their actual occurrence. The Libra/Aries cycle wraps up in March 2023 to make way for the Pisces/Virgo eclipses, the first of which makes its debut in September of 2024. Eclipses unfold in cycles involving all twelve signs of the zodiac and usually occur in pairs about two weeks apart. Never fear eclipses—just think of them as opportunities for growth that allow you to release old patterns. Expect surprises that elicit both positive and perplexing feelings and outcomes. The closer an eclipse is to a planet or point in your birth chart, the greater the importance it has in your life, especially if one of those planets is in the same degree as the eclipse.

On March 25, the first Lunar Eclipse of 2024 falls in Libra and your solar twelfth house of behind-the-scenes activity, recovery from illness or surgery, introspection, mystical and psychic experiences, secrets, and visiting those who are sick or in an institution. Plan some quality alone time if you have been working too many hours, need time to work on plans for the coming year, or want to work on solutions to pressing problems. If you are a writer, use downtime to work on a story outline.

Those of you contemplating a job change can analyze your resume and make appropriate additions or edits.

The year's first Solar Eclipse occurs on April 8 in Aries and your solar sixth house of work, details of your daily routine, health and nutrition, organizational aptitude, relationships with colleagues, and pets. You could have a major overhaul of company practices to implement if you return to work after a significant layoff or reassignment of duties. Do your homework before you begin making changes. Engage support from coworkers and ask for helpful suggestions. Smile and earn the respect of key workers.

The second Lunar Eclipse of 2024 occurs on September 17 in Pisces and your solar fifth house of amusement, children, love, romance, students you coach or teach, adventures, vacation, the entertainment world, sports, your social life, and speculative ventures. This highly active house will bring a surprise or two this year, especially if you are in the midst of letting go of old habits that erode productivity, such as frittering away time, daydreaming, or being indecisive when a situation calls for action. Don't get worn out from juggling the conflicting actions that peers are taking. Insist on balance. This eclipse helps you heal multiple aspects of fragile relationships.

October 2 is the date of the final Solar Eclipse of 2024, which occurs in Libra and your solar twelfth house of hospital visits, recovery from a personal injury or illness, plans in the making that are not ready to be announced, mystical phenomena, secrets, creative writing, and solving mysteries, one of your favorite pastimes. Get ready to implement new products and services that you've had on the drawing board. Have faith in your astute analysis of helpful features that are part of the marketing plan, ensuring the chances of success with proven product integrity. Be proud of the role you play in taking responsibility for boosting confidence and employee morale.

Scorpio | January

Overall Theme

Although you may desire a relaxing vacation, your work agenda has no room until late in the month. Mercury in Sagittarius moves direct on the 1st and calls for a financial meeting as soon as you return to the workplace. The Capricorn New Moon on the 11th has excellent prospects for a lucrative contract with industry partners. Uranus in your opposite sign of Taurus turns direct on the 27th in your solar seventh house of partnerships, opening discussion for prioritizing household projects.

Relationships

Friends may join you for a New Year's Day celebration. You and your partner share customs and favorite foods with guests. Bond with neighbors and siblings on the 11th. Movie night on the 15th gives you a chance to hold your sweetheart's hand tightly. Book that mini vacation on the 24th and enjoy a welcome work break.

Success and Money

Post-holiday sales continue to offer bargains if you need furniture and linens. Use the stash of cash you put away to make quality purchases. Work on an idea for adding value to work procedures on the 15th. Refine your budget for 2024 by mid-month and obtain your partner's approval.

Pitfalls and Potential Problems

Avoid overspending on January 8, when price tags could be mismarked. Aspects for the January 25th Full Moon in Leo work against a productive meeting with your boss. Wait until the 29th.

Rewarding Days

1, 11, 15, 24

Challenging Days

3, 8, 16, 25

Scorpio | February

Overall Theme

Prior to the Lunar New Year of the Dragon, which begins on February 10, grab some red envelopes at the store, slip some cash into them, and put prosperity vibes in motion when you hand them to guests at a celebratory meal. After the Aquarius New Moon on the 9th, begin a household makeover project.

Relationships

A family outing works best for you on the 11th, when a daylong excursion to see exhibits of interest fascinates loved ones of all ages. Why not let the day end with a long, leisurely dinner to allow members to talk about their favorite exhibits? Treat workmates to Valentine's Day treats on February 13 or 14.

Success and Money

Networks are a huge part of this month's success cycle when you learn of openings in fields of interest from professional organizations early in the month. On the 25th, a friend could be recruiting and making a competitive announcement for a prestigious research opening that offers challenging responsibilities and a salary raise. Most of the planets are making favorable aspects to your Sun this month.

Pitfalls and Potential Problems

Avoid haggling over the price of electronics on the 4th, when you're unlikely to encounter a reasonable sales associate. Research products online so you have comparisons to show the next vendor. On the Virgo Full Moon on February 24, a friend seems more on edge than usual at a lunch date. Say nothing.

Rewarding Days

3, 11, 13, 25

Challenging Days

4, 9, 21, 24

Scorpio | March

Overall Theme

Play it cool this month when Pluto in early Aquarius aligns with several fixed signs this month, including Venus and Mars in Aquarius and Jupiter and Uranus in Taurus. Your social life could bring invitations from siblings, neighbors, or your boss. Attend to personal pampering and relaxation on March 18 by booking an overnight trip for special care.

Relationships

A relative might make a wedding or engagement announcement around March 5. Single Scorpios could meet a prospective love interest after the Pisces New Moon on March 10. Your significant other is open to a romantic dinner and night out on March 20. Enjoy the closeness and a chance to talk without interference. Call an out-of-town relative after March 18.

Success and Money

A meeting with your boss may surprise you, but it puts a smile on your face when you learn that you may be a key figure in an office realignment that requires your analytical experience in the planning stage. With the exception of March 3 and 17, the money picture looks good for you all month. Talk to financial experts for tips on building savings.

Pitfalls and Potential Problems

Family members may be disappointed on the 7th when you announce that a major recreational purchase will be postponed due to economic conditions. The year's first Lunar Eclipse falls in Libra and your solar twelfth house on the 25th, a day when apprehension you have been feeling surfaces and reminds you to check critical work.

Rewarding Days

5, 10, 18, 20

Challenging Days

3, 7, 17, 19

Scorpio | April

Overall Theme

The Aries New Moon on the 8th marks the year's first Solar Eclipse and occurs in your solar sixth house of daily routines and work environment. Give some thought to engaging with a new coworker who could be a potential love interest. Be discreet about behavior and the active grapevine that misses nothing. The year's first full Mercury retrograde period begins on the 1st in Aries and your solar sixth house. The planet of communication moves direct on the 25th, favoring completion of a key project section.

Relationships

A nearby sibling may visit you around the 3rd and talk to you about estate matters involving parents. If you don't have answers, suggest that your sibling engage your parents directly, unless you want to be an intermediary. Children are a delight on the 5th. Wine and dine your sweetheart on April 10.

Success and Money

On April 28 you learn that a performance bonus is headed your way, allowing you to revive plans for a household improvement. Be sure to express gratitude to your supervisor. Confer with your partner about this windfall and how you can maximize savings to cover any cost overruns.

Pitfalls and Potential Problems

The Full Moon on the 23rd in Scorpio and your solar first house could drain you of energy. The best medicine is a good night's sleep. Steer clear of persistent telemarketers on April 12.

Rewarding Days

3, 5, 10, 28

Challenging Days

4, 9, 12, 23

Scorpio | May

Overall Theme

The transiting Taurus Sun opposes yours for the first half of the month, releasing inner pressure to make life changes that affect you and your partner. When the New Moon in Taurus occurs in your solar seventh house of partnerships on the 7th, you realize that transitions cannot be rushed. That new person you met may simply be a diversion after all, and you feel much more secure with familiarity. Avoid confusion.

Relationships

Bond with your partner on May 7 to recreate the spark you share. If you walk away prematurely, you'll never know what was driving your insecurity. Schedule playtime with your significant other around the 12th to discuss deep feelings and sort through conditions that led to the emotional rift that is on the mend. Say yes to a sibling who invites you to a Memorial Day gathering on May 27.

Success and Money

You discover that a desire to vacation at a distant location will satisfy your interest in exploring the architecture that so many beautiful regions offer. Make reservations for July using the travel money you set aside. Consider job offers after May 21.

Pitfalls and Potential Problems

Examine contracts closely if you are negotiating details early this month. Pluto turns retrograde on the 2nd in Aquarius and your solar fourth house of home. Look closely at clauses that could alter the outcome of your desired work, especially those related to material substitutions due to shortages of goods.

Rewarding Days

3, 7, 12, 27

Challenging Days

2, 10, 15, 24

Scorpio | June

Overall Theme

Enjoy the solid support of Gemini planets in your solar eighth house of joint assets and income that accompany the New Moon in Gemini on June 6. You could be treated to a monetary surprise with Mercury, Venus, and Jupiter pulling the strings and boosting your threshold of optimism. Play your best numbers on lottery tickets.

Relationships

Meet with new members of the work team early on the 3rd to provide insight into how the work environment operates. You and your spouse share a loving evening on June 5 when you set aside the work you took home and focus on intimacy. Cousins may spend a delightful weekend with your family around June 23, taking in local sights of interest that you thoughtfully suggest.

Success and Money

Team members praise your organizational style and compliment materials you have developed and shared to take the guesswork out of operational procedures. The management hierarchy notes the feedback and acknowledges your performance during the week of June 10. Jupiter's recent entry into Gemini and your solar eighth house boosts bonus options and supports debt reduction.

Pitfalls and Potential Problems

The Full Moon in Capricorn and your solar third house on the 21st has you staying close to home on the Summer Solstice. Play cards or board games with neighbors. Arrange backyard activities and snack food for children, too. Saturn in Pisces turns retrograde on June 29 in your solar fifth house, which could affect plans with your children due to weather conditions.

Rewarding Days

1, 5, 23, 27

Challenging Days

7, 11, 21, 29

Scorpio | July

Overall Theme

The Moon and Jupiter in Gemini line up on the 3rd in your solar eighth house, providing an ideal date to arrive at a desirable vacation destination to mark the Fourth of July holiday. When Mercury and Venus meet in Leo after mid-month, you could be tempted to purchase a piece of expensive jewelry for your partner. Drop a subtle hint to determine their interest.

Relationships

The Sun in Leo and your solar tenth house at the end of the month increases interaction with your supervisor or members of the management team. Professional networking increases after July 12, with scheduled meetings and meals requiring your presence. Local relatives make plans to visit you after July 21 and request the presence of a few old friends at a gathering.

Success and Money

The week of the 15th brings welcome feedback about successful business expansion and the possibility of extra hires with the creation of new positions to cover the volume of work. After the 30th, an income boost comes in the form of a bonus or raise. Put aside extra cash for home improvements or gifts.

Pitfalls and Potential Problems

Neptune in Pisces and your solar fifth house goes retrograde on July 2 right ahead of the Fourth of July holiday. Expect the possibility of rain or stormy weather if you are on vacation. July 9 and 10 could be dicey, with transiting Mars and Uranus in Taurus in hard aspect to your solar tenth house upsetting the flow of work expected.

Rewarding Days

2, 6, 12, 30

Challenging Days

9, 10, 23, 26

Scorpio | August

Overall Theme

Mercury makes swift moves this month, turning retrograde in Virgo on the 5th and resuming direct motion in Leo on August 28. The busy pace of your work environment has subgroups meeting to exchange information and collaborators absorbed in analyzing anticipated outcomes. At home base, consider giving your front entry a face-lift.

Relationships

The New Moon in Leo and your solar tenth house on August 4 spotlights your growing workload and frequent contact with your manager as you determine a strategy to allocate tasks to other staff members. Based on the current demands on your time, it could be August 25 before you and your partner have a chance to spend an enjoyable day together.

Success and Money

A noticeable gift you have is assessing the workload and recruiting adequate staff to share the tasks. You could be asked to apply for an upcoming managerial position. Cash flow continues to grow. Schedule a medical exam after August 29. Shop for auto insurance in September if your carrier announces an increase in rates.

Pitfalls and Potential Problems

The Full Moon in Aquarius and your solar fourth house of home on the 19th impacts household members. More than one could display a quarrelsome attitude. Let complainers work it out without interference. Keep your eye on prices while shopping on August 14, and don't pay more for goods without comparing costs.

Rewarding Days
3, 4, 23, 25

Challenging Days
6, 14, 19, 20

Scorpio | September

Overall Theme
Your solar fifth house of children and romance is one of the busiest areas in your chart this year. Now the final Lunar Eclipse of 2024 joins transiting Saturn and Neptune in Pisces here on September 17, bringing attention to your relationships with lovers, children, and matters related to this complex house.

Relationships
You could renew bonds of friendship on Labor Day, September 2, by reuniting with old contacts from school or sports teams. Siblings could join you on the 13th for a casual dinner at a favorite eatery, sharing personal family and career news. Reserve September 15 for family night dining and a movie.

Success and Money
Focus on sprucing up your home's exterior this fall. Whether you add new shutters, replace the roof, or landscape the grounds before winter sets in, an ideal time to contact a vendor is the week of September 15. Get at least three estimates in writing. Consider running the first PTA fundraiser if you have a child in school.

Pitfalls and Potential Problems
Uranus goes retrograde on the 1st in Taurus and your solar seventh house and may delay your plans for starting a business partnership venture. Don't sign contracts on September 17, when the Lunar Eclipse in Pisces opposes Mercury. Self-consciousness could surface after a colleague makes a critical remark at work around the 20th.

Rewarding Days
2, 13, 15, 21

Challenging Days
1, 17, 20, 27

Scorpio | October

Overall Theme

Jupiter goes retrograde on October 9 in Gemini and your solar eighth house of joint income and debts. Review loan and credit card balances to make sure they are paid up-to-date. If you have a computer or smart TV on order, it may have to be returned because you receive the wrong model. Connect with friends and plan enjoyable fall outings.

Relationships

The Solar Eclipse on October 2 occurs in Libra and your solar twelfth house of secrets. You may suddenly start receiving multiple texts and emails from romantic prospects. Venus in your sign in harmony with Mars in Cancer makes you more attractive to potential suitors. If you are an unattached Scorpio, October 15 is an ideal day to meet a prospective partner.

Success and Money

Congratulate yourself on paying off your credit cards and maintaining a low percentage of their use. You'll be glad you did so when you apply for a loan and receive an attractive borrowing rate. Plan a visit via video chat with a relative in a distant location.

Pitfalls and Potential Problems

After a long retrograde period that began in early May, Pluto stations to move direct on October 11 in the last degree of Capricorn. After finishing its journey in that sign, Pluto moves back into Aquarius on November 19, where it looks closely at your solar fourth house of home and family to identify any evidence of people who are stuck in unproductive patterns.

Rewarding Days

2, 8, 15, 23

Challenging Days

7, 9, 13, 25

Scorpio | November

Overall Theme

The New Moon in your sign on November 1 energizes your passion for holiday preparations. During this action-oriented month, you and your partner send invitations to cherished guests, decide on the menu, purchase party favors, shop early for nonperishable items, and decorate your home.

Relationships

Thanksgiving falls late in the month this year on the 28th, yet some guests start arriving more than a week early, especially parents living at a distance. Your holiday gathering will likely be a festive and warm event, with siblings and their families and a few close friends joining you for a lovely meal.

Success and Money

Saturn in Pisces moves direct in your solar fifth house of children and romance on November 15, a few days before you receive a pay raise that fills you with gratitude. You are pleased that you worked extra hours to complete a work assignment ahead of the due date. You opt to donate meals to worthy charities that support individuals short on holiday cash.

Pitfalls and Potential Problems

The intense Taurus Full Moon on November 15 in your solar seventh house of close relationships gives you a good reason to turn in early to snuggle with your loving partner. If you are traveling over the Thanksgiving holiday, be sure to leave before Mercury in Sagittarius goes retrograde on the 25th to minimize potential delays.

Rewarding Days

1, 8, 19, 30

Challenging Days

7, 10, 17, 25

Scorpio | December

Overall Theme

What a way to end the year, with two New Moons, a Full Moon, Neptune moving direct in Pisces and your solar fifth house of children and creativity on the 7th, and Mercury stationing to move direct on December 15 in Sagittarius and your solar second house of earned income. Shopping may claim your attention early in the month as you seek a few holiday bargains. Filter impulse spending.

Relationships

Children's activities may dominate the first seven days of December, featuring school holiday programs and helping the little ones shop for gifts and treats for the family. Confirm airport pickups for holiday travelers by December 9. A festive dinner invitation from friends adds holiday sparkle around the 22nd and provides you with creative ideas for entertaining annual visitors.

Success and Money

Profits are up in certain investment accounts when you note increases in numbers around December 14. You feel secure and ready to celebrate the season, having had a jump on holiday preparation and shopping. The fine work performance you delivered in 2024 netted rewards for outstanding contributions. Enjoy them as you buy gifts for the community angel tree or a similar charitable cause.

Pitfalls and Potential Problems

Mars turns retrograde on December 6 in Leo and your solar tenth house of profession, possibly slowing down implementation of a highly anticipated work initiative. Passionate outbursts from your spouse may catch you off guard on December 12. Wait until the edge is off the anger before discussing the issue.

Rewarding Days

5, 9, 14, 22

Challenging Days

2, 6, 12, 21

Scorpio Action Table

These dates reflect the best—but not the only—times for success and ease in these activities, according to your Sun sign.

	JAN	FEB	MAR	APR	MAY	JUN	JUL	AUG	SEP	OCT	NOV	DEC
Move	11		5					2			19	
Romance		11		10		5	2		21	15		
Seek counseling/ coaching		13			27			23				22
Ask for a raise			20				30					
Vacation	24				12				3			9
Get a loan				28		23				8	1	

Sagittarius

The Archer
November 22 to December 21

♐

Element: Fire

Quality: Mutable

Polarity: Yang/masculine

Planetary Ruler: Jupiter

Meditation: I can take time to explore my soul

Gemstone: Turquoise

Power Stones: Lapis lazuli, azurite, sodalite

Key Phrase: I understand

Glyph: Archer's arrow

Anatomy: Hips, thighs, sciatic nerve

Colors: Royal blue, purple

Animals: Fleet-footed animals

Myths/Legends: Athena, Chiron

House: Ninth

Opposite Sign: Gemini

Flower: Narcissus

Keyword: Optimism

The Sagittarius Personality

Strengths, Talents, and the Creative Spark

Jupiter is the ruler of your sign, a hallmark of prosperity that describes your luck and fortune. No wonder you embrace a world that is larger than life. The sign of the Archer is a mutable fire member of the zodiac and the natural ruler of the ninth house of the higher mind, religion, spirituality, the clergy, advanced education, law, publishing, in-laws, foreigners, religion, and travel to distant places. With Jupiter leading the way and giving you the space you desire to explore your options, you attract a variety of adventures at home, at work, and in distant locales. You like rich, deep colors like dark blues, browns, purples, and dark green shades. You seek the truth in whatever interests you and are often the one who asks those probing questions when you hear new facts that pique your interest. You want to absorb as much material as you can to expand your consciousness and satisfy your passion for life. Individuals who know you describe you as being very straightforward, freely expressing your opinion and doing so often. Critics claim you stun them with your bluntness when you deliver exceptionally candid remarks. You merely thought you were giving them what they wanted when they asked for your opinion.

Going on a mission is symbolic of your adventure-loving lifestyle. You may start at a young age as a cultural exchange student or an athlete on scholarship. Many of you enjoy traveling and select careers or assignments where hitting the road is a requirement, such as a sales representative, a filmmaker or associate who goes on location to shoot scenes, or a professor-at-large who contracts with different universities every few years. You may also pursue an education at a military academy that assures you of assignments at diverse duty stations to build credentials for increasingly responsible positions. Yours is a sign that almost always has expertise in more than one career field.

Intimacy and Personal Relationships

You enjoy companionship. In fact, you prefer going places and seeing sights with a close friend rather than venturing out alone. Your charming personality makes you popular with friends, coworkers, neighbors, and most of the people you meet. Along with your pleasing manner and an engaging sense of humor, you have an intuitive sense of what drives others. Not surprisingly, you receive numerous social invitations that keep your calendar full. Despite that, you really prefer to hang out with your best friends when you have feelings to share or problems to solve. While some of you marry young, most Sagittarians like to play the field and often find the perfect partner through shared, one-of-a-kind encounters that lead to a powerful relationship with a best friend who ultimately becomes your mate. A partner wins your heart by sharing untraveled paths, eating exotic foods in faraway places, keeping a flexible schedule so you can incorporate impromptu trips into a demanding career routine, and being open to long-distance moves when job transfers offer life-enriching experiences. The air signs, Gemini, Libra, and Aquarius, along with fire signs Aries and Leo make compatible partners. You'll reach boredom quickly if you bond with stay-at-home types or partners who want to control your freedom. If you are a parent, you bond strongly with children, keeping an eye on their educational and sports progress and encouraging them to develop the skills that drive their passion. When your plate is filled with too many distractions, you may be lax in keeping up with children's interests, so be sure to build shared time into part of each week.

Values and Resources

In recent years you have come to value security, something that seldom worried you before unless a sudden event blew up and turned your life upside down. If you have experienced a hurricane or tropical storm that destroyed your neighborhood in recent years, you understand the environmental strain that calls for adaptability and rebuilding the structures that once kept you safe. You like variety in routines, careers, food choices, electronic media, and entertainment. You enjoy relationships with others that go back many years, even if you seldom see these individuals. Texting keeps you linked and up-to-date on evolving circumstances. You believe that you can meet up with a key figure from your past and pick up where you left off without missing a beat. Expanding your consciousness through education is a key goal that you advocate for personal growth and for your cherished family.

Blind Spots and Blockages

Time management is often a problem when distractions get in the way of completing assignments or focusing on priorities. Work associates say you have trouble getting to work or meetings on time. Individuals you see socially or professionally have similar complaints about your disregard for scheduled events when you arrive late for dates, doctor appointments, parties, and automobile tune-ups. You don't see yourself as being rude or selfish and often feel that too much is made of this habit, because you do show up eventually and your work quality is well above average. Managers laud your speech-writing skills and your animated delivery that rouses the audience, yet you may ignore the time allotted for your presentation and cut into time set aside for additional speakers, fueling resentment from team members. Your spouse says you spend too much time after dinner on electronic exchanges instead of bonding and unwinding at the close of the day. You don't like keeping calendars and often ignore electronic alarms on your phone that remind you of a scheduled obligation. Take the time to tweak your operating style by compiling status information weekly to keep your tasks and assignments current.

Goals and Success

Jupiter, your sign ruler, brings out the teacher in you in roles that make others appreciate your diversity and the artful way you present information to others. A number of professions suit your skills, such as book narrators, cruise directors, sales representatives, tour guides, and travel agents. You place high value on the benefits of placing exchange students in homes to assimilate both cultural and academic topics. Ever seeking new experiences, you have likely done a bit of job-hopping in your quest for the perfect career. You may sign on with agencies who cater to placing workers, from support staff to executives, in temporary positions with schedules that may be full- or part-time. The writers among you may take a long sabbatical to pen a novel or take time off to study for a legal degree. You have learned to juggle money admirably to cover expenses when you make interim employment arrangements that limit salary. Due to your many interests and talents, you pack in a great deal of knowledge that you share in several careers in your lifetime. Wise investments help you survive in leaner times.

Sagittarius Keywords for 2024
Beliefs, benefits, bounty

The Year Ahead for Sagittarius

Partnership growth plays a starring role in moving you toward a successful outcome in 2024. At the start of the year, Jupiter finishes up

204 Llewellyn's 2024 Sun Sign Book

ongoing business in Taurus and your solar sixth house of work and health, leaving you fully prepared to move to a new level of responsibility and use your talent to shine in your profession. Also present in your employment arena is provocative Uranus in Taurus, proving that unpredictability has been a constant threat to smooth operations since 2018. On May 25, Jupiter moves into Gemini and your solar seventh house of close business and personal relationships, where evolving conditions in both arenas await your approval and committed participation. If collaboration appeals to you, you may be offered a partnership in a desirable firm. You could also decide to resign from a current position and pursue your own business. Those of you in love may take steps to the altar to change your marital status. Saturn in early Pisces makes its way through your solar fourth house of home and family, where you'll find routines that are out of alignment and in strong need of adjustment as household members wander in and out of living in your residence. Also present in your solar fourth house is spiritually oriented Neptune in late Pisces, reminding you to invoke a calmer state of mind when you return from your frequent travels.

The dwarf planet Pluto has had the longest transit of the current outer planets in Capricorn and your solar second house of income and assets since 2008. This year the planet of transition does its work removing blocks and nudging stuck places as it moves into Aquarius and your solar third house of mental integrity on January 20. Develop a new plan to clear your mind of angst. Four eclipses occur this year, starting with a Lunar Eclipse on March 25 in Libra and your solar eleventh house of friendship, groups, and goals and ending with the last Solar Eclipse of 2024 in the same house on October 2. The first Solar Eclipse occurs on April 8 in Aries and your solar fifth house of children, romance, and risk-taking, and the last Lunar Eclipse of the year falls on September 17 in Pisces and your solar fourth house of home, base of operation, and family, starting a new eclipse cycle for the next year and a half.

Jupiter

After Jupiter, the planet of growth and expansion, made a rapid transit through Aries and your solar fifth house of children and their interests, amusements, entrepreneurial endeavors, recreation, risk-taking, romance, sports, and vacations, and favorably aspected every degree of your sign in 2023, it moved into Taurus and your solar sixth house of work that same year. Despite Jupiter sharing space with disruptive Uranus in Taurus, you realized considerable gains in work accomplishments, improved your health by getting more rest, strengthened collaboration with colleagues, and implemented work-arounds to compensate for lingering staff shortages. You begin 2024 with a much more organized work environment, and your mind is overflowing with innovative ideas. On May 25, Jupiter moves into Gemini and your solar seventh house of partners, where destiny awaits you in the form of a solid love relationship and possibly a marriage as well as emerging opportunities, or you may form a partnership with another dedicated professional who handles the financial details while you sell the product or service. Steady income will fuel your dream of entrepreneurship. Breathe deeply and internalize success. The planet of expansion moves retrograde on October 9 and turns direct in Gemini on February 4, 2025. Sagittarians born during the first twenty-one degrees of your sign benefit the most from this life-changing transit.

Saturn

At the onset of 2024, Saturn, the taskmaster, continues its transit through Pisces and your solar fourth house of home, family members, base of operation, parents, domestic matters, room renovation, and conditions surrounding the lives of those residing in your home. What might this planet demand at this time? For starters, you could be prompted to recognize that certain family members are stuck in unproductive routines that limit personal growth. If a member has returned home in the aftermath of a job loss, lingering upheaval as a result of the pandemic, economic strain, or illness, it could be time to suggest the merits of seeking steady employment and a return to living independently. Coach them by offering to review and critique a resume, suggest firms that are hiring and looking for compatible credentials, or pay for a seminar that focuses on returning to work after an employment gap. If family illness is an issue, make sure the person seeks help from appropriate medical professionals.

Remember that Neptune is in Pisces and your solar fourth house, too, adding an element of hazy thinking that can obstruct a clear path to implementing solutions. The mission Saturn presents you with this year is to bring the household into equilibrium, minimize confusion about priorities, organize schedules, and help family members claim their power outside of the confines of the nest. Applying the strength of your skills to influence current conditions will make a difference in restoring harmonious conditions in your home. Saturn's retrograde period begins on June 29 and ends on November 15. Those born between November 24 and December 12 see the most activity during this cycle.

Uranus

Few planets have the power to inflict sudden chaos into your world than a hard strike from Uranus, which advances this year to late Taurus in your solar sixth house of work, daily routines, health, nutrition, organizational acumen, pets, coworkers, and your approach to accomplishing assignments. This house has received considerable attention over the last few years, with eclipses in Taurus adding unexpected drama to the stability of the work scene. If you have any planets in Taurus in your birth chart, the impact may have been greater, resulting in a higher percentage of layoffs, firings, a reduction in hours, or a cut in pay. The explosive and unpredictable planet transits the later degrees of Taurus in 2024, forming a stressful aspect to the Sun of Sagittarians born between December 9 and 20. Although Uranus enters 2024 in retrograde motion, it goes direct on January 27. The chaotic planet will station to move retrograde on September 1 and resume direct motion on January 30, 2025. Be sure your personal behavior is exemplary at the workplace and refrain from carrying on a flirtation with a staff member, repeating destructive gossip, or marginalizing another's contributions. Use your love of music by finding a side job playing your favorite instrument, composing a song, or singing in an established choir.

Neptune

A key sector in your chart in 2024 is your solar fourth house of home and foundation, where Neptune is moving through late degrees of Pisces while it scrutinizes the state of domestic matters, your family, parents, scheduled work on household improvement projects, and the behavior of people who live with you. Show compassion to those who are recovering from a loss of status, a physical or mental illness, economic hardship, or job loss. If you have personally lost ground due to similar circumstances and have been reluctant to take action, stop the daydreaming and use your fine analytical skills to identify the best approach to offer assistance to others while healing your own psyche. This year these matters and more get the spotlight because Neptune is not the lone planet in this house, sharing the company of Saturn in

Pisces and joined by a Lunar Eclipse in Pisces on September 17 that is very close to Neptune's transiting degree. If you were born between December 17 and 21, Neptune's transit will more meaningfully affect you, giving you a good jolt from the chills of truth running through your auric field and alerting you to approaching change. This year Neptune goes retrograde on July 2 in the last degree of Pisces and stations to move direct on December 7. Release your masterful teaching skills and put the balm of understanding to work in your home.

Pluto

Since 2008, Pluto has occupied Capricorn and your solar second house of assets, income, money you earn and how you spend it, the value you place on resources, and what you are willing to invest in higher education or developmental coursework to give your skills a competitive edge in the employment arena. Along the way, you may have been hanging on to some destructive financial habits that feed either a poverty consciousness that makes you feel sure there is never going to be enough money or an extravagant gene that keeps telling you to spend because the money will just show up and you'll be able to pay off the debt. You've been hanging on to these and other beliefs about money for a long time. In its final passage through your solar second house, Pluto is here to make sure you get the message to act responsibly and have a fiscal management plan that includes a savings account for emergencies and a retirement account that keeps your money safe for the future and allows you to enjoy what you earn without splurging until you are broke. Make sure you no longer carry the baggage related to a fear of poverty. Pluto wants to know you are ready to claim your financial power through the regeneration tools left in your care. On January 20, Pluto moves out of rigid Capricorn and shifts into humanitarian Aquarius and your solar third house of mental outlook and negotiation. Pluto turns retrograde on May 2 in Aquarius and moves direct on October 11 in late Capricorn. Those of you with birthdays between November 21 and 24 experience harmonious vibes from this early Aquarius transit. The planet of rebirth moves into Aquarius for good on November 20 for a multi-year run in the sign of futuristic analysis.

How Will This Year's Eclipses Affect You?

This year's four eclipses, two lunar (Full Moon) and two solar (New Moon), are ready to generate intense periods that start to manifest a few months before their actual occurrence. The Libra/Aries cycle wraps up in March 2023 to make way for the Pisces/Virgo eclipses, the first of which makes its debut in September of 2024. Eclipses unfold in cycles involving all twelve signs of the zodiac and usually occur in pairs about two weeks apart. Never fear eclipses—just think of them as opportunities for growth that allow you to release old patterns. Expect surprises that elicit both positive and perplexing feelings and outcomes. The closer an eclipse is to a planet or point in your birth chart, the greater the importance it has in your life, especially if one of those planets is in the same degree as the eclipse.

Prepare yourself for 2024's first Lunar Eclipse on March 25 in Libra and your solar eleventh house of associations, friends, groups, goals, humanitarian interests, and dreams. If your birth chart has planets in this house, you are challenged with exploring new possibilities for developing networks, finding a better fit for your interests, deciding what types of groups have philosophies compatible with yours, and determining how much time you want to devote to ad hoc assignments versus a permanent place in an organization that earns your commitment.

On April 8, the first Solar Eclipse of the year arrives in Aries and your solar fifth house of children and their interests, adventure, entertainment, romance, social encounters, sports, speculation, and vacations. New encounters in your love life may appear out of the blue. You will be bombarded with social invitations and may find it hard to keep up with all of them. Children's needs could become more demanding due to school and sports involvement.

On September 17, you'll greet the second Lunar Eclipse of the year in Pisces and your solar fourth house, bringing your full attention to family action in your home. An eclipse here can showcase conditions around specific family members and movement of residents into or out of your home, and uncover situations that affect the peace and harmony in your home. Conversely, you may sell or buy a home, give your residence an external makeover, or enter the field of real estate.

The site of the final Solar Eclipse of 2024 on October 2 is Libra and your solar eleventh house of friends, associates, professional colleagues, members of groups that share your interests, and the humanitarian perspective of business enterprises. You could be selected to lead a group, increase membership in a favorite organization, run for political office, or raise funds for a worthy charity. Enthusiasm mounts as you discover the passion you have for creating a new enterprise.

Sagittarius | January

Overall Theme

You start the year off with career prospects looking promising and your money picture looking bright when the Capricorn New Moon rises in your solar second house of income on January 11. Mercury goes direct on January 1 in Sagittarius, giving those of you applying for jobs or loans a chance to start the paperwork early in the month. After Uranus in Taurus goes direct on the 27th in your solar sixth house, you should be ready to do business.

Relationships

Mercury and Venus in your sign early in January pull you closer to your significant other when you make plans for dinner and date nights and romantic encounters. Quality family time looks enjoyable around the 14th, when everyone gathers and shares plans for the coming year. Make suggestions for sharing a vacation week that appeals to all.

Success and Money

Your wallet is fatter because holiday cash has left you in good shape for funding a large household purchase. Early in the month your boss suggests meeting with you once a week to discuss implementing new operating procedures that are not yet ready to be announced. You develop new respect for your employer's thoughtful approach.

Pitfalls and Potential Problems

Those of you working in direct sales of retail goods may notice high absenteeism when you return to work on January 2. Gossip among those who come to work suggests that low pay and meager benefits are affecting morale. Anticipate turnover in coming months.

Rewarding Days

1, 11, 14, 27

Challenging Days

2, 16, 21, 25

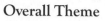 # Sagittarius | February

Overall Theme
Not one retrograde planet shows up this month to disrupt the flow of your work or entertainment schedule. Family members are upbeat and ready to ditch the winter blues with a weekend escape to a snowy wonderland that reflects the magic of Neptune's aura of fantasy. If you can't get to a resort, go ice skating or make a snowman.

Relationships
Children are in for a cultural treat when you plan a dinner outing to celebrate the Lunar New Year of the Dragon sometime between the 10th and the 14th. Buy your own decorations or favors and don't forget to put a cash gift in red envelopes to wish participants a prosperous new year. Red is the color for Valentine's Day, too. Make it a double celebration.

Success and Money
The compatible New Moon in Aquarius and your solar second house of earned income on the 9th opens doors that highlight your superb analytical skills, putting new assignments up for grabs if you are interested. Look for extra money in your paycheck around the 20th after performance acknowledgments from company administrators surface.

Pitfalls and Potential Problems
Your intuition is on target when you notice around February 1 that a usually upbeat friend seems evasive and gives you the cold shoulder. Tension escalates when you attend a meeting on the 9th and get nowhere attempting to find the cause of the frustrating freeze. After you learn that the cost of an auto repair is off the charts, you tell your partner the bad news on the 17th.

Rewarding Days
9, 14, 20, 25

Challenging Days
1, 17, 22, 24

Sagittarius | March

Overall Theme

The New Moon rises in Pisces and your solar fourth house of home and family on March 10, when Daylight Saving Time begins. Household activities and interactions with residents claim most of your free time this month while you manage cleaning and repair projects in your home. Call your favorite charity by March 13 to pick up furniture and goods that are no longer needed.

Relationships

The best day to visit grandparents is March 10, when playfulness and lightheartedness fill your guest-ready home. Interactions with workmates intensify the week of March 11 as assignment deadlines sweep in, calling for an all-out team effort to stay on track. Venus and Mars in compatible Aquarius send charming date material your way around March 16 if you are available.

Success and Money

Monetary talk fills your solar seventh house of partners now as you examine growing pooled resources. Look at the possibilities after the 16th and analyze the amount of debt you can eliminate within six months. An associate introduces you to individuals who share your passion for travel on March 25, the day of the first Lunar Eclipse of the year, occurring in Libra and your solar eleventh house of friends.

Pitfalls and Potential Problems

A strained relationship between you and a sibling calls for a heartfelt talk to heal the pain. If you meet on March 7, neither of you may be willing to acknowledge your part in the rift. Wait a week or two for better communication options and meet on neutral ground.

Rewarding Days

5, 10, 13, 16

Challenging Days

3, 7, 20, 26

Sagittarius | April

Overall Theme

Mercury turns retrograde in Aries on the 1st and moves direct three weeks later on April 25. Sit out this slowdown period by finishing assignments you are already working on and waiting until the direct station date to sign important documents, begin new projects, or take a vacation.

Relationships

A gathering of your nearby relatives takes place on April 6, when the clan arrives at your residence for a potluck dinner and games. Lunar activity includes a Solar Eclipse on April 8 in Aries and your solar fifth house of lovers, recreation, and your social life, suggesting that an intimate relationship is growing. Share the depth of your commitment with your partner.

Success and Money

On April 2 you may be gathering interest quotes from your favorite banker for a home loan. Compare rates with at least two other enterprises before making a decision and monitor Mercury's retrograde motion before finalizing the loan. Donate meals to a well-run food pantry during the last weekend of April.

Pitfalls and Potential Problems

If you are interested in initiatives related to community activities, you are likely to attend a meeting around April 4 to learn specific information about planned growth. Hidden information comes to light by the 23rd.

Rewarding Days

2, 6, 8, 10

Challenging Days

4, 9, 12, 21

Sagittarius | May

Overall Theme

When Jupiter moves into Gemini on May 25 in your solar seventh house of partnerships, personal and business relationships get full attention as you focus on the strengths that make them meaningful and the gratitude you have for the enthusiastic pursuit of a long-term commitment. Open the door wide and welcome this prosperity cycle.

Relationships

A family member bubbles over with passion after joining a sports team and requests your attendance at games to show you the level of achievement gained. Around May 8, consider submitting an award nomination for a colleague who has demonstrated outstanding performance. You'll be glad to have the Memorial Day holiday off on May 27 to relax and bond with family and friends.

Success and Money

The New Moon on May 7 that falls in Taurus and your solar sixth house of daily routines and work favors camaraderie among coworkers and shows an upswing in performance quality, with the team taking pride in accomplishments. If you manage an office, you learn that funding for new equipment has been approved and you share the news with teammates.

Pitfalls and Potential Problems

Pluto in early Aquarius makes a station to move retrograde on May 2 in your solar third house of education, delaying your search for classes that are most helpful to the career path you are pursuing. The May 23rd Full Moon in your sign gives you a chance to rest and regroup from overactivity in your social life.

Rewarding Days

3, 8, 9, 27

Challenging Days

2, 11, 15, 23

Sagittarius | June

Overall Theme

It will likely be another banner month for you in the relationship department when the Gemini New Moon on the 6th lines up with Jupiter in Gemini in your solar seventh house of partnerships. Pluto in Aquarius sends a friendly vibe from your solar third house of communication to let you know that the great uniter, love, is on the scene and all you have to do is embrace it with the partner of your dreams.

Relationships

Go out to eat with your partner and children on June 1 and ask close neighbors to join you for a casual meal in a lively environment. Work with business collaborators on June 6 to identify attention-getting concepts that breathe new life into your work agenda. Plan an outing to a local park on June 27.

Success and Money

Take advantage of sales and free delivery on household goods and sundries around June 23, when you receive outstanding service from an online vendor. Check another site for a Father's Day gift and keep your prosperity streak going.

Pitfalls and Potential Problems

The Capricorn Full Moon on the 21st opposes the Sun, Mercury, and Venus, limiting options for finding sales on gear and clothing for an upcoming vacation. Stoic Saturn moves into retrograde motion on the 29th in Pisces and your solar fourth house, possibly delaying vacation plans when final touches are needed on a critical work project.

Rewarding Days

1, 6, 23, 27

Challenging Days

3, 11, 21, 29

Sagittarius | July

Overall Theme

Picnics drive celebrations in the period after July 2, a favorable vacation week. Check out what your local community is doing to celebrate the Fourth of July. Obtain information for your family and join the festivities, scoping out the activities that interest them most.

Relationships

Relatives visit this week to see sights of interest and to celebrate Independence Day. Take the savvy shoppers among them out on the Cancer New Moon of July 5 to visit boutiques and apparel shops that offer unusual creations. Have a drink and a light dinner with a good friend after work on the 12th to start off the weekend on a relaxing note.

Success and Money

Many Sagittarians have a keen interest in architecture, complemented by their feng shui preference for locating master bedrooms at the back of the home and away from disturbing energy (shars). Look at real estate if you're contemplating a home purchase on July 6, when the Moon trines Saturn in harmony with Mars and Venus.

Pitfalls and Potential Problems

Transiting Neptune turns retrograde on July 2 in the last degree of Pisces and your solar fourth house of home. Be sure you disconnect hoses from outside water sources if you are going on vacation and avoid leaving the washing machine running when you leave home.

Rewarding Days

5, 6, 12, 30

Challenging Days

3, 9, 13, 23

Sagittarius | August

Overall Theme

This month Mercury goes retrograde in Virgo on August 5. It moves back into Leo on August 14 and goes direct on the 28th. The New Moon in Leo, a sign that is compatible to yours, makes a statement on August 4 in your solar ninth house of travel, hoping to tempt you into packing your bags for a rejuvenating getaway.

Relationships

Early in the month you'll hear from long-distance relatives looking to link up with you at your location or theirs for a summer visit. Friends invite you and your family for an outing on August 9 that may include a state park, historical site, or amusement park. Rapport among all of you makes the outing enjoyable from start to finish. Take time for romance on the 23rd.

Success and Money

Your Sagittarius gambling streak surfaces at just the right time this month when several of your lucky numbers bring a small windfall after a lottery drawing on August 23. Your team and another group of employees share responsibility and management of a long-term project. The experiment receives noteworthy praise on August 25 for the outstanding suggestions the teams propose.

Pitfalls and Potential Problems

A child may be disappointed over failure to make the team after not being selected to represent the school during tryouts around August 22. The event is highly competitive and could be attainable for the student with more practice. Offer constructive counsel.

Rewarding Days

4, 9, 23, 25

Challenging Days

6, 14, 22, 26

⋌ Sagittarius | September ⋌

Overall Theme

Occurring appropriately in your solar tenth house of career and organizational environment, the New Moon in Virgo on Labor Day, September 2, reminds you of how grateful you are to be appreciated for your commitment and dedication to work you enjoy and leadership you admire. Whenever you have doubts, all you have to do is think about the value of your benefits.

Relationships

The final Lunar Eclipse of the year occurs in Pisces and your solar fourth house of home and family on September 17 and calls attention to the dynamics you share with others in your home. Intimacy with your love partner is likely on September 26, when romantic talk flows freely and mental compatibility draws you closer than ever.

Success and Money

Finalized contracts make you feel secure when they are signed on September 15 and shore up your expectation that the year will continue to bring you a prosperous, rewarding cycle. Others call your gift of humor a welcome relief to break the ice in meetings or when negotiations reach an impasse. Purchases around the 26th bring the deals you desire.

Pitfalls and Potential Problems

You have an uneasy feeling on September 6 about attending a meeting that has a loose agenda. You ignore your intuition and go anyway, only to be dumped on by members concerned about financial shortfalls. Mixed aspects on September 20 could result in disappointment over an entertainment venue that falls short of the high ticket price.

Rewarding Days

2, 25, 15, 26

Challenging Days

6, 17, 20, 27

♐ Sagittarius | October ♐

Overall Theme

Home base could undergo a loss when transiting Jupiter in Gemini moves retrograde on October 1 after lobbing a hard aspect toward transiting Saturn in Pisces, possibly resulting in the failure of a major appliance. Saturn's retrograde movement in your solar fourth house of home reminds you to check connections on appliances and outdoor lighting to avoid storm damage to your property.

Relationships

A Solar Eclipse occurs on October 2 in Libra and your solar eleventh house, shaping new directions for friendships, a membership application with a prestigious group, or humanitarian work for a deserving charity. Surprises, excitement, and delight over delivery of new furnishings lift your spirits on October 15.

Success and Money

Pluto turns direct on October 11 in Capricorn and your solar second house of earnings. Next year's salary projections are available, and you're delighted to learn that you'll receive a healthy boost in income. A relaxing Sunday outing with your partner on the 13th prepares you for Monday's nonstop request for assistance from coworkers getting acclimated to new equipment or procedures.

Pitfalls and Potential Problems

On the 20th, don't be surprised if your partner, who has no interest in watching a newly released film you want to see in the theater, sleeps through the entire movie. Next time ask a friend or sibling to attend. The Full Moon in Aries on October 17 sends mixed messages to dating couples in the form of strained communication.

Rewarding Days

2, 8, 15, 23

Challenging Days

4, 17, 20, 25

⤢ Sagittarius | November ⤢

Overall Theme

Just thinking about parties and seasonal festivities gives you an adrenaline rush, Sagittarius. You look for signs of merriment everywhere that represent diverse cultures. Invite favorite people to participate in holiday traditions. Saturn turns direct in Pisces on the 15th in your family-oriented solar fourth house, allocating bonus money for hosting holiday gatherings.

Relationships

Even if you're hosting a Thanksgiving meal, start the day by serving meals to individuals at a local soup kitchen. Your own holiday feast could include traveling visitors, siblings, in-laws, parents, and a few coworkers and friends. Fill the table with food made from cherished recipes, inviting guests to devour savory dishes. Then give thanks for the special love that binds hearts together with gratitude.

Success and Money

Synchronicity clicks on November 8 when you get news that a performance bonus is coming your way to acknowledge milestone achievements. Enjoy the extra cash, setting some aside for holiday gifts, entertainment, and a donation to your favorite charity. A salary raise could be announced around November 19.

Pitfalls and Potential Problems

Mercury goes retrograde in Sagittarius on November 25, so travel to your holiday destination could be affected. The Thanksgiving Day Moon in Scorpio in your solar twelfth house clashes with Mars in Leo in your solar ninth house. Don't let post-election political discussions mar the peaceful spirit of the day. Humor is still the best medicine. Turn on the music and dance.

Rewarding Days

1, 8, 15, 19

Challenging Days

7, 13, 17, 25

Sagittarius | December

Overall Theme

Beliefs are a major driver of your spiritual life and an essential part of the holiday season. You'll be reminded of how deeply you have internalized customs and traditions after Neptune turns direct on December 7 and inspires you to start a new ritual. Why not make it about children by focusing on their feelings and the activities they enjoy that make them truly happy?

Relationships

This month, two New Moons occur, the first in Sagittarius on December 1 and the second in Capricorn on December 30. Party season brings you invitations from December 7 through the 23rd that you'll share with neighbors, family, partners, and close friends. Over the weekend of the 6th, visit local connections who will be away over Christmas.

Success and Money

Lift the holiday spirits of children without homes by gifting them with food, toys, or clothing. Ask a child or a friend to accompany you. Grateful eyes are often the only thank-you needed. Leave 2024 with gratitude for achieving personal growth. Spread cheer and optimism in 2025.

Pitfalls and Potential Problems

Mars stations to move retrograde on the 6th in Leo and your solar ninth house, possibly affecting transportation plans. Neptune in Pisces turns direct on December 7, followed by Mercury in Sagittarius on December 15. Simultaneously, the Full Moon in Gemini occurs on December 15, suggesting you avoid travel on that date.

Rewarding Days

7, 9, 14, 23

Challenging Days

6, 11, 15, 21

Sagittarius Action Table

These dates reflect the best—but not the only—times for success and ease in these activities, according to your Sun sign.

	JAN	FEB	MAR	APR	MAY	JUN	JUL	AUG	SEP	OCT	NOV	DEC
Move								4		15		
Romance		14	16		9		6				19	14
Seek counseling/ coaching			13	10			12			2	8	
Ask for a raise	27	25		8	8				2			
Vacation						1		23				7
Get a loan	11					23			26			

Capricorn

The Goat
December 21 to January 20

♑

Element: Earth

Quality: Cardinal

Polarity: Yin/feminine

Planetary Ruler: Saturn

Meditation: I know the strength of my soul

Gemstone: Garnet

Power Stones: Peridot, onyx diamond, quartz, black obsidian

Key Phrase: I use

Glyph: Head of a goat

Anatomy: Skeleton, knees, skin

Colors: Black, forest green

Animals: Goats, thick-shelled animals

Myths/Legends: Chronos, Vesta, Pan

House: Tenth

Opposite Sign: Cancer

Flower: Carnation

Keyword: Ambitious

The Capricorn Personality

Strengths, Talents, and the Creative Spark

When it comes to implementing your goals in life, no sign matches your impeccable preparation for developing them and making sure they meet your objectives. You appear to be born ready to make your mark in the world, even if you typically hold back some of your energy until after age thirty. You put a high premium on knowledge and experience. Saturn rules your sign and plays a lead role in attracting you to a variety of challenges in matters of fame, reputation, and influence. The ambitious mountain goat symbolizes your approach to work and accepting responsibility when you set out on a path to achieve your goals and move far ahead of the competition. Troubleshooting, problem-solving, and movement encompass a considerable part of your day. Yours is the third earth sign of the zodiac (along with Taurus and Virgo) and the natural occupant of the tenth house of career, status in life, ambition, authority, father figures, bosses, government, maturity, recognition, and the path to success. Admirers often comment that you are driven by the desire to improve yourself both mentally and physically on your quest to realize cherished goals. Capricorn rules the bones, hair, joints, knees, skeletal system, skin, and teeth. Your colors are black, dark blue, most dark shades, grays, navy, slate, pine green, and brown.

As one who is thoroughly organized, you research facts before presenting them and lay them out efficiently and logically so that others can easily follow the gist of your ideas. You maintain high performance standards through your considerable accomplishments, making you the ideal candidate for leadership and management roles. Authorities count on you, and colleagues recognize the strength of your expertise and rely on your institutional memory to guide the mission, the project, or the acquisition of the skills needed to get the work done. You often inject a bit of your wit and acerbic humor to ease the tension that can creep into the work environment.

Intimacy and Personal Relationships

Many who know you are not aware of your romantic and passionate heart and the depth of your feelings. That's because you control your outer demeanor and appear more formal than most, often earning the reputation of one who is cold and unemotional. You actually prefer a partner who makes you feel emotionally secure in the love you share, and that includes passion and affection along with loyalty and mutual respect. You're known for dating partners who are very level-headed and don't make waves, even if they don't have what it takes to make your heart sing. Once your heart chakra awakens, you make up for lost time by pursuing a love match that awakens your sensual side and brings you the true love you desire. A Cancer, your opposite sign, is often the perfect match for you since you both share cardinal energy and have a flair for getting things done without sacrificing your relationship. The other earth signs, Taurus and Virgo, are also fine partnership candidates, along with water signs Scorpio and Pisces. Unless there are a good number of compatible aspects in your charts, Aries and Libra may not be the easiest love connections. Home life is a hub of activity, with the emphasis on scheduling appointments, meetings, and family events with children and other relatives. Friends are welcomed as family and invited to participate in holiday gatherings. Your biggest challenge is to maintain balance at home, leaving your workaholic tendencies behind.

Values and Resources

Authority figures, including father figures, heads of state, bosses, and government officials, gain your deepest respect. You get along well with all the VIPs in your organization because they see how beautifully you take responsibility for maintaining high standards of conduct while meeting goals and work deadlines. Autonomy means the world to you and the executives who hire you value your need for it, making a supervisory or leadership role the perfect outlet for your style. As a self-starter, you begin by organizing the talent pool in your large or small circle of authority with a well-developed plan that covers the bases, follows a timeline, and showcases the efficacy of the team. While you enjoy the glory of recognition for a job well done, you believe in passing the credit for achievement down the line to all who have a hand in successful outcomes. You value the contributions of employees of all ages and are turned off by criticisms of youth or practices of ageism. You show gratitude for those who have your back in challenging times and reciprocate by loyally supporting them when the need arises.

Blind Spots and Blockages

The common complaint about you from family, friends, and colleagues is that you work too much and sacrifice leisure time for inflexible dedication to your job. Most critics say you expect too much of yourself and sometimes of others, who may not have the stamina to work twelve-hour days. You can be impatient when another's work style is not a good match for yours and may fail to hide your disappointment when the outcome is flawed. Instead of stepping in and doing the work yourself, you are better off discussing the problems privately and suggesting a solution while reframing your expectation of the bottom line. Sometimes colleagues point out that your tone of voice becomes harsh and your body language reflects your feelings of disappointment. Salaries and awards are another sore spot for team members who feel you can be miserly when recommending raises or bonuses. By seeking counsel from qualified coaches, you can learn to let go of the rigid outlook that you have a tendency to hang on to for far too long.

Goals and Success

Vitality perks up and so does your visibility with higher authorities when you invent a solution to a persistent work problem that saves money, time, and the need to hire extra talent to execute plans effectively. You're ready to lobby for executive buy-in by taking the stage to present the details of your plan, answer questions, and show the cost-effectiveness of smarter ways to do business. Strategically, you usually seem steps ahead of the competition because you appear ready to implement well-thought-out plans that benefit the organization and further your career goals. You excel in positions that offer a variety of tasks that call for your expertise in the analysis of the situation, communication, organizational alignment, personal contact with others, problem-solving, and implementation of a workable timeline. Look for opportunities in 2023 to build credibility and find happiness in your chosen field of expertise.

Capricorn Keywords for 2024
Achievement, ambition, award

The Year Ahead for Capricorn

In transition year 2024, you will be juggling a busy schedule that encompasses new life phases, with the cardinal signs dominating the year's eclipses in your solar tenth house (two in Libra on March 25 and October 2) of ambition, authority, career, and responsibility and your solar fourth house of home, family, and foundation of life (a Solar Eclipse in

Aries on April 8). The third eclipse of the year occurs in Pisces on September 17, a Lunar Eclipse in your solar third house of communication, neighbors, siblings, and transportation. If one of these eclipses falls in a degree that directly aspects your Sun or other Capricorn planets, major life changes may be unfolding. If you've been hoping for a reprieve from delays in important business or personal matters, you may find relief when Mercury in Sagittarius turns direct on January 1 in your solar twelfth house and gives you the go-ahead to reveal new goals and plans. Capricorns who have been recuperating from illness or surgery may expect a return to good health when Jupiter in Taurus favorably aspects your Sun while transiting your solar fifth house. Supporters of your work contributions could be unusually active from May 25 onward, when Jupiter moves into Gemini and occupies your solar sixth house of organization and work environment for the remainder of 2024.

Another planet that is occupying Taurus and your solar fifth house is Uranus, which turns direct on January 27. Unpredictable conditions are sure to pop up this year until the erratic planet finally leaves Taurus in 2025, minimizing the waves of conflict that stem from people connected with your solar fifth house, such as children, coaches, and lovers. Occupying your solar third house along with the September Lunar Eclipse are Saturn and Neptune in Pisces, which may contribute to delays in contracts, local travel, purchases of vehicles or electronic products, and clear communication. Neptune occupies late degrees of Pisces this year, stimulating your interest in pursuing educational classes that support career goals and spiritual interests. At long last, Pluto in Capricorn, which has stimulated your solar first house of adventure, assertiveness, innovation, passion, and self-image since 2008, is crossing the finish line of its long passage in this sign. If you are ready to unload unwanted baggage, now is the time to unpack it before you get a glimpse of how Pluto will behave when it moves into Aquarius on January 20 in your solar second house of assets, income, and what you value in life. This transformative planet will energize members of your sign born between January 19 and 21. Rejoice and embrace the freedom you have as you release painful hurts from the past.

Jupiter

In 2023, Jupiter forges ahead in compatible Taurus and your solar fifth house of children and their interests, entrepreneurial endeavors, recreational pursuits, romantic partners, and travel opportunities.

One or more of these pursuits is likely to become Jupiter's beneficiary, endowing you with positive, healthy relationships, clearer insight into creative business ventures, and taking to the skies or seas to enjoy long-distance downtime via exciting, invigorating trips. Solve any lingering problems with others and make plans to schedule events and excursions, get engaged, or start a business while Jupiter's transit accelerates the momentum in your social life. Uranus in Taurus gets close to Jupiter around mid-April, stimulating unexpected activity if you have planets located around the 21st degree of Taurus. On May 25, Jupiter moves into Gemini, focusing interest on your solar sixth house of daily environment, health, nutrition, and your expertise in organizing your work life. This transit gives you the limelight and showcases the talent you have to affect career expansion and win the support of those who count on your performance to get the job done. You'll feel better physically, too, when a buildup of self-confidence elevates your spirits. Capricorns most affected by the Jupiter-in-Gemini transit in 2024 are those born between December 21 and January 12.

Saturn

Your solar third house of communication, contracts, neighbors, relatives, and transportation is one of the busiest houses in your solar chart in 2024. Saturn in early degrees of Pisces makes an attempt to organize the mixed messages and confusion that transiting Neptune in Pisces sends periodically to scramble the meaning of correspondence, delay the mail, interfere with online messages that go to spam, and prevent expeditious responses to questions. Those of you experiencing this situation are growing weary of the frequency and level of inconvenience delaying responses. Saturn urges you to address all correspondence and legal documents and keep them safe until you can analyze and act on the next steps. If you don't, you'll be correcting your work once or twice, missing out on registration for courses you desire or contract deadlines, and potentially jeopardizing the relationships you have with cousins, neighbors, and siblings who think you are avoiding them. Adding to the drama is the last Lunar Eclipse of the year in Pisces on September 17, which could produce a windfall or a setback, depending on its relationship to the rest of your birth chart and the level of achievement you attain in your work. Capricorns most affected by this transit are those born between December 25 and January 10.

Uranus

Another house with high visibility in 2024 is your solar fifth house of adventure, dating, children's interests, recreation, reasoned risk-taking, romance, and sports. How many of these themes have been subjected to shakeups, unplanned activity, or directions that have nose-dived? Is it possible that Uranus, the planet of chaos, has made its presence known in this highly social house over the past year? Even though Jupiter in Taurus is in this same house for the first five months of 2024, all may not be calm and trouble-free. Uranus starts the year in retrograde motion and goes direct on January 27, keeping a brisk pace through September 1, when it turns retrograde again and remains so until January 30, 2025. The erratic behavior associated with Uranus is sure to influence the condition of relationships and activities connected to this house. What conditions have come up that had you scrambling to make a decision, disrupted your plans, or changed your course of action? Expect additional diversions this year, such as deciding to marry, leaving your job when a plum offer comes along, starting a business, or taking a long sabbatical from a high-pressure job. Capricorns born between January 1 and 20 may experience significant activity in this house.

Neptune

As Neptune in Pisces continues its slow, dreamy pace through your solar third house of mental activity, it is sure to create diversions that tempt you to daydream, study art instead of analyzing contracts, play word games, and solve jigsaw puzzles. Residents of work and home may have told you that they attempted to communicate with you at times but you did not seem to hear them. You were probably zoned out and deep in the infamous Neptune fog. If you are wondering what happened to your hard-driven ambition, it is not gone but has made a detour into more entertaining pursuits after a bout of burnout. Are there any siblings you have tuned out or neighbors you have been ignoring or find hard to understand? Opt for a get-together to catch up and lend a friendly ear to renew your bonds. If you are a Capricorn writer, the perfect time to start a new project is between January 1 and July 1. Neptune is headed for completion of its cycle this year after spending the last thirteen years in your solar third house. Capricorns born between January 15 and 20 begin to embrace the energy of this spiritual planet that urges you to claim ownership of the intuitive gifts you were born to master.

Pluto

Have you noticed anything different occurring in your life since Pluto entered Capricorn and your solar first house back in 2008? A presence in your solar first house for such a lengthy time creates a subtle awareness of the need to clear the air of feelings not expressed, pent-up anger, physical disorders that affect health, and toxic people who have become fixtures in your life often because you avoided addressing the pressure they created when they dumped their problems on you instead of taking responsibility for solving them. Feel lighthearted when you realize that the pressing burdens you have felt are about to fade from the list of daily demands. Often this situation comes about because key people leave your circle via moves, breakups, divorces, transfers, or death. Relationships may suddenly deepen or come to an end.

While Pluto is in the last few degrees of Capricorn this year, those of you born during the last few days of your sign are likely to undergo major changes. Expect surprises and mixed feelings in the outcomes. The transformer planet aids in remodeling your body through diet, exercise, and a healthier lifestyle. No doubt this slow-moving planet has aided you in forming good habits to replace the bad ones you accumulated over the years. On January 20, Pluto enters Aquarius and your solar second house of income and resources. It turns retrograde in Aquarius on May 2 and goes direct in the last degree of Capricorn on October 11, affecting Capricorns born between January 18 and 21 the most. Those of you with your Sun at 0–2 degrees of your sign may feel a mild shift when Pluto enters Aquarius. From September 2 to November 19, Pluto occupies 27–29 degrees of Capricorn before turning the karma cleaning over to analytical Aquarius on November 20 for good.

How Will This Year's Eclipses Affect You?

This year's four eclipses, two lunar (Full Moon) and two solar (New Moon), are ready to generate intense periods that start to manifest a few months before their actual occurrence. The Libra/Aries cycle wraps up in March 2023 to make way for the Pisces/Virgo eclipses, the first of which makes its debut in September of 2024. Eclipses unfold in cycles involving all twelve signs of the zodiac and usually occur in pairs about two weeks apart. Never fear eclipses—just think of them as opportunities for growth that allow you to release old patterns. Expect surprises that elicit both positive and perplexing feelings and outcomes. The closer an eclipse is to a planet or point in your birth chart, the greater the importance it has in your life, especially if one of those planets is in the same degree as the eclipse.

Give a big welcome to 2024's first Lunar Eclipse on March 25 in Libra and your solar tenth house of authority, ambition, career, and leadership. Expect to learn considerable information related to members of your management team's senior executives and priorities that are unfolding in the organization's agenda. Welcome new employees to the workplace and engage in friendly, professional communication.

On April 8, the first Solar Eclipse of the year arrives in Aries and your solar fourth house of home, family, residents living at home base, and the physical attributes of your dwelling. An eclipse in this house often reflects a new beginning in some facet of your intimate environment. Your attitude toward others and the quality of relationships make a difference in how well you take care of household duties, share meals together, and engage in bonding time to enjoy amusements, vacations, and special events as a family. Expect revelations about new directions some family members may be taking. Review personal goals and assess how well they fit the course of action you would like to explore in 2024.

When your solar third house is the site of the second Lunar Eclipse of the year on September 17, you'll greet this lunation in Pisces by giving avid attention to education, the quality of your communication style, your growing interest in spirituality, your desire for local travel, interactions with neighbors and community interests, and bonding with siblings. With Neptune present near the eclipse degree, your mind could experience intensified psychic insight and a greater volume of dreams. Transiting Saturn in Pisces adds stability to the ultimate analysis.

The final Solar Eclipse of 2024 occurs on October 2 in Libra and your solar tenth house of administrators, company heads, advancement, and career choices. Your savvy business sense puts you in the limelight and brings you solutions to pressing workplace problems, resulting in conflict-free outcomes that promote greater team harmony. Changes in routines may have occurred since the March 25th Lunar Eclipse in this house. If financial support was lacking, an influx of cash has since made funding for new projects viable. An eclipse in this house often brings a promotion or bonus for professional achievement, so enjoy the awards. You earned them.

Capricorn | January

Overall Theme

Concentration peaks by mid-month. Your mind works overtime as Mercury moves into Capricorn, offering clear signals to proceed with plans for the year ahead. Count on receptivity for your bright ideas when you present them to your work team. Don't be surprised if you're asked to work on a plan to implement them.

Relationships

Out-of-town visitors may linger over the first week of January, giving you extra time to bond. Enjoy the company of a good but hard-to-reach friend on the 6th. The 15th is a perfect night for informal dining and games with neighbors. Warm your partner's heart with a January 24th date night, enjoying favorite cuisine and sharing signature dishes with gusto.

Success and Money

If you are away when the new year starts, savor every moment of your much-deserved extended holiday. Buy lottery scratchers when the New Moon is in your sign on January 11 and see what the lunar energy does to ignite your winning streak. Spend holiday gift cash on a few of your favorite things at sales around the 19th.

Pitfalls and Potential Problems

January 3 could be a bust for holding a successful meeting with key staff still on holiday leave. Household harmony in the family wanes around the 16th when you cancel entertainment plans. Uranus in Taurus turns direct on the 27th, potentially uncovering a conflict in planned activities for the upcoming weekend when some invitees will be unable to attend.

Rewarding Days

1, 6, 15, 24

Challenging Days

3, 16, 21, 26

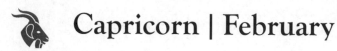 # Capricorn | February

Overall Theme

Squeeze in time for a nice weekend trip this month, taking advantage of the many earth-sign planets that favor your chart. If that doesn't work for you, schedule a day trip the whole family can enjoy since no planets are retrograde now. You could use a break and your family will love you for surprising them with an unplanned adventure.

Relationships

February has a sociable tone that is perfect for bonding with neighbors at a community Valentine party on the 14th. Bring some sweets to treat attendees. Celebrate the beginning of the Lunar New Year of the Dragon on the 10th with siblings. Ask everyone to pop some cash into a red envelope to seed the year with a prosperous beginning. Invite guests to draw an envelope from the bag before leaving the gathering.

Success and Money

Your partner may accompany you on a long-distance business trip to a resort location on the 20th that allows you to take extra time to enjoy a break after the organizational agenda ends. The New Moon in Aquarius on the 9th could reveal promotion potential for you, along with news about a new project that has high-level financial backing awaiting approval.

Pitfalls and Potential Problems

On February 1, you may learn that certain team members are unhappy with assignments. Gather facts before making suggestions to your boss to reassign employees. Review your financial portfolio on February 22 to make sure you are not overextended in a questionable investment. Correct the balance judiciously.

Rewarding Days

7, 10, 14, 20

Challenging Days

1, 8, 22, 24

Capricorn | March

Overall Theme

The March 10th New Moon in Pisces corresponds to the beginning of Daylight Saving Time. As a lover of lush, green landscapes and beautiful flowers, your thoughts turn to lawn and garden preparation after the last frost occurs. The Vernal Equinox on March 19 marks Aries's entry into the zodiac, followed by the first Lunar Eclipse of 2024 on March 25 in Libra and your solar tenth house of career.

Relationships

Satisfying interactions with members of a professional group affirm your commitment to a worthy humanitarian initiative on March 2. Romance with your significant other is in the stars on the 13th after you agree on where to put assets to work on household improvements. Intimacy becomes a priority for the next several days.

Success and Money

An ideal date to meet with your boss to discuss staffing solutions is March 16, after you have analyzed talent management qualifications. Home improvement or mortgage loans are a likely possibility on the 21st after credit checks validate creditworthiness. Begin projects before Mercury goes retrograde on April 1.

Pitfalls and Potential Problems

You may feel unsettled by a friend's behavior on March 1. Rather than leave a puzzling issue on the table, offer to discuss any matters that affect you and air them out. On March 26, staffing issues could surface that necessitate meeting with your boss to make plans to identify skills that are needed to cover all positions.

Rewarding Days

2, 13, 16, 21

Challenging Days

1, 8, 20, 26

Capricorn | April

Overall Theme

With the spotlight on your home in April, later-born Capricorns won't appreciate Mercury going retrograde in Aries on April 1 in the middle of planned negotiations. The communication planet turns direct on the 25th, freeing up energy to take action in early May. Avoid signing important home-related documents and contracts this month. Stay close to home to monitor loan terms.

Relationships

In April, the Sun, Venus, and Mercury all spend time in Aries and your solar fourth house of home. Each member of your household could have a vested interest in the outcome of home projects or the sale of your house if you are planning a move. The Solar Eclipse in Aries on the 8th makes you vulnerable to overlooking important contract wording.

Success and Money

This month you're preoccupied for a variety of reasons centering around home base, such as repairs, remodeling, landscaping, or marketing for resale. Children's interests and romance claim your attention around April 10. Make entertainment and dining reservations for these special people and treat them to venues they enjoy. Speak loving words to your partner.

Pitfalls and Potential Problems

Table spending on April 4 no matter how tempting the offer. Work issues could exhaust you on the 12th, favoring extra rest over the weekend. On the 22nd, organizational demands could create chaos. Nip complaints in the bud and examine the most critical ones before acting. Around the 23rd, buy dinner for a friend who needs support.

Rewarding Days

6, 8, 10, 29

Challenging Days

4, 12, 22, 23

Capricorn | May

Overall Theme

Capricorns have contracts on their minds this month, whether for personal or business transactions. Pluto in Aquarius stations to move retrograde on May 2 in your solar second house of assets and income, giving you the incentive to compete for promotions. The New Moon in Taurus on the 7th stimulates your solar fifth house of romance, bringing a potential partner your way if you are single.

Relationships

Siblings connect with you on May 3 to discuss upcoming plans. Children's interests claim your attention on the 8th. How delightful that Mother's Day, May 12, features the Moon in nurturing Cancer, giving you a strong reminder of the maternal influences in your life. Strong Jupiter aspects on that day give you the incentive to go the extra mile to honor the treasured mothers in your life.

Success and Money

A work colleague presents an innovative idea for collecting valuable project data to accelerate completion of analytical work. Keep this person in mind for a team assignment that will roll out in the last quarter of the month. Venus and Uranus in Taurus could present you with an unexpected financial windfall in mid-May. Enjoy the limelight you've earned.

Pitfalls and Potential Problems

Transits are tricky for you from May 23 to the 25th, when the Full Moon in Sagittarius on the 23rd hides out in your solar twelfth house of seclusion. Jupiter enters Gemini and your solar sixth house on the 25th opposite the Full Moon. Wait a few days before making staffing assignments or purchasing electronic equipment.

Rewarding Days

3, 7, 8, 12

Challenging Days

1, 10, 23, 25

Capricorn | June

Overall Theme

With a heavy emphasis on planets in Gemini and your solar sixth house this month, you could fall in love all over again with your career and current assignments. The New Moon in Gemini on the 6th falls here, too, a strong indicator that a lead for a promotion or an offer for a new job is in the wind. Assignments keep you confined to local travel, but you're okay with exploring nearby venues.

Relationships

Enjoy networking with professional colleagues the week of June 3, when shared information excites you with its potential to benefit not only you but also others on your team. Wait for announcements about positions opening up. Bond with children on June 4 and with your romantic partner on June 10.

Success and Money

You are very pleased with the state of your checkbook due to a recent raise. Work contracts undergoing revisions may lead to salary increases for you and members of your work team in the negotiation stage. Optimism beams from within as you consider the possibilities. Encouragement from management authorities is a strong motivator that meshes with your goals.

Pitfalls and Potential Problems

Dates with romantic partners may be canceled on June 3 or 7. To avoid cancellations, don't book travel that starts on June 13, when the Moon in Virgo opposes Saturn in Pisces. Although Saturn turns retrograde on June 29 in Pisces and your solar third house, you'll be able to complete contract proposals if they are signed by the 27th.

Rewarding Days

2, 4, 6, 10

Challenging Days

3, 7, 13, 25

Capricorn | July

Overall Theme

Your patriotic soul thrives on summer festivities related to venues that celebrate our nation's birthday. The holiday week gets off to a rousing start with the Moon conjunct Mars in Taurus that favors the Sun, Venus, and Saturn in water signs. Enthusiasm to participate in traditional customs flows through your veins.

Relationships

The New Moon in Cancer on the 5th reflects your partner's buoyant mood as you host a gathering of favorite friends and relatives. Strengthen family ties and extend an invitation to new people in your neighborhood. You and your partner may travel for a few days around the 6th to get away for relaxation.

Success and Money

An upbeat exchange with your manager regarding job performance excellence gives you an optimistic boost regarding upward mobility in the company. Jupiter in Gemini transiting your solar sixth house supports the positive environment and team spirit at your daily work site. On the 30th, you may be assigned to a new project when the Gemini Moon lands on Jupiter, signaling a shift in work responsibilities.

Pitfalls and Potential Problems

Harsh words may be exchanged by a disgruntled employee on July 3. Neptune's station to move retrograde on the 2nd is an indication of potential confusion, followed by a personnel change. Make sure you don't overreact to the blowup. Don't let the cat out of the bag on the 19th if confidential information comes your way that is not ready for company-wide distribution.

Rewarding Days

5, 6, 12, 30

Challenging Days

3, 9, 19, 24

Capricorn | August

Overall Theme
Mercury goes retrograde in Virgo and your solar ninth house on August 5, suggesting you start your vacation with your partner a few days earlier to avoid travel delays. August 3 looks good. This month's activity centers around socializing, good relationships with the management team, and harmony at home base.

Relationships
Your romantic partner has your full attention for most of the month, claiming your time at sporting events or on vacation, date nights, or shopping trips. Include children on a trip to a favorite amusement park. By the end of the month, you could be purchasing new furniture to outfit a bedroom or a child's play area.

Success and Money
Mars and Jupiter in Gemini energize your workplace this month, increasing activity and emphasizing your role in keeping productivity moving at a desirable pace. On the 11th, accept a meal invitation from a friend whose professional interests match yours and exchange information on industry opportunities that may be a good collaborative match.

Pitfalls and Potential Problems
Avoid heavy spending on August 5 and on the Aquarius Full Moon of the 19th, when you could be throwing away your hard-earned cash on inferior goods or uninspiring venues. Entertainment could be disappointing or canceled. Those of you who like to gamble should avoid temptation on those days. Mercury turns direct on August 28 in Leo and your solar eighth house, allowing you to tap savings for a large purchase.

Rewarding Days
3, 9, 11, 23

Challenging Days
5, 10, 12, 19

Capricorn | September

Overall Theme

The New Moon in Virgo on Labor Day, September 2, showcases your solar ninth house of travel. Instead of looking for extra work, why not take to the skies and do a bit of bucket-list travel? If you can't leave right away, snag a bargain and book your trip so you and your partner can plan a leisurely vacation to a sought-after spot while the price is right.

Relationships

Connect with relatives at a distance to make plans for late-year holiday visits. Firm up business travel with affiliates in different countries. Savor the intimacy and affection shared with your romantic partner and head for a lush beach resort around September 25. Hosting visiting family members on the night of the September 17th Lunar Eclipse in Pisces lets you savor memories of happy times shared in the past as you create new ones.

Success and Money

Shopping for a loved one on the 15th could be costly. Be glad your recent raise left you with extra cash to cover escalating expenses. By the end of the week, you could be replacing a kitchen appliance. Feel grateful that you put bonus money in your emergency fund.

Pitfalls and Potential Problems

Your solar fifth house of children, romance, and vacations is where Uranus, the planet of upheavals, goes retrograde in Taurus on September 1. Keep an eye on the safety of children involved in sports, especially around the 22nd, when Uranus conjoins the Moon.

Rewarding Days

2, 17, 19, 25

Challenging Days

1, 12, 15, 22

Capricorn | October

Overall Theme

This month highlights the state of your finances and personal ambition. The final Solar Eclipse of 2024 falls on October 2 in Libra and your solar tenth house, highlighting career, promotion potential, organizational stability, and rapport with team members. Prosperity-oriented Jupiter stations to move retrograde on October 9 in Gemini and your solar sixth house of work, suggesting a need to validate sufficient funding for planned expenses.

Relationships

Executives and workplace contacts get priority attention now. Major shifts in the direction of work call for combining resources and adjusting the work plan. A cousin or sibling seeks advice on a personal matter mid-month. Be receptive and expect to talk more than once. Being harmoniously on the same page strengthens rapport between you and your partner.

Success and Money

Numerous talks with members of your management team pave the way for an offer of a new position. Be sure that it's what you want and the salary increase meets your expectations. Enjoy high praise from supervisory personnel, passing on compliments to subordinate staff who go the extra mile to meet goals.

Pitfalls and Potential Problems

Jupiter's slowdown on the 9th is a sign to check the workplace status quo to determine complete coverage of assignments, ensuring that no employee has a burdensome workload. Slow-moving Pluto moves direct on October 11 in Capricorn and your solar first house of personal interests, reminding you that you are only weeks away from shedding the remaining baggage uncovered during this transit.

Rewarding Days

2, 5, 11, 23

Challenging Days

4, 9, 17, 20

Capricorn | November

Overall Theme

Although Saturn in Pisces is still retrograde as the month begins, it won't dampen your spirits to put cheer into holiday preparations. Your home could be the site of a Thanksgiving feast on November 28, with a guest list likely to include family, friends, and neighbors who are about to be overwhelmed by the details you develop to deliver this exquisite feast.

Relationships

Work colleagues meet for a Thankful Thursday meal around the 7th, sharing an early holiday gathering in gratitude for outstanding support all year. Celebrate Thanksgiving with passion and show your generous spirit to all who attend. Your elegant dining table complements the aroma of beautifully prepared food that fills the air.

Success and Money

How caring you are to donate money and dinner accompaniments to shelters and food pantries before November 8 to supply food for those without funds. Plan your holiday menu and start baking treats early. Engage your children to help make cookies or candy. Consider ordering a medley of pies from your favorite bakery to take some of the labor away from hosting duties.

Pitfalls and Potential Problems

On the 10th, avoid awkward verbal exchanges with relatives or neighbors who display tension over holiday preparation that overwhelms them. Send them home with an inviting plate of treats. Saturn in Pisces turns direct on the 15th, while Mercury turns retrograde in Sagittarius on the 25th, alerting you to check flight schedules if you are traveling.

Rewarding Days

7, 8, 19, 28

Challenging Days

10, 13, 17, 25

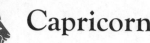 # Capricorn | December

Overall Theme

December is a power month with the array of planets present. Celebrate two New Moons, the first in Sagittarius on December 1 and the second in Capricorn on December 30. Those of you traveling for the holidays get the all-clear on December 22 when the Moon in Virgo visits your solar ninth house. A local getaway is possible the week of the 9th thanks to a promotional vacation offer.

Relationships

Complete holiday gift shopping for your mate on December 5. Invite siblings to festive gatherings on the 9th. Plan a night out with your partner on the 17th, expressing your love and gratitude for the strength of your relationship. Parents and in-laws may arrive to celebrate Christmas after the 22nd. Their presence brings back thoughts of memorable childhood celebrations.

Success and Money

The state of your finances makes you smile after the 5th, when extra income arrives in your paycheck. For some it is a holiday bonus, while for others it represents a performance award or gift. Your boss could take leave for the holiday on the 23rd and place you in charge of operations through the 31st—another opportunity to demonstrate leadership.

Pitfalls and Potential Problems

Mars in Leo moves into retrograde motion on December 6, cautioning you not to make unplanned withdrawals from savings accounts. Neptune in Pisces stations to move direct on the 7th, followed by Mercury turning direct in Sagittarius opposite the Gemini Full Moon on the 15th—a day to steer clear of travel.

Rewarding Days

5, 9, 22, 23

Challenging Days

6, 7, 12, 15

Capricorn Action Table

These dates reflect the best—but not the only—times for success and ease in these activities, according to your Sun sign.

	JAN	FEB	MAR	APR	MAY	JUN	JUL	AUG	SEP	OCT	NOV	DEC
Move		10				4			2			9
Romance	24		13		12			3	25	23		
Seek counseling/ coaching	15			6			30				28	
Ask for a raise		7			8		12			2		
Vacation				10				11				22
Get a loan			21			10					8	

Aquarius

The Water Bearer
January 20 to February 18

≋

Element: Air

Quality: Fixed

Polarity: Yang/masculine

Planetary Ruler: Uranus

Meditation: I am a wellspring of creativity

Gemstone: Amethyst

Power Stones: Aquamarine, black pearl, chrysocolla

Key Phrase: I know

Glyph: Currents of energy

Anatomy: Ankles, circulatory system

Colors: Iridescent blues, violet

Animals: Exotic birds

Myths/Legends: Ninhursag, John the Baptist, Deucalion

House: Eleventh

Opposite Sign: Leo

Flower: Orchid

Keyword: Unconventional

The Aquarius Personality

Strengths, Talents, and the Creative Spark

As the fourth of the fixed signs of the zodiac and the natural occupant of the eleventh house of associations, friendships, goals, groups, your employer's resources, humanitarian endeavors, motivations, and new trends and unorthodox methods of setting them, you make a bold statement through sudden revelations or change. The symbol for Aquarius is the Water Bearer, the prototype of optimism. As the third air sign, you thrive on communication as a powerful vehicle to deliver your analytical perspective. Uranus, your planetary ruler, provides prolific opportunities that allow you to experience a variety of social settings, adding futuristic insight to your sphere of influence. Those of you with planets in the eleventh house of your birth chart display your creative tendencies and demonstrate how you wish to share them with diverse groups. Over the years I have noted that Aquarians with a strong showing of planets in this house often have an astrologer or two in their circle of friends or connections. In fact, a fair number of Aquarians are astrologers.

High on your list is problem-solving, whether to aid humanitarian endeavors or develop complex technical expertise in software development, financial strategies, or management systems. You are insightful networkers, with a gift for putting the right mix of talent on teams to maximize the output of quality work. Using your inventive style, your prominence among analytical signs gives you a knack for improving relationships on the local or world stage. Outgoing Aquarians seldom limit the number of opinions they form and display no fear in expressing them in a convincing manner. To intensify your energy, wear or surround yourself with colors that perk up your auric field, such as brilliant or electric blues, indigo, sky blue, and ultramarine with lightning-white accents. Your sign rules the ankles, blood pressure, calves, hemoglobin, legs from the knees to the ankles, shins, body tremors, and wrinkles.

Intimacy and Personal Relationships

Along the way to finding the perfect love partner, you flirt your way across the romantic playing sphere, keeping your independence intact for as long as possible. Since Aquarius is the universal sign of friendship, it makes sense that you have an abundance of acquaintances yet very few close friends. You may go through many partners before finding the one who is a keeper and helps you shed your aura of detachment. Your wish list must include a love interest who thrives on talking but especially loves to listen to your lengthy and often witty discussions on how to detail your car, find the right accountant, or score comp tickets to entertainment or sports venues. You are attracted to those who are different, so it is no surprise that you may find magnetic appeal with a member of your opposite sign, Leo. The other two air signs, Gemini and Libra, are also compatible since communication is an important driver for the relationship to survive. Clashes could occur with Taurus and Scorpio, who may stifle your spirit with possessiveness or jealousy.

Values and Resources

Information flows your way from diverse sources, opening up possibilities for life-changing occurrences that alter your world from the inside out. You learn to release personal fear by guiding others through difficult situations in which they seem stuck. If an organization has the need for a shakeup, your expertise as a change agent could be the vehicle to analyze the status quo and get the innovative juices flowing again via a company rebirth. People who know you describe you with a fascinating array of personal traits ranging from conservative, traditional, conventional, politically correct, and friendly to dogmatic, eccentric, impersonal, rebellious, and stubborn. At various times in your life you own every one of these characteristics. You value privacy, keeping most friendships on an impersonal level, and divulge personal information reluctantly. Challenging assignments attract your attention. Your astute analytical abilities send headhunters your way with multiple job offers, which you willingly accept until the next rung on the ladder of success beckons with another prestigious position.

Blind Spots and Blockages

Keep your eyes open when applying for positions so you don't wind up accepting a job that is only moderately attractive to you. Regret sets in quickly when you find that another's management style clashes with yours and the autonomy you expected is a mirage. The result is that you could fritter away valuable time on less important experience builders, wallow in anger, become depressed, or transfer your disappointment to personal relationships that crumble over time. Observers say you often become openly critical when you have stayed too long in failing career or romantic relationships. Part of you knows the professional relationship is going to result in moving on. When the intimate relationship fades, you still may want to be the gregarious Aquarius who stays friends despite the realization that the love is gone. The worst scenario is feeling trapped and becoming cynical. Seek counsel in anger management.

Goals and Success

The choices you make in life emanate from your strong desire for change. You often move far from home to achieve success by relocating to distant cities or to other countries. Your expectations about yourself reflect many different possibilities and motivate you to broaden your perception of humanity. You take pride in your many affiliations, which can lead you to run for office, head up task forces or think tanks, or set up impartial panels to assess emerging civic and environmental issues. Your personable nature blends in seamlessly with the work cultures of most organizations, displaying versatility and a seasoned set of analytical skills. You are joiners and your insight is cut out for making working conditions viable for those employed in the fields of charity and fundraising, cybersecurity in the banking and finance industries, electronics manufacturing and technology, management development, politics, talent acquisition, and diverse avenues of training. Your insightful mind gives you a flair for identifying fraudulent schemes that undermine integrity in established organizations, including funds mismanagement, identity theft, and complex information breaches. An impersonal approach gives you the ability to champion the underdog by analyzing personal, organizational, and social problems that stand in the way of achieving progressive promotions that improve mobility in career ladders. In this important transition year, build camaraderie with your diverse contacts.

Aquarius Keywords for 2024
Choice, community, consultation

The Year Ahead for Aquarius

How appropriate for your change-oriented sign that in 2024, Pluto leaves Capricorn and your solar twelfth house of healing and dreams, dumping old baggage and leaving it behind for good. On January 20, Pluto intrepidly moves into Aquarius and your solar first house. It retrogrades back into Capricorn on September 1 before moving into

Aquarius for good on November 19. Through 2043, Pluto in your sign will rally around conditions affecting people that are reflective of the birth of the American Constitution, which was written the last time Pluto was passing through Aquarius (from 1778 to 1798). Expect a huge number of reorganizations during this twenty-year transit, both in your personal life and in the prevailing universal power centers. Get ready to ditch those dogmatic blind spots.

Mercury turns direct on January 1 in Sagittarius and your solar eleventh house of friendships, professional contacts, and goals, giving you the signal to proceed with plans you have on the drawing board. Your solar fourth house of home, family, and foundations hosts Jupiter in Taurus as the year begins, paving the way for smoother household transactions and better rapport with family members. On May 25, benevolent Jupiter moves into Gemini for the rest of the year in your solar fifth house, benefiting interactions with children, love interests, entrepreneurial connections, and travel companions. Expect to spend more time enjoying amusements and recreational activity. Uranus in Taurus also occupies your solar fourth house of home this year and turns direct on January 27 after creating conditions over the previous year that probably resulted in a surprising turn of events, unexpected visitors, or storm conditions that may have affected your house's condition.

This year, two planets occupy Pisces and your solar second house of income, assets, and self-development. Saturn in early degrees of Pisces calls attention to the need to develop a personal spending budget, while Neptune, the planet of illusion, does its best to tempt you with must-have goodies on which to spend your hard-earned dollars. In 2024, four eclipses will affect your chart, two lunar and two solar. These eclipses will occur in Libra and your solar ninth house of long-distance travel and higher education (one lunar and one solar), Aries and your solar third house of communication (a Solar Eclipse), and Pisces and your solar second house of earned income (a Lunar Eclipse).

Jupiter

Jupiter, the most welcome prosperity planet, entered Taurus and your solar fourth house of home on May 16 of last year and is making a rapid trip through this sign, where it accentuates family relationships and provides a vehicle to increase income through starting a home-based business or a plan to work on company assignments remotely. Inheritances are often distributed when Jupiter transits this house.

Sometimes you sell and/or buy a home or remodel it. You may either start a family or add a new baby to your existing one. Those of you born between January 25 and February 18 benefit most from this transit. On May 25, Jupiter moves into Gemini and your solar fifth house, placing a premium on children's needs and school events, your social life (including your love life, which may move into high gear, especially if you are single), students you coach or teach, recreational interests, and vacation trips. Aquarians born between January 20 and February 11 are most likely to benefit from this year's Jupiter-in-Gemini transit. During Jupiter's retrograde period, which lasts from October 9 to February 4, 2025, spend time planning vacations, reviewing children's educational interests, scheduling games if you coach a team, or competing in healthy fitness events. Decide whether traditional employment suits you best or you want to start your own consulting business this year. Follow your intuitive hunches to launch your next steps.

Saturn

Last year Saturn wrapped up a two-and-a-half-year transit through Aquarius and your solar first house of action, assertiveness, decision-making, health, and individuality. The taskmaster planet made you edgy and ready to get on with plans. Now your solar second house of income and spending options is a hub of activity, with Saturn in Pisces there sending additional responsibilities your way to maintain integrity and consistency in the quality of financial undertakings. You may have noticed an increase in activity related to the need to replace household furnishings and appliances, vehicles, and the school where children receive their education. If you are working on self-development, some of your money may be going toward a degree or a certification in career-enhancing subject matter. Changing transportation needs may make the purchase of a new vehicle for the household a mandatory expense. The burden is on you to be cautious, especially since Neptune in Pisces, a planet that often contributes to glossing over details in favor of a quick fix, occupies this same house this year. Don't be caught off guard in any financial transactions. A Lunar Eclipse here in September may also bring you an unexpected windfall that boosts your income. Saturn's transit of Pisces most affects Aquarians born between January 23 and February 9. Saturn's retrograde phase begins on June 29 and ends on November 15. For greatest success, create a budget and set spending goals that are affordable and meet your needs in proportion to your income.

Uranus

This year starts off with retrograde Uranus in Taurus and your solar fourth house of home and family, where it has been creating erratic scenarios since 2018 in its quest to get you to notice that other possibilities exist to help you manage your home and the temperamental people who live there. More than one family relationship has likely undergone strain in the form of blowups, unemployment, health flare-ups, or romantic breakups. When Uranus goes direct on January 27, you may notice a shift in attitude or the sudden departure of a resident who comes forward to announce unfolding plans. At times, Uranus in your solar fourth house represents damage from weather elements such as earthquakes, tornados, or hurricanes, or damage to the foundational walls of your home. If you had exterior work or remodeling of your home in progress, you may have experienced unplanned delays in completing the work. On a positive note, you may have received gifts, awards, or inheritances that helped to fund your planned work. On September 1, Uranus turns retrograde and remains so until January 30, 2025. Aquarians born between February 9 and 17 feel the most intense impact from this transit. Those of you working from home or another remote location may get clearance to continue your current schedule. Conversely, if you work on company-leased property, you may be told to work from home as the organization implements cost-cutting strategies to save money on office space.

Neptune

In 2024, Neptune in Pisces shares space with transiting Saturn in Pisces in your solar second house of personal income, assets, spending habits, investment in self-development, and the importance of financial clout. You may be weighing your need for material security with your desire for spiritual growth. During this long transit period, you may have had your share of financial opportunities that soured or turned out to be resource sinks despite scheduling consultations with experts. Other potential issues include the purchase of goods made with inferior products that you simply ignored and wrote off as a bad choice. It's time to stop that defeatist thinking before the Neptune haze clouds your vision and you find yourself in a rut of accepting what you don't really want. The next time you order even a package of cinnamon buns from an expensive online vendor and they arrive stale or very different looking from the advertisement, take a picture of the item, phone the vendor, send them the photo, and request a refund. Ignite the spark of your prosperity consciousness to work in your best interests despite the challenges of the world economy. Claim your power. Neptune goes retrograde on July 2 in the last degree of Pisces and resumes direct motion on December 7. This planet connects with your Sun if you were born between February 14 and 18.

Pluto

Aquarius, you have been feeling the hot and hounding breath of Pluto in Capricorn and your solar twelfth house of healing and secrets. The planet of transformation has allowed you to hide away there since 2008, trying to dodge the fallout that holding on to excess baggage creates when you don't shed it. The hand of time catches up with you in 2024 when your dreams and nightmares give way to the reality that Pluto is moving into Aquarius on January 20, putting down roots in your solar first house that last until 2043. You will soon know what it's like to unleash stuck parts of your psyche that have held you back. The action-oriented first house gives you a welcome opportunity to use your finely honed analytical skills to figure out what or who stands in the way of your quest for freedom. You are paying more attention to your health, innovative ideas, passion for life, and individuality. After Pluto emerges from its reflective shelter and moves into early Aquarius on January 20, it turns retrograde on May 2, moves back into Capricorn, then turns direct on October 11. Only those of you born between January 20 and 23 are likely to feel the impact of this Pluto-in-Aquarius transit to your Sun. You'll have greater insight after November 19, when Pluto finally bids adieu to Capricorn and occupies Aquarius for good. Meanwhile, assess the quality of your treasured goals and the inner places you would most like to liberate. What happened earlier this year that has you searching for the truth? Which anger issues are troubling? Know that this Pluto transit means business and will keep on reminding you to clear the air.

How Will This Year's Eclipses Affect You?

This year's four eclipses, two lunar (Full Moon) and two solar (New Moon), are ready to generate intense periods that start to manifest a few months before their actual occurrence. The Libra/Aries cycle wraps up in March 2023 to make way for the Pisces/Virgo eclipses, the first of which makes its debut in September of 2024. Eclipses unfold in cycles involving all twelve signs of the zodiac and usually occur in pairs about two weeks apart. Never fear eclipses—just think of them as opportunities for growth that allow you to release old patterns. Expect surprises that elicit both positive and perplexing feelings and outcomes. The closer an eclipse is to a planet or point in your birth chart, the greater the importance it has in your life, especially if one of those planets is in the same degree as the eclipse.

Your solar ninth house is the site of the first Lunar Eclipse of 2024, which falls on March 25 in Libra, putting the spotlight on your higher mind and advanced education, foreign countries and cultures, in-laws and relatives at a distance, philosophy, politics, religion, publishing, writing, and long-distance travel. Make sure applications and transcripts are submitted on time if applying to schools, and make solid travel plans to avoid cancellations. Consider accepting either a foreign assignment or a transfer to a different work location if it meets career goals.

The year's first Solar Eclipse occurs on April 8 in Aries and your solar third house of communication, community interests, contracts and leases, education, mental acuity, local travel, neighbors, siblings, technology, and transportation. Compare prices and request bids on work or vehicle purchases, and review documents thoroughly before signing. Be sure to update your resume if applying for a new assignment.

The site of the second Lunar Eclipse this year is Pisces and your solar second house of assets, income, salary requirements, what you value, how you spend your money, and self-development on September 17. This eclipse encourages you to fully address any salary concerns or money issues that need attention. Diligently develop a budget you can monitor that covers all expenses. Shop the competition when making large purchases. With an eclipse in your solar second house, visualize a win or cash bonus coming your way.

The year's final Solar Eclipse occurs on October 2 in Libra and your solar ninth house of colleges, educational advancement, foreign interest and cultures, in-laws, long-distance travel for business or pleasure, publishing, writing, and legal matters. Put your focus on cherished goals that you had to put on hold as a result of economic downturns and the rising cost of doing business. Travel again to fulfill your wish list or if your job calls for visits to remote locations. Some of you may take time off to complete a course or earn a degree. Enjoy a growth period that allows you to use your fine mind to better the working conditions for humanity through astute analysis of existing structures. Let positive self-talk drive your spirit and enjoy the new prosperity cycle.

Aquarius | January

Overall Theme

The January 11th New Moon in Capricorn and your solar twelfth house in company with departing Pluto in Capricorn helps you release any remaining baggage you have been holding on to during this long transit of the planet of extraction, which has aided you in shedding secrets and letting go of fears. Uranus turns direct on the 27th in Taurus and your solar fourth house of home, allowing you to resume plans with household members that have been on hold.

Relationships

Invite football fans for a cordial New Year's Day brunch to view the Rose Bowl Parade and watch a game. Get ready for crunch time at work when most employees return from leave the week of January 8 and listen to your manager's outlook for business growth in 2024. Single Aquarians could hear from a former flame who proposes rekindling your relationship around the Leo Full Moon on the 25th.

Success and Money

You're in good shape financially heading into the new year thanks to a promotion and generous gifts from relatives. Saving extra cash has paid off. With Neptune in Pisces and your solar second house of earned income, don't be tempted to splurge on post-holiday sales. Your best shopping days are January 14 and 15.

Pitfalls and Potential Problems

If you are still away on January 3, check travel arrangements in case a flight for a leg of your journey gets canceled. A working lunch meeting scheduled for January 8 could be postponed due to unavailability of key employees.

Rewarding Days

1, 6, 11, 14

Challenging Days

3, 8, 16, 21

Aquarius | February

Overall Theme

In February, Mercury gives you a voice to communicate your innovative ideas in your professional circle. Take advantage of a month where all the planets are in direct motion to get your message across to executives, staff, and members of professional groups. Some of you may hold a wedding celebration on February 10, which marks the beginning of the Lunar New Year of the Dragon. Plan a feast that includes your favorite cuisine and invite guests to participate in your good fortune.

Relationships

Agreeable interactions with management staff around February 3 include assignment discussions that could lead to a decision when a new position opens up. Siblings plan a Valentine's Day party that includes children, parents, and a few close relatives. Workmates celebrate on the 20th with a catered lunch to honor a major accomplishment.

Success and Money

Do your homework if you have an interest in applying for a job opening that comes with a major salary boost. The internal debate centers around whether you are willing to take on the high level of stress that accompanies this demanding position. Management would love to have you.

Pitfalls and Potential Problems

A work matter at a distant location flares up and cannot be settled without a more hands-on approach. Be prepared to travel to resolve the matter after you investigate details and can plan an interactive strategy. You and a friend may not agree on an entertainment venue on February 4. Make alternative plans for February 9.

Rewarding Days

3, 13, 14, 20

Challenging Days

1, 4, 21, 24

Aquarius | March

Overall Theme

Fixed signs dominate the landscape now, with the Moon in Scorpio leading off on March 1. Venus and Mars in Aquarius add romance to your daily life. Contacts are drawn to your magnetic appeal. People you meet may tell you they feel like they already know you. Pluto in early Aquarius joins the gathering in your solar first house, while Jupiter and Uranus in Taurus add tension from your solar fourth house of home.

Relationships

You could attend a social gathering hosted by your boss or a team supervisor on March 2. Accept graciously and enjoy the rapport with other guests, who could become part of your business network. Love is in the air for you and your significant other between March 16 and 21. Make midweek dinner plans with mutual friends around the 20th.

Success and Money

Your boss may send you packing for a visit to a remote satellite office right after the year's first Lunar Eclipse ignites your solar ninth house in Libra on March 25. With your astute analytical skills, you learn enough about the operations in one week's time to develop recommendations that will help the group increase productivity.

Pitfalls and Potential Problems

A dinner with a group of friends on the 3rd could fall flat when two members with radically different opinions try to dominate the discussion and alienate participation from others. Be prepared to hear from diners the next day weighing in on the boorish behavior they witnessed. Maintain neutrality.

Rewarding Days

2, 13, 16, 21

Challenging Days

1, 3, 9, 25

Aquarius | April

Overall Theme

When Mercury in Aries makes a station to turn retrograde on April 1 in Aries, your solar third house could confound logic with bits and pieces of confusing dialogue. Keep a low profile at your workplace on Monday morning, spending time completing mundane tasks instead of starting something new. The Messenger of the Gods resumes direct motion on April 25. Examine work quality before submitting a final product.

Relationships

Cherish the time you spend with siblings during the second week of April when you take the time to catch up on news and the health status of older relatives. Invite those who are in town to participate in a family night of takeout food and games on the 10th.

Success and Money

The Aries New Moon on the 8th is the year's first Solar Eclipse, occurring in your solar third house and emphasizing the quality of life in your neighborhood. You might have successfully initiated improvements in your community that were approved and funded and have made a difference in attracting home buyers to the area. A service award could be in your future.

Pitfalls and Potential Problems

The April 23rd Scorpio Full Moon highlights tension at work when unclear directives skew the meaning of a section of a critical report. Work with the best team of troubleshooters you have to restore integrity. By the 29th, you should have a top-notch report.

Rewarding Days

6, 8, 10, 26

Challenging Days

4, 9, 16, 23

Aquarius | May

Overall Theme

The allure of the New Moon on May 7 in Taurus and your solar fourth house of home makes you curious about what is going on with your relatives near and far and also with immediate family. Plan an event to bring family together between May 3 and 12. Put your focus on scheduling a much-needed home improvement project to begin after May 16.

Relationships

Enjoy the company of your sweetheart on May 9 at an entertainment venue you both enjoy. Have dinner at a trendy restaurant you've had on your radar screen for months. Spend quality time with work colleagues the week of May 12, mapping out your tasks to accomplish the company plan of work. Honor the mothers in your life on May 12.

Success and Money

The financial picture of your checkbook is healthy and allows you to cover bills with no worries. Salary increases have been lucrative. Your next area of interest to improve your holdings involves increasing the amount of money you add to retirement. Explore options with your banker around May 3, paying attention to your savings portfolio.

Pitfalls and Potential Problems

On May 2, Pluto in an early degree of your sign turns retrograde in your solar first house for a six-month slowdown. What concerns are leaving a bad feeling in the pit of your stomach? Those of you born between February 11 and 14 may be mulling whether to accept a recent job offer, reluctant to give up the security of a predictable future.

Rewarding Days

3, 7, 9, 12

Challenging Days

2, 10, 15, 25

Aquarius | June

Overall Theme

Jupiter's recent entry into Gemini and your solar fifth house marks an anniversary. It's been twelve years since the prosperity planet last spent time here improving conditions in your social life with people including children, lovers, innovative entrepreneurs, and those you teach, coach, or travel with. Let the excitement begin with the lineup of compatible Gemini planets this month, starting with Mercury, Venus, Jupiter, and the June 6th New Moon.

Relationships

Set aside June 1–8 as the ideal time to vacation with family or your significant other. Romance and adventure are in the air. Book time at a new destination that offers amenities the entire party will enjoy. Reunite with a loved one who lives out of town on June 15 and 16. Celebrate Father's Day with parents and siblings if possible.

Success and Money

Shop wisely for a travel package offering perks such as extra meals, daily excursions, and park passes. Don't agree to a funding increase for additional staff hires while you are away from your place of business. Ask for a full report and review it when you return. By June 27, you should have enough information to make the call.

Pitfalls and Potential Problems

An argument over company finances surfaces around June 13, leaving decision-makers at an impasse over funding extra equipment. Viewpoints on both sides seem fair. Saturn in Pisces turns retrograde on June 29 in your solar second house of earned income and assets, leaving you on the fence about making an additional investment in household furnishings.

Rewarding Days

1, 4, 6, 27

Challenging Days

11, 13, 16, 29

Aquarius | July

Overall Theme
Favorable planetary alignments involving the Moon and Jupiter in Gemini indicate that your Fourth of July holiday will be at home base. Order a complete menu from your favorite caterer to feed visiting guests traditional favorites while they celebrate the nation's birth. Put sparklers on the cake and insect-proof your backyard if watching fireworks from your deck or patio.

Relationships
Work priorities right after the holiday mean that you're in charge of responding to queries about task priorities right through July 10 while key staff remain on vacation. By the 12th, you'll be on your way to a distant location to enjoy leisure time at the invitation of a close friend. Share a favorite pastime with your children at the end of the month and have fun creating cherished memories with them.

Success and Money
Unified teamwork makes it possible to exceed goal completion ahead of the estimated date. You supplied astute analysis of the findings, pleasing the management team and receiving acknowledgment for a job well done. Dine with members of a think tank network around July 27.

Pitfalls and Potential Problems
On July 2, Neptune in Pisces goes retrograde in your solar second house of income just ahead of the Fourth of July holiday. Turn off outside water valves if you plan to travel. A child could come down with a cold or cough-related ailment right ahead of vacation departure time. Pack medical supplies to avoid searching for a pharmacist in transit.

Rewarding Days
5, 12, 27, 30

Challenging Days
2, 13, 19, 24

Aquarius | August

Overall Theme

Mercury moves retrograde on the 5th in Virgo and your solar eighth house of joint income and debt, completing its cycle on August 28, when the messenger planet resumes direct motion in Leo. Stay current on financial transactions, loans, interest rate increases, and payment details. Don't sign new loan papers while Mercury is retrograde.

Relationships

The Leo New Moon shines a light this month on partnership matters on August 4, one of the best days to spend quality time with your sweetheart affirming feelings and pursuing favorite interests. After making exciting plans to spend quality time at a relaxing resort, leave for a vacation on August 9. Entertain neighbors on August 23, including those who have recently moved into your community.

Success and Money

August 3 favors reorganizing household papers, paring back what you no longer need and setting up clear files that make it easy to find important documents. You may curry favor with your boss around August 11 when your quarterly accomplishment report highlights operational cost savings. The management team applauds you.

Pitfalls and Potential Problems

The Aquarius Full Moon in your solar first house on August 19 aligns well with Jupiter in Gemini and favors relaxing activity at home base. Conflicts with retrograde Mercury in Leo and Venus in Virgo could reveal underlying tension with your partner over spending limitations on a remodeling project. Table discussion of the matter until mid-September.

Rewarding Days

3, 4, 9, 11

Challenging Days

5, 12, 14, 26

Aquarius | September

Overall Theme

Another planet heads for retrograde territory when Uranus in Taurus and your solar fourth house makes a station on September 1 and keeps this erratic profile going through the end of January 2025. Those of you with late Aquarius birthdays will be most aware of this transit. Look to the final Lunar Eclipse of the year on September 17 in Pisces and your solar second house of income for unusual activity related to your financial status.

Relationships

Work with financial experts after September 2 to explore mortgage or home equity line of credit rates if you are in the market. Rapport with lender networks and accountants is cordial and informative, and you are gaining insight into workable options for sound money practices.

Success and Money

Having a superior credit rating gives you advantages when choosing bankers, credit cards, and personal or mortgage loans. Congratulations on doing all you can to raise your credit profile. Remember not to apply for credit you don't need or put charges on every card you carry. Visualize prosperity during this positive money cycle.

Pitfalls and Potential Problems

Uranus turns retrograde on September 1 in Taurus and your solar fourth house of home and family, creating sudden shifts in activity for certain household members. Retrograde Neptune in your solar second house conjunct the September 17th Lunar Eclipse in the company of retrograde Saturn in Pisces cautions you to be extremely careful engaging in financial transactions to protect your assets.

Rewarding Days

2, 13, 15, 18

Challenging Days

1, 17, 20, 27

Aquarius | October

Overall Theme

Compatible Jupiter in Gemini goes retrograde on October 9 in your solar fifth house of children, romance, entertainment, speculation, and travel, greatly influencing the timing of related plans. The final Solar Eclipse of 2024 occurs on October 2 in Libra and your solar ninth house of higher education, publishing, and long-distance contacts, opening up the possibility that you'll be traveling more than usual in the coming months.

Relationships

Expect stepped-up activity with children's teachers, tutors, or coaches who manage sports teams. Attend parent-teacher meetings, support the fundraisers, and attend games to cheer for your children as team members. Invite friends over for game night on October 8.

Success and Money

Enjoy the spotlight in your career sector this month when your record of accomplishment raises your profile in the performance arena. Management suggests you look deeply at what facets of work or positions you're willing to consider. The most promising dates for discussion fall between October 5 and 23. Book December travel dates now to get the best fares.

Pitfalls and Potential Problems

Pluto's direct motion resumes in Capricorn on October 11 after a long retrograde period in both Aquarius and Capricorn. The planet of transformation returns to Aquarius for good on November 19, targeting regeneration of your assertiveness, innovative ideas, and passionate expression. Steer clear of a telephone argument with a sibling on October 17, when careless words could hit a sore spot.

Rewarding Days

2, 5, 8, 23

Challenging Days

9, 17, 20, 25

Aquarius | November

Overall Theme

Saturn's move into direct motion in Pisces on November 15 aids your solar second house of income when a check you were expecting arrives in time to facilitate holiday shopping. Painting interior rooms at home base makes everything sparkle and shine for an extra holiday glow. Prepare for stepped-up activity around family gatherings, visits, phone calls, and text messages. Buy food staples and party supplies for upcoming holiday meals.

Relationships

Review the menu and showcase your finest china on the elegant table you set for the Thanksgiving feast. Immediate family, parents, nearby relatives, and your boss could share your dinner table. Invite a few coworkers or friends who live too far from family to travel home.

Success and Money

The New Moon in Scorpio shines in your solar tenth house on November 1, reminding you to be grateful for the secure and satisfying employment you have and the career that motivates your passion for life. Donate a generous gift to a favorite shelter to purchase food and clothing for those with few resources. Buy items for your community food bank.

Pitfalls and Potential Problems

Spend carefully on the 10th, especially if you are shopping in crowded stores that are short on help. Check receipts carefully. Power outages on the 13th could disrupt Internet, cable, and phone services. Mercury in Sagittarius turns retrograde on the 25th, possibly delaying the arrival of Thanksgiving travelers.

Rewarding Days

1, 3, 15, 19

Challenging Days

4, 10, 13, 25

Aquarius | December

Overall Theme

December's first New Moon falls in compatible Sagittarius and your solar eleventh house on December 1, providing the perfect Sunday to finalize holiday plans. By the time the second New Moon this month appears in Capricorn on December 30, you'll be ready for solid downtime after the whirlwind pace of holiday visiting.

Relationships

Friends with children gather to bake cookies around December 1 after a visit to Santa. A get-together with cousins and siblings on December 10 brings kin together for a cheerful dinner. Every moment of your visit to see parents starting on the 23rd sparkles with nostalgia and memory-making magic.

Success and Money

Mall stores compete for attention from last-minute shoppers around December 9. Pre-holiday sales net you several attractive bargains. Everyone on your gift list has been covered. You look forward to seeing happy faces as they open holiday presents that match their wishes.

Pitfalls and Potential Problems

Just as Mars turns retrograde on December 6 in Leo and your solar seventh house of partnerships and the Moon arrives in your sign, you get word of bad weather moving in and decide to stay home for the evening. Weather reports confirm your wise decision. A Full Moon in Gemini and your solar fifth house of children and creativity rises on Sunday morning, December 15, while Mercury goes direct in Sagittarius and your solar eleventh house of friendships in the midafternoon.

Rewarding Days

1, 9, 10, 23

Challenging Days

6, 11, 15, 28

Aquarius Action Table

These dates reflect the best—but not the only—times for success and ease in these activities, according to your Sun sign.

	JAN	FEB	MAR	APR	MAY	JUN	JUL	AUG	SEP	OCT	NOV	DEC
Move		13				1		9		2		10
Romance	1	3	21	26	9		30		2		3	
Seek counseling/ coaching							5				1	
Ask for a raise		3			12			11		5		
Vacation			16			6						23
Get a loan	14			6					18			

Pisces

The Fish
February 18 to March 20

♓

Element: Water

Quality: Mutable

Polarity: Yin/feminine

Planetary Ruler: Neptune

Meditation: I successfully navigate my emotions

Gemstone: Aquamarine

Power Stones: Amethyst, bloodstone, tourmaline

Key Phrase: I believe

Glyph: Two fish swimming in opposite directions

Anatomy: Feet, lymphatic system

Colors: Sea green, violet

Animals: Fish, sea mammals

Myths/Legends: Aphrodite, Buddha, Jesus of Nazareth

House: Twelfth

Opposite Sign: Virgo

Flower: Water lily

Keyword: Transcendence

The Pisces Personality

Strengths, Talents, and the Creative Spark

Born under the fourth mutable sign of the zodiac, you're known for demonstrating flexibility. Adaptability suits your complex nature. Your symbol is the dual fish, swimming up and downstream as a gesture of compassion that adds refined texture to your water sign element. Those dreamy Pisces eyes gaze out from a mind that highly values personal privacy. Who could know that when you actually need to share the most, you swim in the opposite direction, seeking retreat until you figure out a workable path. Since you shun confinement, few who know you understand that freedom means the world to you, despite this particular characteristic being closely affiliated with your sign. A good number of you celebrate time alone, especially if your Sun falls in the sixth or twelfth house of your birth chart. Neptune, the planetary ruler of your sign, is the natural occupant of the twelfth house of seclusion, retreat, and regrouping. Your dominion here covers extensive confidential matters, including behind-the-scenes activity, confinement, convents, escapism, healing, hidden enemies, meditation, mysticism, psychic mediumship, recovery, secrets, and trysts.

Known for your sensitivity and compassion, you are interested in assisting the underdog and encouraging optimism in others. You help others turn their lives around through your generosity, helping them find housing, acting as a sounding board for airing their problems, or donating to charities that purchase food and supplies for those in need. You are often a Secret Santa, privately sending a gift to someone in need. Many of you run charities, manage fundraisers, or work in a variety of medical institutions. You are a natural in showing intuitive insight, especially now that Neptune is transiting your sign. Although many of you gravitate toward religion and may opt for a vocation in the clergy, a greater majority of you describe your participation as more spiritual than religious.

Intimacy and Personal Relationships

You are a huge fan of happy endings and relish the romantic side of love stories that cover the details from the initial meeting of soulmates to the progression leading to commitment and how the couple enjoyed those golden years as partners. When you make a deep connection with a partner, you're in it for life, even if the "music" stops playing. You may hang on far too long to a lost cause, but when you're gone, you're gone and aren't hesitant to remarry when the next sublime partner comes along. The search for your soul mate is unending. Looks and physical attraction are strong factors in playing the mating game. Idealistic Pisces may fall in love at first sight with a Taurus or Capricorn, or possibly with a member of your opposite sign, Virgo. The two other water signs, Cancer and Scorpio, are partnership-worthy, but Geminis and Sagittarians may give off erratic vibes that are a turnoff for the harmonious environment you prefer. You let evidence of peevish behavior go for a longer time than most, but once you discover that a significant other is dishonest, your tolerance level dissolves, especially if you have fire or earth planets in your birth chart. Children mean the world to you, and you wholeheartedly support their interests. Your biggest fault is not letting them spread their wings to demonstrate independence on the road of life. Cut the cords to let them fly and see what the universe has in store.

Values and Resources

Empathy and compassion are two characteristics that you routinely demonstrate as a sign ruled by Neptune. You go out of your way to find the right words to comfort others when you sense they need it most. Generosity is another trait. Out comes your wallet to treat others to a meal when you feel your best friend could use a break from cooking, a colleague experiences a death in the family, or your hardworking sibling might appreciate dining in a fine restaurant that serves delicious cuisine where you can both enjoy a relaxing meal. You may also be an avid gift giver who enjoys surprising loved ones on birthdays and holidays. Nothing bothers you more than a taker. Those who neglect to thank you aggravate your sense of justice, and you think of these individuals as selfish and inconsiderate. Over time, you're likely to remove these people from your gift list. Positive feedback is a treasure that gives you a motivational high. You value recognition from a boss who appreciates your dedicated performance, openly acknowledges how much your contributions benefit the work team, and presents you with a monetary reward or promotion.

Blind Spots and Blockages

Annoyance sets in when others direct you to take a class in subject matter that bores you, and you don't easily hide your disdain for what you dislike. When you feel like you have the skills to do your job well, you resent pressure to enroll in coursework that you feel wastes your time. Critics say you reject integrating new technology into your work routines or learning new systems programs. You may be caught off guard when your boss makes comments about stepping up your game to learn new applications to ensure that consistency in use of practices is even across the board. Instead of complying, you've been known to deliver a defensive response that often leaves others thinking you have a short fuse that rejects cooperation. Your typical response to receiving undesirable assignments is to crawl into the Neptune fog and daydream until the deadline arrives and you burn the midnight oil rushing to finish.

Goals and Success

Talent seems to radiate from you in a variety of forms. Many of you excel in the healing arts and may be employed as a bodyworker, massage therapist, psychologist, Reiki master, or nurse. A number of you are experts in more than one field of metaphysics, which may include using clairvoyance, mediumship, numerology, psychic phenomena, runes, or tarot readings. It's not unusual for you to incorporate these modalities into your professional practices, to the enjoyment of clients or patients. A love of music captures the hearts of enthusiastic Pisces who enjoy mood music, dance, and playing musical instruments. Pisces tend to be aficionados of mysteries, watching movies and TV shows and reading detective novels. They faithfully follow crime-solving shows based on true events, often becoming mesmerized by court cases, trials, and sentencing details. Acting and writing poetry or prose are other talents. Along with using these gifts, many of you have considerable expertise in accounting and enjoy crunching numbers and balancing the books.

Pisces Keywords for 2024
Aid, appeal, awe

The Year Ahead for Pisces

Activity in your solar first house is seldom more stimulated than it is in 2024, Pisces, when you start off the year hosting transiting Saturn in your sign, reminding you to assess the level of stamina you have for managing the stepped-up responsibility that comes your way. Saturn usually arrives with a restriction or two that stifles creativity and innovative expression while it teaches you a lesson about laying the groundwork for implementing practical solutions to emerging problems. You'll also continue to host Neptune, your ruling planet, in Pisces and your solar first house, a planetary transit that has been guiding your spiritual conscience since 2011. Neptune has considerably advanced in its journey to open your fertile mind to trust in your beautiful heart. Be on the lookout for the presence of this year's second Lunar Eclipse, which graces this house in Pisces on September 17, opening up yet another cycle of spiritual growth and awareness for the next eighteen months. Three other eclipses make a statement this year as well. The first occurs on March 25 in Libra and your solar eighth house of joint finances, debt, estates, savings, karmic matters, and regeneration. Next, a Solar Eclipse in Aries lands in your solar second house of income and assets on April 8, calling attention to how you use your personal resources. The final eclipse of 2024 is a Solar Eclipse on October 2 in Libra and your solar eighth house of other people's money, investments, and wills.

If prosperity appeals to your senses, then settle back while Jupiter in Taurus brings lucrative contracts, educational courses, a healthier mindset, and smoother transportation experiences your way when it occupies your solar third house of communication through May 25. On that day, Jupiter moves into Gemini and your solar fourth house of home, family, and household activity, where it stimulates the rapport among family members, aids in healing those who have been ill, and brings skilled artisans your way to give you fair estimates on sprucing up your home. Erratic Uranus in Taurus keeps you hopping in your solar third house of communication, neighbors, siblings, and local travel as it continues the final phase of its cycle in this demanding space. At long last, Pluto in reform-oriented Capricorn says goodbye to your solar eleventh house of goals and friendships and moves into Aquarius and your solar twelfth house, looking for a way to heal emotional hurts.

Jupiter

Last year Jupiter headed for Taurus on May 16 in your solar third house of communication, community activities, local travel, mental health, neighbors, siblings, and transportation, intent on bringing calmer dynamics to this demanding hub of activity. In 2024, Jupiter completes its Taurus journey before heading into Gemini on May 25 in your solar fourth house of home and family for the rest of the year. While at your base of operations, Jupiter may influence expanding your space through remodeling or redecorating projects, installing stunning landscape, or giving your home's façade a makeover via painting, stonework, or a new roof. The entrepreneurs among you may start your own business after recovering from a few years of erratic schedules and shifting workspace. Those who live with you seem to shine with greater enthusiasm and a sense of cooperation that gives off a contented vibe, allowing all to get along and enjoying harmony and straightforward talk in the home. Possibly one or more of your household members may move out of your home this year. If you are giving your house a face-lift with a move in mind, your plan should be successful. The planet of growth and prosperity moves retrograde in Gemini on October 9 and turns direct on February 4, 2025. Those of you born between February 19 and March 11 see the most action during this cycle.

Saturn

Saturn in Pisces starts its first full year in your solar first house of action, assertiveness, health, individuality, innovation, and self-image, leaving you with lots of work to do on inner and outer levels to eliminate constraints and develop more freedom in making life choices that reflect your goals. Many of you opt to work on the exterior of your body to reshape the contours, change the style or color of your hair, or revamp your wardrobe. Saturn holds individuals to high standards of conduct when performing work or setting goals. This restrictive planet leans on you to dig for facts, listen, and analyze the information you uncover. You have opportunities to review commitments. Saturn pulls on the reins to curb impulsive actions or make hasty decisions that divert you from your goals. Help yourself chill out with a routine meditation program and exercise. This year both Neptune and a Lunar Eclipse land in Pisces and your solar first house, adding a triple layer of complications to sort through that might seem overwhelming at times. You're in charge, so don't fear change. Pisces born between February 19 and March 7 relate strongly to this year's transit. Give yourself time to digest the implications instead of rushing to make changes and becoming overly anxious. In 2024, Saturn goes retrograde on June 29 and moves direct on November 15.

Uranus

Uranus in Taurus starts off the year in retrograde motion, going direct on January 27. The planet of the unexpected has been transiting your solar third house of community, communication venues, electronics, local travel, siblings, technology, and the state of your mind since 2018. Although Taurus is a sign compatible with your Pisces Sun, you have had more than your share of cable, telephone, and Internet disruptions over this long passage of time. Facets of communication, including development of contracts, hiring employees, writing material for publications and procedural manuals, and ordinary conversations, have been subject to disruptions, erratic schedules, canceled travel, and conflicts that added inconvenient tension to the smooth execution of plans. Uranus is often an indicator of harsh weather conditions such as earthquakes and tornadoes. The unpredictable planet stations to move retrograde on September 1 and remains so until January 30, 2025. If your birthday falls between March 8 and 18, you are likely to experience notable activity from transiting Uranus this year.

Neptune

The principal sphere of demand for you this year is your solar first house, where transiting Neptune is joined by Saturn all year, along with a Lunar Eclipse on September 17. Neptune continues to influence your health and physical body, action, assertiveness, innovation, passion, self-image, and temperament. You have learned many lessons from this planet since its arrival here in 2011, sending creative, inspirational, and romantic energy your way to help you explore the depths of your soul and the spiritual gifts you nurture there in your sacred, quiet space. Your first house may be the storehouse of psychic and intuitive knowledge that you manifest when you are looking for solutions to the problems of life. You may remember your dreams in the most minute detail and keep a notebook at your bedside to record them. You may already be a psychic medium or work with the psychological meaning of dreams as a profession. If not, don't be surprised if clear opportunities come your way this year and you consider an alternative career. Find Neptune's soft spot by using compassion and understanding to draw people in your life into serious discussions to sort out the discomfort associated with the Neptune fog. With the presence of both Saturn and the September 17th Lunar Eclipse in Pisces here, you'll have more than one mystical situation to interpret. Protect yourself from those who display negative energy and manipulative behavior. Those of you born between March 14 and 19 see the most activity this year as Neptune travels in late degrees toward completion of this long cycle. Neptune goes retrograde on July 2 in the last degree of Pisces and stations to move direct on December 7.

Pluto

You could be heavily involved in the countdown as Pluto in Capricorn heads for the exit gate after occupying your solar eleventh house of friendships, groups, and goals since January 2008. You have been forced to change your goals, eliminate friends from your circle, and give up long-held memberships to clubs and organizations based on the nagging hints you received from Pluto's insistent prodding. Surely you are ready to move into another dimension of your awareness by now. This year you may no longer desire to remain in the employment of a company that is not putting enough resources into helping humanity tackle social problems. You could be networking with new affiliates to find the perfect job that allows you to raise the stakes for those in society who need more support. Bravo if you choose to accept a new position or retire. On January 20, Pluto enters Aquarius and your solar twelfth house of seclusion. Could more soul-searching lie ahead? Pluto turns retrograde on May 2 in Aquarius, moves back into Capricorn on September 1, and stations to move direct on October 11 in the last degree of Capricorn and your solar eleventh house. On November 19, Pluto returns to Aquarius for good, anchoring your solar twelfth house and the discretionary information you have locked away regarding your dreams, health, relationships, secrets, and desire for renewal. Those of you born between March 18 and 20 relax your breathing when Pluto moves into Aquarius. Congratulations on embracing new directions.

How Will This Year's Eclipses Affect You?

This year's four eclipses, two lunar (Full Moon) and two solar (New Moon), are ready to generate intense periods that start to manifest a few months before their actual occurrence. The Libra/Aries cycle wraps up in March 2023 to make way for the Pisces/Virgo eclipses, the first of which makes its debut in September of 2024. Eclipses unfold in cycles involving all twelve signs of the zodiac and usually occur in pairs about two weeks apart. Never fear eclipses—just think of them as opportunities for growth that allow you to release old patterns. Expect surprises that elicit both positive and perplexing feelings and outcomes. The closer an eclipse is to a planet or point in your birth chart, the greater the importance it has in your life.

Greet 2024's first Lunar Eclipse on March 25 in Libra and your solar eighth house of joint income and debt, investments, savings and retirement accounts, estates, inheritances, wills, sex, birth, death, rebirth, your psyche, and regeneration. If you have planets in this house in your birth chart, expect that they may be stimulated and send a few surprises your way. Dreams may become prophetic, allowing you to solve a few of life's mysteries. Money could improve for you and your partner. Shopping for mortgages, loans, and interest rates could require careful scrutiny before committing to the terms. Contact reliable lenders.

On April 8, the first Solar Eclipse of the year arrives in Aries and your solar second house of assets, salary, money you earn or spend, self-development funds, and how you prefer to spend disposable income. If your salary has decreased or you have lost your job, you may be working with a headhunter to identify a suitable new position. Be sure to polish your resume, do your homework related to availability of qualification-matched job posts, and look into new avenues of employment that may bring you more satisfaction. Take a certification course to bring new qualifications to your field of expertise.

Get ready for the anticipated sign change that accompanies the second Lunar Eclipse of 2024 on September 17 when the lunation appears in Pisces and your solar first house. First-house matters cover your most obvious assets, such as personal appearance and self-image, and describe assertiveness, your character, individuality, personality, and the passion you demonstrate in life. Eclipses challenge you to work on your goals and develop a plan to describe interests and objectives. Disagreement with a loved one could be an issue. An eclipse in romantic Pisces often leads to a surprise proposal or elopement.

Two weeks later, on October 2, the final Solar Eclipse of 2024 occurs in Libra and your solar eighth house of partnership income, debt, and savings. You could be surprised by a sudden windfall from an inheritance or lottery win. Undoubtedly you have made financial changes since the March 25th Lunar Eclipse occurred by analyzing the strength of your assets, making changes to increase savings and decrease credit card usage, or paying down debt. Since eclipses in money houses raise income potential, you or your partner may have received a promotion or raise. Your increased knowledge of money management leads to greater stability and success.

Pisces | January

Overall Theme
You become serious about your goals this month with Saturn in Pisces giving you a nudge to keep your eye on what you most want to accomplish in 2024. With Mercury going direct on January 1 in Sagittarius and your solar tenth house, career prospects gain importance on your quest to showcase capabilities. If a job search interests you, update your resume and apply for a desirable opportunity after Uranus in Taurus goes direct on the 27th.

Relationships
Enjoy an out-of-town visit on the 6th with relatives who wine you and dine you over a three-day period. A longtime friend comes to town around the January 11th New Moon in Capricorn and lures you away from your mounting workload for just enough time to reconnect. Purchase tickets for an entertainment venue your children will enjoy around January 24.

Success and Money
You could please management by presenting a favorable financial report for last year's activity. You could also win points with your boss if you offer to write sections of the annual report that relate to your areas of expertise. Ask for input from other team members Treat your love partner to an elegant dinner on January 29.

Pitfalls and Potential Problems
Don't spend holiday cash on the 3rd, when sales are likely to be come-ons. Allure is there but not the quality you want for the goods offered. Nasty rumors may upset family members on January 21. Discreetly research the source to rule out a reason to worry.

Rewarding Days
6, 11, 24, 29

Challenging Days
3, 16, 21, 26

Pisces | February

Overall Theme

Go ahead and dream big while you anticipate personal and professional growth as your birthday cycle draws closer. The alignment of the Pisces Sun, Saturn, and the Moon on February 10 puts you at your charming best and able to convince others that plans you have for the coming year are in your best interest.

Relationships

Attend a meeting of a professional group that is looking to engage members to work on a timely project on February 7. If you are available, look into details and enjoy the challenges. Shop for a gift on February 13 for your sweetheart. Devote bonding time with your significant other on Valentine's Day. Schedule a date night on February 25, when romance fills your heart.

Success and Money

The first week of February is ideal for volunteering your services for a worthy cause that could increase fundraising prospects. Your current budget looks like it covers all the monthly necessities. The New Moon in Aquarius on the 9th might be a good night to order in for family members who may be gathering for a celebration of the start of the Lunar New Year of the Dragon on the 10th.

Pitfalls and Potential Problems

It would not be wise to use your primary credit card to charge a large purchase on February 1. Consider a small loan instead. This is one of those days when the infamous Neptune fog could cloud your judgment. A dinner date scheduled for the 22nd would work out more advantageously on the 25th.

Rewarding Days
7, 10, 13, 25

Challenging Days
1, 4, 22, 24

Pisces | March

Overall Theme

Interactions with diverse people populate your calendar this month. The focus early on is with groups and responsibilities that unite you in work. Visit art galleries or museums early in the month. Around March 13, you could learn more about your neighborhood's plan for scheduling spring cleaning and planting in community areas.

Relationships

Meet friends for lunch on March 5 and talk with an old classmate after dinner. Neighbors host a potluck or informal gathering around the 13th. If you have time, offer to bring your favorite recipe. It just might be the crowd favorite. When the Pisces New Moon shows up in your solar first house on the 10th, single members of your sign begin to encounter potential love partners at upcoming social events.

Success and Money

The year's first Lunar Eclipse occurs in Libra and your solar eighth house on March 25 and motivates you to get a handle on accounting records to make sure you file your income tax return on time. Attend school meetings on the 18th if you have children and volunteer your time.

Pitfalls and Potential Problems

Mixed planetary aspects on March 12 suggest that you table decisions about surgery or medical tests until the 21st, when planets are compatible with your objectives. Keep a cool head on March 20 if work projects hit a few snags that can be clarified by asking responsible parties for a timeline update.

Rewarding Days

5, 13, 18, 21

Challenging Days

3, 12, 20, 26

Pisces | April

Overall Theme

For the first time in 2024, a planet turns retrograde. Mercury starts off the month by going retrograde in Aries and your solar second house of purchasing power on April 1. Three weeks later, on April 25, this messenger planet turns direct. You may not benefit from signing loan papers or buying a car this month, but doing comparison shopping will give you a better option for the vehicle you eventually choose.

Relationships

Most relationships are cordial this month. April 2 is ideal for joining forces with others for mutual purposes. Getting together to generate interest in supporting a purpose or mission brings satisfactory results to a social cause that could benefit greatly through improving funding conditions. Reserve April 10 to bond with a sibling.

Success and Money

The Aries Solar Eclipse on the 8th in your solar second house of earned income and assets gives birth to a series of career discussions with the management team. Reorganizing proposals are on the table that identify new positions. Your skill set is a good fit for one or more of them. Be sure to show an interest in applying if the affiliated responsibilities and salary match your interests.

Pitfalls and Potential Problems

Obey the rules of the road and the timing of traffic signals if you are driving on April 22–23. Communication could be frustrating at home base on the 12th when one of the parties is not focused on details you would like to share. Don't take signs of anger personally.

Rewarding Days

2, 8, 10, 28

Challenging Days

9, 12, 22, 23

Pisces | May

Overall Theme
If you're looking for a reason to take a short trip out of town, plan a getaway on the 8th or 9th if possible. Sublet a friend's place for a few days if it's available to give yourself a few relaxing days in the sun. Right around the middle of the month, work activity gets very demanding as deadlines converge and an intense schedule emerges.

Relationships
Enjoy Mother's Day, May 12, with a gathering of children, siblings, and parents. The Moon in Cancer with harmonious planetary aspects that day encourages you to honor the special mothers in your life. If you are a mother, enjoy the tributes. Work demands fill your calendar the second half of May starting around the 15th.

Success and Money
Saturn in your sign has been funneling additional responsibilities your way since mid-January. Your expertise in managing projects is getting considerable buzz from organizational contacts. Part of the demand on your time has involved training staff. A promotion or bonus could be coming your way. What will you say when you receive an offer for a new job?

Pitfalls and Potential Problems
On May 2, Pluto in early Aquarius makes a station to move retrograde in your solar twelfth house, urging you to clean out your files, organize important papers, and shred multiple copies of old reports that have no meaning in your life today. Celebrate the reclaimed space when you eyeball the empty shelves and file drawers.

Rewarding Days
3, 8, 9, 12

Challenging Days
10, 11, 15, 24

Pisces | June

Overall Theme

Home base is the main focus of activity all month. Jupiter in Gemini transits your solar fourth house of home, drawing attention to getting your house in pristine condition to entertain traveling visitors. The New Moon in Gemini on the 6th harmonizes with Jupiter in early Gemini, an ideal day to bond with friends and meet new ones who share common interests.

Relationships

Relatives from out of town arrive for a visit around June 6. Enjoy the love and laughter when local family members join you, too. Find diversions for younger children who are excited by the reunion with grandparents. Recognition for accomplishment brings inner joy. Show support for a good friend's success by celebrating at a brunch on June 23.

Success and Money

You discover that salary and interest earnings are up this month when you take inventory of your finances on June 2. Purchase clothes for the family to wear to an upcoming wedding or formal event. Praise runs high on June 10 when performance accomplishments exceed goals and elevate team spirit.

Pitfalls and Potential Problems

With Saturn in Pisces going retrograde in your solar first house on June 29, you'll be grateful to get a break when transiting Mercury and Venus in Cancer in your solar fifth house send comic relief or romance your way. The Capricorn Full Moon on the 21st opposes the Sun, Mercury, and Venus, possibly delaying plans for much-anticipated weekend entertainment.

Rewarding Days

2, 6, 10, 23

Challenging Days

7, 13, 21, 29

Pisces | July

Overall Theme

Holiday fun and games are what you experience in your solar fifth house of entertainment, recreation, and vacations this month when the compatible New Moon in Cancer beams its joyful rays on your plans on July 5. Be glad that compatible Venus in Cancer and Mars and Uranus in Taurus are present to boost your spirits as you celebrate the Fourth of July holiday and visit local attractions.

Relationships

Hoping to avoid traffic jams, visitors may begin to arrive on July 1 to share the holiday festivities with you. Plan events that guests of all ages will enjoy. Decorate bicycles, front porches, and garages with streamers and fly the flag proudly. A favorable time for a week's vacation is July 1–9, when the planets favor recreation.

Success and Money

Investments, savings, and retirement accounts show rising numbers this month. The credit goes to your wise management of funds. You have the available cash to cover vacation week without going into debt. Be proud of the contributions you have made to increase productivity in your work group.

Pitfalls and Potential Problems

Transiting Neptune turns retrograde in the last degree of Pisces on July 2 in your solar first house of activity and passion. A household visitor or resident may complain of stomach discomfort on the 4th after binging on too much holiday fare. Late-day confusion on the 19th could result in taking work home for the weekend.

Rewarding Days

1, 5, 12, 30

Challenging Days

2, 13, 19, 24

Pisces | August

Overall Theme

Mercury, the great communicator, goes retrograde in Virgo on the 5th, backs up into Leo on the 14th, and stations to move direct in Leo on August 28. Love planet Venus occupies Virgo for most of the month in your solar seventh house of partners, sending a few romantic vibes your way. The Leo New Moon on August 4 energizes the quality of productivity needed to support a hectic workweek.

Relationships

Collaboration with key workmates in early August makes a difference in producing desired results in task accomplishment. Talk to a banker on the 9th to discuss lending rates if considering a home refinance. Visitors arrive on August 11 to tour local venues and parks.

Success and Money

This month you're looking at successful training programs that have helped key supervisory staff assimilate new procedures in the workplace. Now it's time to schedule this training for remaining employees so that information and practices are fully incorporated into daily routines. Newly purchased equipment is part of the transition to a more efficient operating system.

Pitfalls and Potential Problems

A hard aspect to the Sun from transiting Saturn in your sign on the 10th may lead to an exchange of words that sound harsher than intended. Pause and offer a clarifying explanation to the other party. With Mercury retrograde, misunderstandings are not unexpected.

Rewarding Days

4, 9, 11, 23

Challenging Days

10, 12, 14, 26

Pisces | September

Overall Theme
Don't be surprised if you feel a bit drained of energy with the Sun in Virgo for most of the month. It's a Pisces thing to want to recharge your batteries in September by taking a relaxing vacation. Why not travel with your partner? The New Moon on Labor Day, September 2, is in Virgo and your solar seventh house of close relationships, highlighting an enjoyable phase for Pisces.

Relationships
Your romantic partner may suggest a date for Labor Day that includes chowing down at a holiday party or accepting an invitation with business partners to honor work accomplishments. If you are single, leave for vacation to a favorite getaway spot on the 13th accompanied by a friend or romantic interest.

Success and Money
Excellent verbal and written communication gives you a leg up on the competition when management announces that job openings will post after September 21. Enjoy this productive cycle and be sure to list your assets that support the team and successful project management. Show your enthusiasm for the support you are receiving to apply for upcoming positions.

Pitfalls and Potential Problems
When Uranus in Taurus goes retrograde on September 1, Labor Day plans could be affected by travel delays for many. Leave later. Don't get into a debate on the 11th over personal opinions with someone who is "always right." The final Lunar Eclipse of the year occurs on September 17 in Pisces and your solar first house, energizing your passion and vitality.

Rewarding Days
2, 13, 18, 21

Challenging Days
1, 11, 17, 20

Pisces | October

Overall Theme

Jupiter in Gemini makes a station to move retrograde on October 9 in your solar fourth house of home, creating tension with your Sun. Two days later, Pluto moves direct on October 11 in the last degree of Capricorn and your solar eleventh house of friendships and groups. Challenging transits this month relate to conflicts with authorities in charge of your work organization. Discuss them diplomatically.

Relationships

A Solar Eclipse occurs on October 2 in Libra and your solar eighth house of joint income, highlighting the good health of your savings and retirement accounts. Propose that money you and your partner saved be used to fund a winter vacation. Treat your partner to a music venue around October 23rd.

Success and Money

Recent downtime may have you thinking about the weekly hours you work that keep you scrambling to find time to complete errands and enjoy time for leisure. You may decide to explore employment with companies that offer attractive, more flexible hours, such as a four-day workweek with Fridays off.

Pitfalls and Potential Problems

The Aries Full Moon on October 17 could put a strain on your budget if you are forced to make an unplanned auto repair. Ask the mechanic to give you a complete estimate of necessary repairs to determine what must be done now and what work can wait. Hire temporary staff to cover pressing assignments on October 25.

Rewarding Days

2, 5, 8, 23

Challenging Days

9, 17, 20, 25

Pisces | November

Overall Theme

When the Scorpio New Moon on the 1st occupies your solar ninth house of the higher mind, you are moved by the deep, rich earth of November to manifest your spiritual destiny. A feeling of gratitude encircles your sensitive heart as you spend most of the month remembering loved ones and planning holiday get-togethers. Saturn turns direct on the 15th in Pisces and your solar first house, prompting you to issue invitations.

Relationships

Food banks and shelters make heartfelt pleas for donations to purchase food for the Thanksgiving holiday. Make a donation to organizations that make your gift count. Complete shopping for your dinner menu and surprise honored guests with their favorite dishes. Present a showstopper after-dinner dessert.

Success and Money

Your financial accounts are capable of covering seasonal purchases. Complete shopping for remaining holiday gifts before Mercury in Sagittarius turns retrograde on November 25. Mail any wrapped packages and greeting cards well ahead of the deadlines for on-time delivery. Enjoy news about projected salary increases in 2025. Attend a work-related dinner party on November 3.

Pitfalls and Potential Problems

After attending a party that ended late and included lots of toasting, a little Monday morning crankiness on the 4th might affect members of your work team. Things could get loud at home base on the 17th when the Moon opposes Mercury and receives a harsh aspect from Neptune. Chalk it up to pre-holiday nerves.

Rewarding Days

1, 3, 15, 19

Challenging Days

4, 7, 17, 26

Pisces/December

Overall Theme

Can you remember the last time you saw a planetary lineup featuring a Blue Moon? Two New Moons occur this month, the first in Sagittarius on December 1 and the second in Capricorn on December 30. The Sun, Mercury, and the December 1st Sagittarius New Moon pass through your solar tenth house of career, with harmonious aspects from Mars in Leo and Pluto in Aquarius. Bring on the holidays!

Relationships

Attend a party with a friend on December 7, the same day that Neptune in Pisces goes direct. Party season arrives! Neighbors may host a get-together on the 15th. Meanwhile, family at a distance checks in to give you an arrival date for the upcoming holidays. Bond with your love partner on December 22 at your favorite dining spot.

Success and Money

Accounting projections you made cover hiring adequate staff and funding a higher level of project work. Management praises your performance and encourages you to apply for promotions in the new year. Enjoy the confidence your executive team has bestowed on you. Celebrate the new year with anticipation for future growth and career satisfaction in 2025.

Pitfalls and Potential Problems

The year's final Full Moon occurs in Gemini on December 15 just as Mercury in Sagittarius stations to move direct, a day to be alert to travel changes. December 21 may seem like a long day when you keep finding errors in purchase totals. Check receipts before you leave the premises and double-check online purchases.

Rewarding Days

1, 7, 19, 22

Challenging Days

2, 4, 12, 21

Pisces Action Table

These dates reflect the best—but not the only—times for success and ease in these activities, according to your Sun sign.

	JAN	FEB	MAR	APR	MAY	JUN	JUL	AUG	SEP	OCT	NOV	DEC
Move	6		13		12			11		5		
Romance		25				23			2		19	7
Seek counseling/coaching	24				8		30		13			1
Ask for a raise				28				4			3	
Vacation			18	10			5			23		
Get a loan		13				2						